David Barber

WE WON THE CUP

A celebration for the 100th FA Cup Final

An official publication of the Football Association

Pan Books London and Sydney

First published 1981 by Pan Books Ltd,
Cavaye Place, London SW10 9PG
in association with the Football Association
An official publication of the Football Association
© The Football Association 1981
ISBN 0 330 26401 X
Photoset by Parker Typesetting Service, Leicester
Printed in Great Britain by
Richard Clay (The Chaucer Press) Ltd, Bungay, Suffolk

WE WON THE CUP

Introduction by the Secretary of the FA, Ted Croker

This year will see the one hundredth Football Association Challenge Cup Final played, and as Secretary of the Football Association I am pleased to write an introduction to this book which has been written to mark the occasion.

We Won the Cup contains a report on each of the ninety-nine Cup Finals played since 1872, illustrated with photographs of some of the most memorable moments from those matches, and including a compilation of the results of every tie ever played in the competition proper. These results have never been published before in their entirety.

History

The Football Association Challenge Cup competition was instituted in the 1871–2 season, nine years after the formation of the Association. At a meeting held in the offices of the Sportsman, London, on 20 July 1871 a proposal by C. W. Alcock, Honorary Secretary of the Football Association, 'That it is desirable that a Challenge Cup should be established in connection with the Association, for which all clubs belonging to the Association should be invited to compete', met with favour and was finally approved at a subsequent meeting on 16 October 1871.

The present trophy is actually the third to be played for in the history of the competition. It was made for the Football Association in 1911 by Messrs Fattorini & Sons of Bradford. The cost of this trophy was 50 guineas. It weighs 175 ounces and stands 19 inches high, exclusive of the ebony plinth which has a silver band around it upon which the names of the winners are inscribed.

The club that has won the Cup the greatest number of times is Aston Villa who have carried off the trophy on seven occasions. Only two clubs have won the Cup three times in succession – Wanderers in 1876, 1877 and 1878, and Blackburn Rovers in 1884, 1885 and 1886. The highest score in a Cup Final is 6–0, the score by which Bury beat Derby County in 1903, and the highest score in earlier rounds is Preston North End's 26–0 victory against Hyde United in a First Round match in season 1887–8.

Part of the answer to the question of why the competition has such an appeal to players and spectators alike is to be found in the fact that it is really the most democratic of contests. The giants cannot be sure that they will play teams in their own class; they must be prepared to face the smaller fry and sometimes – indeed, very often – they come down with a resounding crash. There is life and sudden death. This is the spice the Cup offers.

Since the First World War seven First Division clubs have been eliminated from the competition by clubs from outside the Football League. The most recent instance – Wimbledon's famous victory at Burnley in 1975 – occurred in a season in which the then Southern League club had entered the competition at the First Qualifying Round stage and took on Burnley in the Third Round Proper having already accounted for Bracknell Town (3–1), Maidenhead United (4–0), Wokingham Town (2–0), Guildford and Dorking (3–0), Bath City (1–0) and Kettering Town (2–0). McMahon's goal early in the second half at Turf Moor put Wimbledon through to the next round, where there was more glory in store for them as they held the reigning League champions Leeds United to a draw at Elland Road.

Organization

The control and management of the Challenge Cup competition is vested in the Council of the Football Association. The Council has about ninety members representing county associations, clubs in ten regional areas, universities, schools, services, Commonwealth associations and the Football League. The Council has the power to formulate the rules of the competition and to alter or add to the rules as they think fit. The Council appoints a Challenge Cup Committee to control and manage the competition on their behalf and to give decisions on matters arising out of the competition which, according to the rules laid down by the Council, are considered to be decisions of the Council.

The number of entries to the competition has risen steadily from the original fifteen in 1871. In the 1930s and 1940s, except for the war years, over six hundred clubs took part in several seasons. The Football Association realized that the numbers had to be restricted, and now there is a standard of ability and ground facilities which must be reached before a club's entry is accepted.

The Challenge Cup competition is open (i) to all clubs which are members or associate members of the Football Association and take part in a senior competition of an affiliated county association, (ii) to all other clubs which take part in a senior competition of an affiliated county association, (iii) to such other clubs which are members of an affiliated county association as may be approved by the Council and (iv) to Welsh clubs not exceeding fourteen in number.

The competition commences every year in early September with a preliminary round. The remainder of the entries come in at the first qualifying round. Twenty non-League clubs are excused until the fourth and final qualifying round. At the First Round Proper stage the forty-eight clubs of Divisions Three and Four of the Football League enter with the previous season's FA Challenge Trophy finalists and two other selected non-League clubs. The twenty which emerge after the Second Round Proper join with the League clubs from Divisions One and Two, which have been exempted until then, and it continues as a strict elimination contest.

Special magic

There is a special magic which only the Cup Final possesses and, to me, the most important ingredient is of course the players. In the big match — and the FA Cup Final, watched by millions, is undoubtedly the biggest annual football match in the world — success or failure depends on the form of the players on the day. Past reputations seem to mean nothing. One's memories of past Finals invariably centre on individuals, mine particularly on Chris Duffy's great goal for Charlton against Burnley in 1947 when my brother was playing for Charlton. Regrettably I am one of the majority of ex-professionals who never played in a Cup Final. The fourth round was as far as I ever got, but even that is a pleasant memory.

Nevertheless, there is something about the occasion which makes it greater than any team or individual. The same two clubs could be competing in a match a couple of weeks before the big day and attract a tiny fraction of the attention the Cup Final will command. Here's to the next hundred!

1871–2

First Round

WANDERERS v Harrow Chequers wo; Clapham R v Upton Pk 3–0; Crystal Palace v Hitchin 0–0; Maidenhead v Gt Marlow 2–0; Queen's Pk, Glasgow bye; Donington School (Spalding) bye; ROYAL ENGINEERS v Reigate Priory wo; Hampstead Heathens bye; Barnes v Civil Service 2–0

Second Round

WANDERERS v Clapham R 3–1; Crystal Palace v Maidenhead 3–0; Queen's Pk, Glasgow v Donington School wo; ROYAL ENGINEERS v Hitchin 3–1; Hampstead Heathens v Barnes 2–0

Third Round

WANDERERS v Crystal Palace draw; Queen's Pk, Glasgow bye; ROYAL ENGINEERS v Hampstead Heathens 2–0

Semi-Final

WANDERERS v Queen's Pk, Glasgow wo; ROYAL ENGINEERS v Crystal Palace 3–0

WANDERERS **1**
ROYAL ENGINEERS **0**

Wanderers had drawn a hard, goalless semi-final tie with Queen's Park and won a place in the Final only because the Glasgow team could not afford to travel back to London for a replay.

The historic first Final took place at Kennington Oval on 16 March 1872, before a crowd of 2,000. At that time football matches were played without crossbars or goal-nets. There were no free-kicks or penalties, and the pitch markings did not include a centre-circle or a half-way line.

Wanderers gained the first of their five victories in the competition, but it was only by a single goal scored by Betts, mysteriously playing under the pseudonym 'A. H. Chequer'. Wanderers had the pick of all the best players who had been at the public schools and universities, yet it was the Royal Engineers from Chatham who took the field as favourites at odds of 7 to 4 on. Not for the last time, the favourites went down in the Final. Engineers were particularly unlucky in that Lieutenant Creswell broke his collar-bone after ten minutes – the first recorded accident in football.

Once Betts had scored from an acute angle after Vidal's long dribble had made the opening, the Engineers did well to keep the margin of defeat down to one goal.

C. W. Alcock, Secretary of the Football Association, had been the one to table the resolution to start a Cup competition that he believed would fire interest in the game. Fittingly, it was Alcock who captained Wanderers to victory in the first Final. They had six future internationals in their side, and their best players were probably Hooman of Charterhouse and Vidal, 'the prince of dribblers' from Westminster. The Rev R. W. S. Vidal, who also played for Oxford University, once scored three goals in succession from the kick-off in one match, without an opponent touching the ball – a tribute to his legendary dribbling skills. Wanderers' goalkeeper Bowen was still an outstanding player at thirty-six – no mean achievement in the days when training was unknown and goalkeepers were fair game for the heaviest of charges, whether they had the ball or not.

The first Cup competition had been riddled with byes, exemptions and unfinished ties. Wanderers reached the Final, but Harrow had scratched to them in the first round, and they had failed to win both their quarter-final and semi-final ties.

Wanderers: R. de C. Welch; C. W. Alcock, M. P. Betts; A. G. Bonsor, E. E. Bowen, W. P. Crake; T. C. Hooman, E. Lubbock, A. C. Thompson, R. W. S. Vidal, C. H. R. Wollaston
Royal Engineers: Capt Marindin; Capt Merriman, Lieut Addison; Lieut Creswell, Lieut Mitchell, Lieut Renny-Tailyour; Lieut Rich, Lieut Goodwyn, Lieut Muirhead, Lieut Cotter, Lieut Bogle
Referee: A. Stair (Upton Park)

1872–3

First Round
Clapham R v Hitchin wo; OXFORD UNIV v Crystal Palace 3–2; Royal Engineers v Civil Service 3–0; 1st Surrey Rifles v Upton Pk 2–0; Maidenhead v Marlow 1–0; South Norwood v Barnes 1–0; Windsor Home Pk v Reigate Priory 4–2; Queen's Pk, Glasgow bye; WANDERERS Cup-holders

Second Round
Clapham R v OXFORD UNIV 0–3; Royal Engineers bye; 1st Surrey Rifles v Maidenhead 1–3; South Norwood v Windsor Home Pk 0–3

Third Round
OXFORD UNIV v Royal Engineers 1–0; Maidenhead v Windsor Home Pk 1–0

Fourth Round
OXFORD UNIV v Maidenhead 4–0

Semi-Final
OXFORD UNIV v Queen's Pk, Glasgow wo

WANDERERS **2**
OXFORD UNIVERSITY **0**

As Cup-holders, Wanderers were exempted until the Final in this following year. Their challengers, Oxford University, had received a strange kind of bye in the semi-final when their opponents, Queen's Park, were unable to travel to London to play the tie.

The 1873 Final was staged for the one and only time in the history of the competition at the Lillie Bridge ground, which used to exist close to where famous Stamford Bridge stands now. The match was timed to start at 11 a.m. in order to avoid a clash with the Boat Race being held later the same day.

Wanderers won the Cup again, this time by two goals scored by Kinnaird and Wollaston. Kinnaird, later President of the Football Association, was making the first of his nine appearances in Cup Finals and dribbled through the Oxford team to score a spectacular second goal.

Oxford were able to call upon a number of the best footballers from the public schools, and with players like Vidal, Birley and Ottaway, were bound to make an impact on the competition. They were not at full strength against the Wanderers and perhaps not fully fit either, and they even elected to play without a goalkeeper – Kirke-Smith moving upfield – after going a goal down in a desperate attempt to save the match.

Wanderers: E. E. Bowen; C. M. Thompson, R. de C. Welch; Hon A. F. Kinnaird, L. S. Howell, C. H. R. Wollaston; J. R. Sturgiss, Rev H. H. Stewart, W. S. Kenyon-Slaney, R. K. Kingsford, A. G. Bonsor
Oxford University: A. Kirke-Smith; A. J. Leach, C. C. Mackarness; F. H. Birley, C. J. Longman, F. B. Chappell-Maddison; H. B. Dixon, W. B. Paton, R. W. S. Vidal, W. E. Sumner, C. J. Ottaway
Referee: A. Stair (Upton Park)

1873–4

First Round

OXFORD UNIV v Upton Pk 4–0; Barnes v 1st Surrey Rifles 1–0; Wanderers v Southall wo; Trojans v Farningham wo; Clapham R v AAC wo; Cambridge Univ v South Norwood 1–0; Sheffield beat Shropshire Wand; Pilgrims v Gt Marlow 1–0; ROYAL ENGINEERS v Brondesbury 5–0; Uxbridge v Gitanos 3–0; Maidenhead v Civil Service wo; High Wycombe v Old Etonians wo; Swifts v Crystal Palace 1–0; Woodford Wells v Reigate Priory 3–0

Second Round

OXFORD UNIV v Barnes 2–1; Wanderers v Trojans wo; Clapham R v Cambridge Univ 4–1; Sheffield v Pilgrims 1–0; ROYAL ENGINEERS v Uxbridge 2–1; Maidenhead v High Wycombe 1–0; Swifts v Woodford Wells 2–1

Third Round

OXFORD UNIV v Wanderers 1–0; Clapham R v Sheffield 2–1; ROYAL ENGINEERS v Maidenhead 7–0; Swifts bye

Semi-Final

OXFORD UNIV v Clapham R 1–0; ROYAL ENGINEERS v Swifts 2–0

OXFORD UNIVERSITY **2**
ROYAL ENGINEERS **0**

Major Marindin's Engineers from Chatham were undoubtedly the best team in the country during the first four seasons of the Cup. All their matches were against the leading clubs like the Wanderers or the University sides, and their remarkable record during that period included a goal-tally of 244 for and 21 against. Only three matches out of eighty-six were lost in four years and one of those, unfortunately, was the Final of 1874.

Oxford had always been one of the Engineers' most difficult opponents and they had had many a closely matched contest. Beaten finalists the year before, Oxford again swept through to the Final, where they were clearly superior to the Engineers who were playing well below their best form.

Mackarness sent a loose ball in under the tape following a corner-kick, to give Oxford a 1–0 lead. The Sappers often threatened the Oxford goal, but then Ottaway, Chappell-Maddison and Vidal rushed away with the ball and Patton kicked a second goal for the University very soon after the first.

The teams changed ends again – they were obliged to after every goal – and the Engineers were compelled to defend for some time, and though Renny-Tailyour's shot against a post at the other end gave them a brief respite, it was to no avail.

Oxford University: C. E. B. Neapean; C. C. Mackarness, F. H. Birley; F. T. Green, R. W. S. Vidal, C. J. Ottaway; R. H. Benson, F. J. Patton, W. S. Rawson, F. B. Chappell-Maddison, Rev A. H. Johnson
Royal Engineers: Capt Merriman; Major Marindin, Lieut G. W. Addison; Lieut G. C. Onslow, Lieut H. G. Oliver, Lieut T. Digby; Lieut H. W. Renny-Tailyour, Lieut H. E. Rawson, Lieut J. E. Blackman, Lieut A. K. Wood, Lieut P. G. von Donop
Referee: A. Stair (Upton Park)

1874–5

First Round
ROYAL ENGINEERS v Gt Marlow 3–0; Cambridge Univ v Crystal Palace 2–1; Clapham R v Panthers 3–0; Pilgrims v South Norwood 2–1; Oxford Univ v Brondesbury 6–0; Windsor Home Pk v Uxbridge wo; Wanderers v Farningham 16–0; Barnes v Upton Pk 3–0; OLD ETONIANS v Swifts 3–0; Maidenhead v Hitchin 1–0; Reigate Priory bye; Shropshire Wand v Sheffield wo; Civil Service v Harrow Chequers wo; Woodford Wells v High Wycombe 1–0; Southall v Leyton 5–0

Second Round
ROYAL ENGINEERS v Cambridge Univ 5–0; Clapham R v Pilgrims 2–0; Oxford Univ v Windsor Home Pk wo; Wanderers v Barnes 4–0; OLD ETONIANS bye; Maidenhead v Reigate Priory 2–1; Shropshire Wand v Civil Service wo; Woodford Wells v Southall 3–0

Third Round
ROYAL ENGINEERS v Clapham R 3–2; Oxford Univ v Wanderers 2–1; OLD ETONIANS v Maidenhead 1–0; Shropshire Wand v Woodford Wells 2–0

Semi-Final
ROYAL ENGINEERS v Oxford Univ 1–0; OLD ETONIANS v Shropshire Wand 1–0

Royal Engineers: Capt Merriman; Lieut G. H. Sim, Lieut G. Onslow; Lieut R. M. Ruck, Lieut P. G. von Donop, Lieut C. K. Wood; Lieut H. E. Rawson, Lieut R. H. Stafford, Capt H. W. Renny-Tailyour, Lieut Mein, Lieut C. Wingfield Stratford
Old Etonians: Capt E. H. Drummond-Moray; M. Farrer, E. Lubbock; F. H. Wilson, Hon A. F. Kinnaird, J. H. Stronge; F. J. Patton, C. E. Farmer, A. G. Bonsor, A. Lubbock, T. Hammond. (C. J. Ottaway, W. S. Kenyon-Slaney, R. H. Benson and A. G. Thompson took part in the first match in place of A. Lubbock, T. Hammond, M. Farrer and Capt E. H. Drummond-Moray)
Referee: C. W. Alcock (Wanderers)

ROYAL ENGINEERS **2**
OLD ETONIANS **0** (after a 1–1 draw)

Apart from the Wanderers, the Royal Engineers were the most consistent team in the early years of the competition. Having lost the first Final at the Oval and again in 1874, they won the Cup at last in 1875 after a 1–1 draw.

The Engineers were the first to appreciate that football was essentially a team game. Passing and supporting the player with the ball were as important as dribbling. Their players were fit and fast and, for all their sportsmanship, no suitable opponents for the squeamish.

The Engineers went through the season without a single defeat, but had had little to spare in winning their semi-final with Oxford. In the Final against the Old Etonians they drew the first game at the Oval after extra time.

The match had been remarkable for the strange handicap imposed on the Engineers by the existing rule that teams had to change ends after each goal was scored. This led to their having to play against a gale for most of the ninety minutes.

Etonians won the toss and gained the advantage of the wind at the outset. For forty minutes they tried their utmost to score but the Engineers invariably got the ball away at the critical moment. Their clearances upfield tended to be blown back towards their own penalty-area, and success or failure in the match seemed to depend on whether they could play out the last five minutes of the half without conceding a goal.

In the last seconds Bonsor, using the wind to full advantage, curled his corner-kick round the goalkeeper and through the posts and the teams changed ends. The Sappers, enraged by this cruel stroke of luck, roared on to the attack and immediately scored an equalizer.

Ends were changed again and the fight carried on with renewed energy. Ruck's collision with Etonian inside-forward Ottaway led to the latter being carried off with an injured ankle. This accident more or less made the game equal, allowing for the wind, and it finished after ninety minutes with the score at 1–1.

Following a pre-match arrangement, an extra half-hour was played. Etonians failed to score in the first period with the wind behind them, and the prospects of the Engineers winning looked bright. But the Etonians concentrated solely on defending their goal and successfully kept their opponents out. Several leading Etonians were unable to take part in the replay, but surprisingly the Engineers had some difficulty in winning.

1875–6

First Round
WANDERERS v 1st Surrey Rifles 5–0; Crystal Palace v 105th Regiment 3–0; Sheffield Club v Shropshire Wand wo; Upton Pk v Southall 1–0; Swifts v Gt Marlow 2–0; South Norwood v Clydesdale wo; Royal Engineers v High Wycombe 15–0; Panthers v Woodford Wells 1–0; Reigate Priory v Barnes 1–0; Cambridge Univ v Civil Service wo; Oxford Univ v Forest School 6–0; Herts Rangers v Rochester 4–0; OLD ETONIANS v Pilgrims 4–1; Maidenhead v Ramblers 2–0; Clapham R v Hitchin wo; Leyton v Harrow Chequers wo

Second Round
WANDERERS v Crystal Palace 3–0; Sheffield Club v Upton Pk wo; Swifts v South Norwood 5–0; Royal Engineers v Panthers wo; Reigate Priory v Cambridge Univ 0–8; Oxford Univ v Herts Rangers 8–0; OLD ETONIANS v Maidenhead 8–0; Clapham R v Leyton 12–0

Third Round
WANDERERS v Sheffield Club 2–0; Swifts v Royal Engineers 3–1; Cambridge Univ v Oxford Univ 0–4; OLD ETONIANS v Clapham R 1–0

Semi-Final
WANDERERS v Swifts 2–1; Oxford Univ v OLD ETONIANS 0–1

WANDERERS **3**
OLD ETONIANS **0** (after a 0–0 draw)

The Oval crowd saw the Etonians on top for the first few minutes of a Final that kicked-off twenty-five minutes later than scheduled. Then Wanderers, with the wind at their backs, took the initiative.

There were frequent stoppages for handball in the first half, and Wanderers also forced several corner-kicks without being able to turn them to any account. On the half-hour Edwards, by a dexterous flick, hit a wind-assisted shot only just wide of the Etonians' goal.

Etonians were more prominent in the second half and, following a corner-kick, the ball appeared to be driven through for the first goal. The posts collapsed on impact and the referee (or 'umpire' as he was then called) could not award a goal.

In the replay a week later, again at the Oval, Wollaston scored Wanderers' first after a scramble in front of goal. Their next attack saw a fast run down the field by Heron, and Hughes slamming in the second.

Heron and Hughes made another good run early in the second half and, being well supported, the latter was able to notch another goal for the Wanderers. It was the first year of their 'hat-trick' of Final victories.

Wanderers: W. D. O. Greig; A. Stratford, W. Lindsay; F. B. C. Maddison, F. H. Birley,
C. H. R. Wollaston; H. Heron, F. Heron, J. H. Edwards, J. Kenrick, T. Hughes
Old Etonians: Q. Hogg; E. Lubbock, Hon E. Lyttleton; M. G. Faner, Hon A. F. Kinnaird,
J. H. Stronge; W. S. Kenyon-Slaney, Hon A. Lyttleton, J. R. Sturgis, A. G. Bonsor, H. P. Allene.
(C. Meysey, A. C. Thompson and J. E. C. Welldon took part in the first match in place of
J. H. Stronge, M. G. Faner and E. Lubbock)
Referee: W. S. Rawson (Oxford Univ)

1876–7

First Round
WANDERERS v Saffron Walden wo; Southall v Old Wykehamists wo; Pilgrims v Ramblers 4–1; Panthers v Wood Grange 3–0; Cambridge Univ v High Wycombe wo; Clapham R v Reigate Priory 5–0; Rochester v Union 5–0; Swifts v Reading Hornets 2–0; Royal Engineers v Old Harrovians 2–1; Shropshire Wand v Druids wo; Sheffield v Trojans wo; South Norwood v Saxons 4–1; OXFORD UNIV v Old Salopians wo; 105th Regiment v 1st Surrey Rifles 3–0; Queen's Pk, Glasgow bye; Upton Pk v Leyton 7–0; Barnes v Old Etonians wo; Gt Marlow v Herts R 2–1; Forest School v Gresham 4–1

Second Round
WANDERERS v Southall 6–1; Pilgrims v Panthers 1–0; Cambridge Univ v Clapham R 2–1; Rochester v Swifts 1–0; Royal Engineers v Shropshire Wand 3–0; Sheffield v South Norwood 7–0; OXFORD UNIV v 105th Regiment 6–1; Queen's Pk, Glasgow bye; Upton Pk v Barnes 1–0; Gt Marlow v Forest School 1–0

Third Round
WANDERERS v Pilgrims 3–0; Cambridge Univ v Rochester 4–0; Royal Engineers v Sheffield 1–0; OXFORD UNIV v Queen's Pk, Glasgow wo; Upton Pk v Gt Marlow 1–0

Fourth Round
WANDERERS bye; Cambridge Univ v Royal Engineers 1–0; OXFORD UNIV v Upton Pk 1–0

Semi-Final
WANDERERS v Cambridge Univ 1–0; OXFORD UNIV bye

WANDERERS 2
OXFORD UNIVERSITY 0

In 1877, again on Boat Race day, it was the turn of Oxford University to oppose the Wanderers at the Oval. Though the game went into extra time, it was the Wanderers once more who carried the day with two goals during the extra half-hour.

Oxford had almost taken the lead in bizarre fashion in the fifteenth minute. After something like a rugby scrum in front of the Wanderers' goal, the ball went behind for a corner. Waddington's corner-kick fell neatly into Kinnaird's hands and the Wanderers' custodian very nearly stepped back over the goal-line with the ball.

Wanderers charged the Oxford goal repeatedly, Heron and Wace being continually frustrated by the vigilant Allington. The game went on without any advantage being gained by either team, and the match was declared drawn after ninety minutes. Then, by mutual consent, the teams agreed to play for another half-hour and despite the heavy rain both now played with redoubled energy.

After ten minutes Kenrick made a brilliant run from well inside his own half, successfully avoided a number of challenges and finished by eluding Allington to slide the ball home. In a fierce Wanderers attack soon afterwards Lindsay passed the ball through to make the final score 2–0.

Wanderers: A. F. Kinnaird; W. Lindsay, A. Stratford; F. H. Birley, C. A. Denton, F. T. Green; H. Heron, T. Hughes, J. Kenrick, H. Wace, C. H. R. Wollaston
Oxford University: E. H. Allington; J. Bain, O. R. Dunnell; J. H. Savory, A. H. Tod, E. W. Waddington; P. H. Fernandez, A. F. Hills, H. S. Otter, E. H. Parry, W. S. Rawson
Referee: S. H. Wright (Marlow)

1877–8

First Round

WANDERERS v Panthers 9–1; High Wycombe v Wood Grange 4–0; Barnes v St Marks wo;
Gt Marlow v Hendon 2–0; Sheffield v Nottingham 3–0; Darwen v Manchester 3–1;
ROYAL ENGINEERS v Union wo; Pilgrims v Ramblers 1–0; Druids (Wales) v Shropshire Wand 1–0;
Oxford Univ v Herts Rangers 5–2; Old Foresters v Old Wykehamists wo; Clapham R v Grantham
2–0; Swifts v Leyton 8–2; Old Harrovians v 105th Regiment 2–0; 1st Surrey Rifles v Forest School
1–0; Cambridge Univ v Southill Pk 3–1; Maidenhead v Reading Hornets 10–0; Upton Pk v
Rochester 3–0; Reading v South Norwood 2–0; Remnants v St Stephens 4–1; Hawks v Minerva
5–2; Queen's Pk, Glasgow bye (later withdrew)

Second Round

WANDERERS v High Wycombe 9–0; Barnes v Gt Marlow 3–1; Sheffield v Darwen 1–0;
ROYAL ENGINEERS v Pilgrims 6–0; Druids bye; Oxford Univ v Old Foresters 1–0; Clapham R v
Swifts 4–0; Old Harrovians v 1st Surrey Rifles 6–0; Cambridge Univ v Maidenhead 4–2; Upton Pk v
Reading 1–0; Remnants v Hawks 2–0

Third Round

WANDERERS v Barnes 4–1; Sheffield bye; ROYAL ENGINEERS v Druids 8–0; Oxford Univ v
Clapham R 3–2; Old Harrovians v Cambridge Univ 2–0; Upton Pk v Remnants 3–0

Fourth Round

WANDERERS v Sheffield 3–0; ROYAL ENGINEERS v Oxford Univ 4–2; Old Harrovians v Upton Pk
3–1

Semi-Final

WANDERERS bye; ROYAL ENGINEERS v Old Harrovians 2–1

WANDERERS **3**
ROYAL ENGINEERS **1**

The Wanderers, having won the trophy twice consecutively, assembled perhaps the most powerful team they had ever put on to the field, in the hope of winning the match and the Cup outright at the same time. They were strong favourites at the start and, though the Engineers maintained a gallant uphill struggle throughout the afternoon, Wanderers ran out 3–1 winners in the end.

As soon as Lieutenant Hedley had kicked off for the Engineers the game began to develop into one of the fastest ever witnessed. Morris's head intervened to divert Kinnaird's good shot for a throw-in and when Kinnaird returned the ball into play, Wace hit it across to Kenrick and he drove it in under the tape to give Wanderers a fifth-minute lead.

On restarting, the 'Sappers' made a desperate rush upfield, and, during a determined struggle for possession that followed, Wanderers goal-keeper Kirkpatrick had his arm broken. But, though he must have been in great pain, he refused to leave the field.

Never before had the Wanderers displayed such skill and quickness than on this important occasion; yet the Engineers met their opponents with great resolve, often attacking brilliantly. In the eighteenth minute Wanderers sent the ball out of their penalty-area, Morris hit it straight back, and the ball bobbed about in front of goal before eventually going through for an equalizer. Ten minutes later Wanderers were in the lead again, as one of the Engineers put through his own goal.

The Engineers continued to play with spirit after the interval, but fate was clearly against them. Hedley's 'goal' was disallowed for offside and then, ten minutes into the half, Heron squared the ball from the right for Kenrick to drive it in.

The Cup became Wanderers' property by the rules of the competition. They chose, in fact, to hand the trophy back to the Football Association on the condition that in future it was not to be won outright by any club.

After making history, the Wanderers were never again to appear in the Final. The club which had borne such a great share of the hard work of founding the game had a limited future. Composed as it was of a collection of members of other clubs, it found increasing difficulty in securing players. In September 1878, Kinnaird and other leading players resigned from the Wanderers to play for the Old Etonians.

Wanderers: J. Kirkpatrick; A. Stratford, W. Lindsay; Hon A. F. Kinnaird, F. T. Green, C. H. R. Wollaston; H. Heron, J. G. Wylie, H. Wace, C. A. Denton, J. Kenrick
Royal Engineers: L. B. Friend; J. H. Cowan, W. J. Morris; C. B. Mayne, F. C. Heath, C. E. Haynes; M. Lindsay, R. B. Hedley, F. G. Bond, H. H. Barnet, O. E. Ruck
Referee: S. R. Bastard (Upton Park)

1878–9

First Round
OLD ETONIANS v Wanderers 7–2; Reading v Hendon 1–0; Minerva v 105th Regiment wo; Grey Friars v Gt Marlow 2–1; Darwen v Birch, Manchester wo; Eagley, Bolton bye; Remnants v Unity wo; Pilgrims v Brentwood 3–1; Nott'm Forest v Nottingham 3–1; Sheffield v Grantham 3–1; Old Harrovians v Southill Pk 8–0; Panthers v Runnymede wo; Oxford Univ v Wednesbury Stlls 7–0; Royal Engineers v Old Foresters 3–0; Barnes v Maidenhead 4–0; Upton Pk v Saffron Walden 5–0; CLAPHAM R v Finchley wo; Forest School v Rochester 4–2; Cambridge Univ v Herts R 2–0; South Norwood v Leyton wo; Swifts v Hawks 2–1; Romford v Ramblers 3–1

Second Round
OLD ETONIANS v Reading 1–0; Minerva v Grey Friars 3–0; Darwen v Eagley 4–1; Remnants v Pilgrims 6–2; Nott'm Forest v Sheffield 2–0; Old Harrovians v Panthers 3–0; Oxford Univ v Royal Engineers 4–0; Barnes v Upton Pk 3–2; CLAPHAM R v Forest School 10–1; Cambridge Univ. v South Norwood 3–0; Swifts v Romford 3–1

Third Round
OLD ETONIANS v Minerva 5–2; Darwen v Remnants 3–2; Nott'm Forest v Old Harrovians 2–0; Oxford Univ v Barnes 2–1; CLAPHAM R v Cambridge Univ 1–0; Swifts bye

Fourth Round
OLD ETONIANS v Darwen 6–2; Nott'm Forest v Oxford Univ 2–1; CLAPHAM R v Swifts 8–1

Semi-Final
OLD ETONIANS v Nott'm Forest 2–1; CLAPHAM R bye

OLD ETONIANS **1**
CLAPHAM ROVERS **0**

Nottingham Forest's appearance in the semi-final had brought warning of the rise of the provincial clubs. On this occasion, however, Old Etonians reached the Final at their expense and went on to win the Cup for the first time.

Against Clapham in the Final at the Oval, the Etonians had rather a stiff breeze to contend with, yet still contrived to keep the ball principally in their opponents' half. Clapham held them in check with coolness and good judgement and often looked dangerous in attack themselves, with Growse and Bevington showing up well. There was no score at half-time, but after the break the Etonians proceeded to completely pen their opponents in their own part of the ground. Their goalkeeper, Hawtrey, had scarcely anything to do to keep himself even moderately warm.

In the fifty-ninth minute an enterprising run by Goodhart carried him down the right and into a position from which to centre. The energetic Clerke was on the end of the pass and he shot the ball under the bar.

Loud and prolonged cheering from all parts of the ground greeted the goal that later proved to be the winner. Clapham worked manfully to the end to try and at least equalize matters but were unable to do so.

Old Etonians: J. P. Hawtrey; E. Christian, L. Bury; Hon A. F. Kinnaird, E. Lubbock,
C. J. Clerke; N. Pares, H. C. Goodhart, H. Whitfield, J. B. T. Chevallier, H. Beaufoy
Clapham Rovers: R. H. Birkett; R. A. Ogilvie, E. Field; N. C. Bailey, J. F. M. Prinsep,
F. L. Rawson; A. J. Stanley, S. W. Scott, H. S. Bevington, E. F. Growse, C. Keith-Falconer
Referee: C. W. Alcock (Wanderers)

1879–80

First Round
Blackburn R v Tyne Association 5–1; Turton v Brigg 7–0; Darwen v Eagley 1–0; Nott'm Forest v Notts Club 4–0; Sheffield v Queen's Park, Glasgow wo; Providence, Sheffield bye; Maidenhead v Calthorpe, Birmingham 3–1; Stafford Road v Wednesbury Strollers 2–1; OXFORD UNIV v Gt Marlow 1–0; Birmingham v Panthers wo; Henley v Reading wo; Aston Villa bye; Old Carthusians v Acton 4–1; Hotspur v Argonauts 1–0; Old Etonians v Barnes wo; Wanderers v Rochester 6–0; West End v Swifts wo; Royal Engineers v Cambridge Univ 2–0; Grey Friars v Hanover Ath 2–1; Old Harrovians v Finchley 2–0; Gresham v Kildare 3–0; Upton Pk v Remnants 5–2; Hendon v Old Foresters 3–0; CLAPHAM R v Romford 7–0; Pilgrims v Clarence 5–2; South Norwood v Brentwood 4–2; Mosquitoes v St Peter's Institute 3–1; Herts Rangers v Minerva 2–1

Second Round
CLAPHAM R v South Norwood 4–0; Pilgrims v Herts Rangers wo; Hendon v Mosquitoes 7–1; Old Etonians bye; Wanderers v Old Carthusians 1–0; West End v Hotspurs 1–0; OXFORD UNIV v Birmingham 6–0; Aston Villa v Stafford Road 3–1; Maidenhead v Henley 3–1; Royal Engineers v Upton Pk 4–1; Old Harrovians bye; Grey Friars v Gresham 9–0; Nott'm Forest v Turton 6–0; Blackburn R v Darwen 3–1; Sheffield v Sheffield Providence 3–0

Third Round
CLAPHAM R v Pilgrims 7–0; Hendon bye; Old Etonians v Wanderers 3–1; West End bye; OXFORD UNIV v Aston Villa wo; Maidenhead bye; Royal Engineers v Old Harrovians 2–0; Grey Friars bye; Nott'm Forest v Blackburn R 6–0; Sheffield bye

Fourth Round
CLAPHAM R v Hendon 2–0; Old Etonians v West End 5–1; OXFORD UNIV v Maidenhead 1–0; Royal Engineers v Grey Friars 1–0; Nott'm Forest v Sheffield 2–2 (Sheffield disqualified)

Fifth Round
CLAPHAM R v Old Etonians 1–0; OXFORD UNIV v Royal Engineers 1–0; Nott'm Forest bye

Semi-Final
CLAPHAM R bye; OXFORD UNIV v Nott'm Forest 1–0

CLAPHAM ROVERS **1**
OXFORD UNIVERSITY **0**

Clapham, finding themselves once more at an Oval Final, made up for their disappointment of the previous year with a narrow victory, and so added a new name to the trophy.

The Oxford team that had conquered much-fancied Nottingham Forest in the semi-final immediately took the initiative in the Final. Phillips' early free-kick, given for hands, went within an ace of its intended destination. Then Clapham, recovering their poise after this sudden attack, moved forward in fine style and caused their opponents' backs many anxious moments.

Lloyd-Jones's cross was only cleared to outside-left Ram and his shot came back off a post, Lloyd-Jones tried a shot himself which went over the tape and that proved to be the last noteworthy incident of the half.

Oxford, with the wind, carried all before them in the first few minutes of the second half and immediately forced two corners in quick succession. Play then proceeded so evenly that thoughts of an extra half-hour's play were being entertained. But, with ten minutes to go, King failed to cut out Sparks' cross and Lloyd-Jones rushed up to shoot between the posts.

Birkett, an England international at both football and rugby, moved smartly to save from Childs as Oxford launched a counter-attack, but the Clapham goal was not seriously threatened again.

Clapham Rovers: R. H. Birkett; R. A. Ogilvie, E. Field; A. Weston, N. C. Bailey, H. Brougham; A. J. Stanley, F. Barry, F. J. Sparks, C. A. Lloyd-Jones, E. A. Ram
Oxford University: P. C. Parr; C. W. Wilson, C. J. S. King; F. A. H. Phillips, B. Rogers, R. T. Heygate; G. B. Childs, J. Eyre, F. D. Crowdy, E. H. Hill, J. B. Lubbock
Referee: Major Marindin (Royal Engineers)

1880-1

First Round

Astley Bridge v Eagley 4–0; Blackburn R v Sheffield Providence 6–2; Turton v Britannia Recreation, Brigg 5–0; Sheff Wed v Queen's Pk, Glasgow wo; Sheffield Club v Blackburn Olympic 5–4; Darwen v Brigg 8–0; Aston Villa v Wednesbury Strollers 5–3; Stafford Road, Wolverhampton v Spilsby 7–0; Nottingham v Derby 4–2; Grantham v Birmingham Calthorpe 2–1; Nott'm Forest v Caius College, Cambridge wo; Reading v Hotspur 5–1; Weybridge Swallows v Henley 3–0; Clapham R v Finchley 15–0; Upton Pk v Mosquitoes 8–1; Swifts v Old Foresters 2–1; Herts Rangers v Barnes 6–0; OLD ETONIANS v Brentwood 10–0; London v St Peter's Institute 8–1; Maidenhead v Old Harrovians 1–0; Grey Friars v Windsor Home Pk 3–1; Dreadnought v Rochester 2–1; OLD CARTHUSIANS v Saffron Walden 7–0; Royal Engineers v Remnants 1–0; Rangers v Wanderers wo; Pilgrims v Old Philberdians wo; Gt Marlow v Clarence 6–0; West End v Hanover Utd 1–0; Reading Abbey v St Albans 1–0; Romford v Reading Minster wo; Acton v Kildare 5–0

Second Round

OLD CARTHUSIANS v Dreadnought 5–1; Royal Engineers v Pilgrims 1–0; Rangers bye; Clapham R bye; Swifts v Reading 1–0; Upton Pk v Weybridge 3–0; Darwen v Sheffield 5–1; Sheff Wed v Blackburn R 4–0; Turton v Astley Bridge 3–0; Romford bye; Reading Abbey v Acton 2–1; Gt Marlow v West End 4–0; OLD ETONIANS v Hendon 2–0; Herts Rangers bye; Grey Friars v Maidenhead 1–0; Stafford Road v Grantham 7–1; Aston Villa v Nott'm Forest 2–1; Nottingham bye

Third Round

OLD CARTHUSIANS bye; Royal Engineers v Rangers 6–0; Clapham R v Swifts 2–1; Upton Pk bye; Darwen bye; Sheff Wed v Turton 2–0; Romford v Reading Abbey 2–0; Gt Marlow bye; OLD ETONIANS v Herts Rangers 3–0; Grey Friars bye; Stafford Road bye; Aston Villa v Nottingham 3–1

Fourth Round

OLD CARTHUSIANS v Royal Engineers 2–1; Clapham R v Upton Pk 5–4; Darwen v Sheff Wed 5–1; Romford v Gt Marlow 2–1; OLD ETONIANS v Grey Friars 4–0; Stafford Road v Aston Villa 3–2

Fifth Round

OLD CARTHUSIANS v Clapham R 4–1; Darwen v Romford 15–0; OLD ETONIANS v Stafford Road 2–1

Semi-Final

OLD CARTHUSIANS v Darwen 4–1; OLD ETONIANS bye

OLD CARTHUSIANS **3**
OLD ETONIANS **0**

The Etonians were a side with clever individuals, but Carthusians, wonderfully linked together, convincingly won the last Final to be played between amateur clubs from the south.

Carthusians were the first Charterhouse team to enter the competition, and, led on by Parry and Page, made a rapid succession of attacks on the Etonians' goal, ably defended by Rawlinson.

After half an hour's play, during which the Etonians had several times been lucky not to concede a goal, Carthusians finally scored. Prinsep's long throw was deflected by Wynyard into the goal.

Wynyard 'scored' again within a minute, charging Rawlinson over the line with the ball, but, curiously, the point was disallowed for offside.

The heavier men in the light blue ranks began to tire midway through the second half, and the Carthusians, improving every minute, used quick and accurate passing to switch the play to the opposite end. Rawlinson punched out Page's shot from Prinsep's pass, but Parry followed up to make it 2–0. Almost directly from the kick-off the ball was in the Etonians' goal again, Todd heading through after Page's fine dribble.

The spectators had cheered the winners from start to finish – clearly their victory was a popular one.

Old Carthusians: L. F. Gillett; W. H. Norris, E. G. Colvin; J. F. M. Prinsep, A. J. Vintcent,
W. E. Hansell; L. M. Richards, W. R. Page, E. G. Wynyard, E. H. Parry, A. H. Tod
Old Etonians: J. F. P. Rawlinson; C. W. Foley, C. H. French; Hon A. F. Kinnaird, R. B. Farrer,
J. B. T. Chevallier; W. J. Anderson, H. C. Goodhart, R. H. Macaulay, H. Whitfield, P. C. Novelli
Referee: W. Pierce Dix (Sheffield)

1881-2

First Round
Bootle v Blackburn Law 2–1; Turton v Astley Bridge 2–0; Darwen v Blackburn Olympic 3–1; Bolton Wand v Eagley 1–0; BLACKBURN R v Park Road 9–1; Accrington S v Queen's Pk, Glasgow wo; Aston Villa v Nott'm Forest 4–1; Nottingham v Calthorpe wo; Wednesbury Old Ath v St George's 9–0; Small Heath Alliance v Derby 4–1; Wednesbury Strollers v Stafford Road 3–1; Staveley v Spilsby 5–1; Grantham v Brigg 6–0; Sheffield v Britannia Recreation, Brigg 8–0; Heeley v Lockwood Bros 5–0; Wednesday v Providence 2–0; Gt Marlow v Brentwood 3–1; Reading v Hendon 5–0; West End v Remnants 3–2; St Bartholomew's Hospital v Wanderers wo; Dreadnought v Caius College wo; Pilgrims v Mosquitoes 5–0; Barnes v Rochester 3–1; Old Foresters v Morton Rangers 3–0; Royal Engineers v Kildare 6–0; Old Carthusians v Esher Leopold 5–0; Swifts v Herts Rangers 4–0; Acton v Finchley 4–0; OLD ETONIANS v Clapham R 1–0; Maidenhead v Henley 2–0; Old Harrovians v Olympic 4–2; Romford v Rangers wo; Upton Pk v St Albans 3–0; Hotspur v Union 1–0; Reading Abbey v Woodford Bridge 2–0; Reading Minster v Windsor Home Pk 1–0; Hanover Utd bye

Second Round
BLACKBURN R v Bolton Wand 6–2; Darwen v Accrington S 3–1; Turton v Bootle 4–0; Wednesbury Old Ath v Small Heath Alliance 6–0; Aston Villa bye; Nottingham v Wednesbury Strollers 11–1; Sheff Wed bye; Staveley v Grantham 3–1; Heeley v Sheffield 4–1; Upton Pk v Hanover Utd 3–1; Hotspur v Reading Abbey 4–1; Reading Minster v Romford 3–1; OLD ETONIANS bye; Swifts v Old Harrovians 7–1; Maidenhead v Acton 2–1; Gt Marlow v St Bart's Hospital 2–0; Dreadnought bye; Reading v West End wo; Old Foresters v Pilgrims 3–1; Royal Engineers bye; Old Carthusians v Barnes 7–1

Third Round
BLACKBURN R bye; Darwen v Turton 4–2; Wednesbury Old Ath bye; Aston Villa v Nottingham 4–1; Sheff Wed v Staveley 5–1; Heeley bye; Upton Pk bye; Hotspur v Reading Minster 2–0; OLD ETONIANS v Swifts 3–0; Maidenhead bye; Gt Marlow v Dreadnought 2–1; Reading bye; Old Foresters bye; Royal Engineers v Old Carthusians 2–0

Fourth Round
BLACKBURN R v Darwen 5–1; Wednesbury Old Ath v Aston Villa 4–2; Sheff Wed v Heeley 3–1; Upton Pk v Hotspur 5–0; OLD ETONIANS v Maidenhead 6–3; Gt Marlow v Reading wo; Old Foresters v Royal Engineers 2–1

Fifth Round
BLACKBURN R v Wednesbury Old Ath 3–1; Sheff Wed v Upton Pk 6–0; OLD ETONIANS bye; Gt Marlow v Old Foresters 1–0

Semi-Final
BLACKBURN R v Sheff Wed 0–0, 5–1; OLD ETONIANS v Gt Marlow 5–0

OLD ETONIANS **1**
BLACKBURN ROVERS **0**

A provincial club now managed to reach the Final for the first time, but, unfortunately for Blackburn, the Cup did not travel back to Lancashire. The Etonians, led by Kinnaird in his eighth Final, were prepared for Rovers with their newly won reputation and record of winning thirty-one out of thirty-five matches during the season.

Rovers, playing into a strong wind, were hard pressed to keep their goal intact in the early stages. Macaulay's shot was deflected behind for a corner in the first minute, and then, eight minutes later, Dunn got clear away, outpacing Sharples and M'Intyre, and crossed to Anderson who had moved out to the opposite wing. Amid great cheering, Anderson put the ball through the Rovers' goal.

Blackburn had been upset by the tactics of their opponents, who relied on charges upfield, backed by weight, pace and some fancy kicking, often with both feet off the ground. Superstitious Blackburn were even putting their defeat down to the fact that they had had to change from their normal playing strip owing to a colour clash with that of the Etonians.

Kinnaird celebrated Etonians' victory by standing on his head in front of the Oval pavilion. It was the last time he was to receive a winners' medal.

Old Etonians: J. F. P. Rawlinson; T. H. French, P. J. de Paravicini; Hon A. F. Kinnaird, C. W. Foley, P. C. Novelli; A. T. R. Dunn, R. H. Macaulay, H. C. Goodhart, W. J. Anderson, J. B. T. Chevallier
Blackburn Rovers: R. Howarth; H. M'Intyre, F. Suter; H. Sharples, F. W. Hargreaves, J. Duckworth; J. Douglas, T. Strachan, J. Brown, G. Avery, J. Hargreaves
Referee: J. C. Clegg (Sheffield)

1882–3

First Round

Grimsby v Queen's Pk, Glasgow wo; Lockwood Bros v Macclesfield 4–3; Nottingham v Sheffield 6–1; Phoenix Bessemer v Grantham wo; Sheff Wed v Spilsby 12–2; Nott'm Forest v Brigg Britannia wo; Heeley bye; St George's v Calthorpe 5–1; Walsall T v Staveley 4–1; Stafford Road v Small Heath Alliance 6–2; Aston Villa v Walsall Swifts 4–1; Wednesbury Old Ath v Spital 7–1; Aston Unity bye; Blackburn R v Blackpool 11–1; Darwen Ramblers v South Shore 5–2; BLACKBURN OLYMPIC v Accrington S 6–3; Darwen v Blackburn Park Road 4–1; Church v Clitheroe 5–0; Lower Darwen v Irwell Springs 5–2; Haslingden bye; Northwich Vic v Astley Bridge 3–2; Liverpool Ramblers v Southport 4–0; Eagley v Bolton Olympic 7–4; Bolton Wand v Bootle 6–1; Druids v Oswestry 2–0; Halliwell v Gt Lever 3–2; United Hospitals v London Olympic 3–0; Hanover Utd v Mosquitoes 1–0; Clapham R v Kildare 3–0; Windsor v Acton 3–0; Brentwood v Barnes 4–2; Rochester v Hotspur 2–0; OLD ETONIANS v Old Foresters 3–1; Swifts v Union 4–1; Upton Pk bye; Etonian Ramblers v Romford 6–2; Old Carthusians v Pilgrims 6–0; Old Westminsters v Maidenhead 2–0; Royal Engineers v Woodford Bridge 3–1; Reading bye; Gt Marlow v Hornchurch 2–0; Hendon v West End 3–1; South Reading v Dreadnought 2–1; Reading Minster v Remnants wo; Chatham bye

Second Round

BLACKBURN OLYMPIC v Lower Darwen 9–1; Darwen Ramblers v Haslingden 3–2; Church bye; Darwen v Blackburn R 1–0; Druids v Northwich Vic 5–0; Bolton Wand v Liverpool Ramblers 3–0; Eagley v Halliwell 3–1; Old Carthusians v Etonian Ramblers 7–0; Old Westminsters bye; Royal Engineers v Reading 8–0; Clapham R v Hanover Utd 7–1; Windsor v United Hospitals 3–1; OLD ETONIANS v Brentwood 2–1; Rochester bye; Swifts v Upton Pk 3–2; Hendon v Chatham 2–1; South Reading bye; Gt Marlow v Reading Minster wo; Notts Co bye; Phoenix Bessemer v Grimsby 8–1; Sheff Wed v Lockwood Bros 6–0; Nott'm Forest v Heeley 7–2; Aston Villa v Wednesbury Old Ath 4–1; Aston Unity v St George's 3–0; Walsall T v Stafford Road 4–1

Third Round

BLACKBURN OLYMPIC v Darwen Ramblers 8–0; Church v Darwen 2–0; Druids v Bolton Wand 1–0; Eagley bye; Old Carthusians v Old Westminsters 3–2; Royal Engineers v Clapham R v Windsor 3–0; OLD ETONIANS v Rochester 7–0; Swifts bye; Hendon v South Reading 11–1; Gt Marlow bye; Notts Co v Phoenix Bessemer 3–2; Sheff Wed v Nott'm Forest 3–2; Aston Villa v Aston Unity 3–1; Walsall T bye

Fourth Round

BLACKBURN OLYMPIC v Church 2–0; Druids v Eagley 2–1; Old Carthusians v Royal Engineers 6–2; Clapham R bye; OLD ETONIANS v Swifts 2–0; Hendon v Gt Marlow 3–0; Notts Co v Sheff Wed 4–1; Aston Villa v Walsall T 2–1

Fifth Round

BLACKBURN OLYMPIC v Druids 4–0; Old Carthusians v Clapham R 5–3; OLD ETONIANS v Hendon 4–2; Notts Co v Aston Villa 4–3

Semi-Final

BLACKBURN OLYMPIC v Old Carthusians 4–0; OLD ETONIANS v Notts Co 2–1

BLACKBURN OLYMPIC **2**
OLD ETONIANS **1**

The Olympians somewhat compensated for the disappointment experienced a year ago, when everyone had taken it for granted that Blackburn Rovers would bring the Cup up north. The 1883 Final at one time looked like being a repetition of the previous year's Final, with the Etonians a goal in front and the Olympians playing a similar game to Rovers – very little cohesion, long shots and reckless passing. But they pulled themselves together and in the end fully deserved their victory, having the better of the game overall and running the Etonians off their feet before the match was over.

Inside-left Dunn was proving to be an early handful for the Lancastrians' defence, before Yates relieved the pressure with a snap shot against the Etonian crossbar. After another good run on the left for Old Etonians by Dunn, Goodhart sent the ball over the top when he ought really to have scored.

For some time the play was give-and-take, Olympic indulging in long crossfield passes while their opponents stuck to their close dribbling game. Then Goodhart made amends for his earlier miss, scoring with a terrific shot.

Up to half-time, Olympic, hard though they tried, had been unsuccessful in their efforts to equalize, though the proverbial luck of the Old Etonians saved them on several occasions. Yates dropped the ball on to the Eton bar as he had done earlier and Paravicini and Foley then had to make last-ditch clearances from near the goal-line.

Play in the second half was evenly balanced and, after twenty minutes had elapsed, a grand effort on the part of Olympic ended with Matthews putting a well-directed shot beyond the reach of Rawlinson for the equalizer. Dunn, the best Etonian forward, was hurt at this point and had to retire from the field – a great loss to his side. Olympic began to play with more confidence as a result, and the Eton goalkeeper only just stopped Costley's fine shot in time.

Olympic certainly had the better of the play up to the end of the ninety minutes and Dewhurst, their outside-right, took advantage of the first chance offered in the extra-time period to hammer in a shot that went just wide. The Etonians were tiring fast, and Olympic, with their superior stamina, had matters nearly all their own way in the second period. Yates put in fine diagonal run and crossed hard from the right to Costley who rushed up to score the winning goal.

Blackburn Olympic: T. Hacking; J. T. Ward, S. A. Warburton; T. Gibson, W. Astley, J. Hunter; T. Dewhurst, A. Matthews, G. Wilson, J. Costley, J. Yates
Old Etonians: J. F. P. Rawlinson; T. H. French, P. J. de Paravicini; Hon. A. F. Kinnaird, C. W. Foley, J. B. T. Chevallier; W. J. Anderson, R. H. Macaulay, H. C. Goodhart, A. T. B. Dunn, H. W. Bainbridge
Referee: C. Crump (Wolverhampton)

1883–4

First Round
Grantham v Spilsby 3–2; Rotherham v Spital 7–2; Notts Co v Heeley 3–1; Staveley v Middlesbro 5–1; Lockwood Brothers v Sheffield Club 4–1; Grimsby v Hull T 3–1; Nott'm Forest v Redcar and Coatham wo; Sheff Wed bye; Walsall T v Calthorpe 9–0; Birmingham Excelsior v Small Heath Alliance 3–2; Stafford Road v Aston Unity 5–1; Wednesbury Old Ath v St George's 5–0; Wednesbury T v WBA 2–0; Aston Villa v Walsall Swifts 5–1; Wolves v Long Eaton Rangers 4–1; Derby Midland bye; Blackburn Olympic v Darwen Ramblers 5–1; Blackburn Park Road v Low Moor 6–1; Accrington S v Blackpool 4–1; Padiham v Lower Darwen 3–1; Darwen v Church 1–0; South Shore v Clitheroe 3–2; BLACKBURN R v Southport 7–0; Eagley v Halliwell 5–2; Bolton Wand v Bolton Olympic 9–0; Gt Lever v Astley Bridge 4–1; Rossendale v Irwell Springs 6–2; Bolton v Bradshaw 5–1; PNE bye; Druids v Northwich Vic 0–1; Oswestry v Hartford St John's 7–0; Davenham v Macclesfield 2–0; Manchester v Stoke-on-Trent 2–1; QUEEN'S PK, GLASGOW v Crewe Alex 10–0; Wrexham v Liverpool Ramblers wo; Brentwood v Hanover Utd 6–1; Hendon v Old Etonians 3–2; Mosquitoes v Pilgrims 3–2; Old Westminsters v Chatham 3–0; Romford v Woodford Bridge 3–0; Reading v South Reading 2–0; Upton Pk v Acton 2–0; Old Carthusians v Reading Minster 10–1; Old Foresters v Dreadnought 2–1; West End v Maidenhead 1–0; Clapham R v Kildare wo; Gt Marlow v Hornchurch 9–0; Windsor v Royal Engineers 5–3; Old Wykehamists v Upton Rangers 7–1; Rochester v Uxbridge 2–1; Swifts bye

Second Round
Staveley v Sheff Wed 3–1; Notts Co v Nott'm Forest 3–0; Lockwood Brothers v Rotherham 3–1; Grantham v Grimsby 4–0; Derby Midland v Birmingham Excelsior 2–1; Wednesbury T v Walsall T 6–0; Aston Villa v Stafford Road 5–0; Wednesbury Old Ath v Wolves 4–2; BLACKBURN R v South Shore 7–1; Accrington S v Park Road 3–2 (Accrington disqualified); Blackburn Olympic v Darwen 2–1; Padiham bye; PNE v Gt Lever 4–1; Hurst v Irwell Springs 3–2; Bolton Wand v Bolton 3–0; Eagley bye; Oswestry v Wrexham 4–3; QUEEN'S PK, GLASGOW v Manchester 15–0; Northwich Vic v Davenham 5–1; Romford v Mosquitoes 3–1; Old Westminsters v Hendon 2–1; Brentwood bye; Reading v West End 1–0; Old Foresters v Old Carthusians 7–2; Upton Pk bye; Swifts v Gt Marlow 2–0; Clapham R v Rochester 7–0; Old Wykehamists v Windsor 1–0

Third Round
Notts Co v Grantham 4–1; Staveley v Lockwood Brothers 1–0; Wednesbury T v Derby Midland 1–0; Aston Villa v Wednesbury Old Ath 7–4; BLACKBURN R v Padiham 3–0; Blackburn Olympic bye; PNE v Eagley 9–1; Bolton Wand v Irwell Springs 8–1; QUEEN'S PK, GLASGOW v Oswestry 7–1; Northwich Vic bye; Brentwood v Romford 4–1; Old Westminsters bye; Upton Pk v Reading 6–1; Old Foresters bye; Swifts v Clapham R 2–1; Old Wykehamists bye

Fourth Round
Upton Pk v PNE 1–1 (PNE disqualified); QUEEN'S PK, GLASGOW v Aston Villa 6–1; Northwich Vic v Brentwood 3–0; Notts Co v Bolton Wand 2–2, 2–1; BLACKBURN R v Staveley 5–1; Blackburn Olympic v Old Wykehamists 6–0; Swifts v Old Foresters 2–1; Old Westminsters v Wednesbury T 5–0

Fifth Round
QUEEN'S PK, GLASGOW v Old Westminsters 1–0; BLACKBURN R v Upton Pk 3–0; Notts Co v Swifts 1–1, 1–0; Blackburn Olympic v Northwich Vic 9–0

Semi-Final
QUEEN'S PK, GLASGOW v Blackburn Olympic 4–0; BLACKBURN R v Notts Co 1–0

BLACKBURN ROVERS **2**
QUEEN'S PARK **1**

The 1884 Final had resolved itself into an international contest without precedent. A 12,000 crowd at the Oval, the largest at any Final so far, gathered to see the climax of a competition which had that year attracted a record entry of 101 clubs. Blackburn Rovers won the first of three successive Finals, two of them against this Glasgow club which was virtually the Scottish international side.

Understandably, Rovers had the crowd on their side, but they looked anything but at home during the first twenty minutes. After this early period of uncertainty, however, Rovers set to work in earnest and played superbly to the end. In the second half the Scotsmen were completely outplayed.

The match produced three goals all of which were scored in the fifteen minutes before half-time. First Brown crossed from the left and Sowerbutts had only to apply the gentlest touch to help the ball between the posts: 1–0 to England.

Rovers always looked likely to increase their lead, and, after Gillespie had sent the ball to the left, Forrest obliged with a hard shot just under the bar. They threatened to go further ahead, but then Anderson forced a corner, took it himself, and, following a bout of passing around the Rovers goal, Christie neatly side-footed the ball past Arthur and notched a goal for the Scotsmen.

Blackburn Rovers: H. J. Arthur; J. Beverley, F. Suter; H. M'Intyre, J. Hargreaves, J. H. Forrest; J. M. Lofthouse, J. Douglas, J. Sowerbutts, J. Inglis, J. Brown
Queen's Park: G. Gillespie; W. Arnott, J. MacDonald; C. Campbell, J. J. Gow, W. Anderson; W. W. Watt, Dr Smith, W. Harrower, D. S. Allan, R. M. Christie
Referee: Major Marindin (Royal Engineers)

1884–5

First Round
Wednesbury Old Ath v Derby Midland 2–1; St George's, Birmingham v Aston Unity 5–0; Aston Villa v Wednesbury T 4–1; Walsall Swifts v Stafford Road Works 2–0; Walsall T v Derby Co 7–0; Derby St Lukes v Wolves 4–2; Birmingham Excelsior v Small Heath Alliance 2–0; WBA v Junction Street School 7–1; Nott'm Forest v Rotherham 5–0; Sheffield Club v Lockwood Brothers 3–0; Staveley v Notts Rangers 4–1; Sheff Wed v Long Eaton Rangers 1–0; Heeley v Notts Wand 1–0; Notts Co v Notts Olympic 2–0; Spital bye; Bolton Association v Astley Bridge wo; Darwen Old Wand v Higher Walton 4–1; Lower Darwen v Halliwell 4–1; Darwen v Bradshaw 11–0; Bolton Wand v Preston Zingari (not played); Fishwick Ramblers v Darwen Ramblers 2–0; Chirk v Davenham 4–2; Druids v Liverpool Ramblers 6–1; Crewe Alex v Oswestry 2–1; Leek v Northwich Vic 4–3; Wrexham Olympic v Goldenhill 1–0; Macclesfield v Hartford St John's 9–0; QUEEN'S PK, GLASGOW v Stoke-on-Trent wo; Newtown v Stafford Rangers wo; Lincoln C v Hull T 5–1; Grimsby T v Grantham 1–0; Redcar v Sunderland 3–1; Middlesbro v Grimsby District wo; Newark v Spilsby 7–3; Blackburn Olympic v Oswaldtwistle R 12–0; Accrington S v Southport 3–0; Low Moor v Park Road wo; Church v Hurst 3–2; BLACKBURN R v Rossendale 11–0; South Shore v Rawtenstall wo; Witton v Clitheroe wo; Old Carthusians v Acton 7–1; Upton Pk v West End wo; Reading v Rochester 2–0; Gt Marlow v Royal Engineers 10–1; Hotspur v Uxbridge 3–1; Old Wykehamists v Maidenhead 3–0; Dulwich v Pilgrims 3–2; Old Foresters v Hoddesdon 8–0; Hanover Utd v Reading Minster 1–0; Hendon v Clapham R 6–0; Chatham v Windsor wo; Romford v Clapton 3–2; Swifts v Old Brightonians 3–0; Brentwood v Barnes 2–0; South Reading v Casuals 4–1; Old Westminsters v Bournemouth R 6–0; Old Etonians v Luton Wand 3–1; Henley bye

Second Round
Walsall Swifts v Derby St Lukes 1–0; St George's, Birmingham v Birmingham Excelsior 2–0; Aston Villa v Walsall T 2–0; WBA v Wednesbury Old Ath 4–2; Sheffield Club v Spital 4–1; Nott'm Forest v Heeley 4–1; Notts Club v Staveley 2–0; Sheff Wed bye; Darwen v Fishwick Ramblers 2–0; Darwen Old Wand v Bolton Association 7–2; Lower Darwen bye; Druids v Newtown 6–0; Chirk v Wrexham Olympic 4–1; QUEEN'S PK, GLASGOW v Crewe Alex 2–1; Leek v Macclesfield 5–1; Middlesbro v Newark 4–1; Grimsby T v Redcar 3–1; Lincoln C bye; Church v South Shore 3–2; Southport v Low Moor 3–1; BLACKBURN R v Blackburn Olympic 3–2; Witton bye; Old Wykehamists v Hotspur 2–1; Upton Pk v Reading 3–1; Old Carthusians v Gt Marlow 5–3; Chatham v Hendon 1–0; Hanover Utd v Old Foresters 2–1; Romford v Dulwich 3–0; Old Westminsters v Henley 7–0; Swifts v South Reading 3–2; Old Etonians v Brentwood 6–1

Third Round
WBA v Aston Villa 3–0; Walsall Swifts v St George's, Birmingham 3–2; Nott'm Forest v Sheff Wed 2–1; Notts Club v Sheffield Club 9–0; Lower Darwen v Darwen Old Wand 4–2; Darwen bye; QUEEN'S PK, GLASGOW v Leek 3–2; Druids v Chirk 4–1; Grimsby T v Lincoln C 1–0; Middlesbro bye; BLACKBURN R v Witton 6–1; Church v Southport 10–0; Old Wykehamists v Upton Pk 2–1; Old Carthusians bye; Chatham v Hanover Utd 2–0; Romford bye; Swifts v Old Westminsters 2–1; Old Etonians bye

Fourth Round
Old Carthusians v Grimsby T 3–0; Nott'm Forest v Swifts 1–0; WBA v Druids 1–0; QUEEN'S PK, GLASGOW v Old Wykehamists 7–0; Church v Darwen 3–0; Chatham v Lower Darwen 1–0; Notts Club v Walsall Swifts 4–1; BLACKBURN R v Romford 8–0; Old Etonians v Middlesbro 5–2

Fifth Round
Old Carthusians v Chatham 3–0; Old Etonians bye; Nott'm Forest bye; QUEEN'S PK, GLASGOW bye; WBA bye; Notts Club bye; BLACKBURN R bye; Church bye

Sixth Round
Nott'm Forest v Old Etonians 2–0; QUEEN'S PK, GLASGOW v Notts Club 2–2, 2–1; BLACKBURN R v WBA 2–0; Old Carthusians v Church 1–0

Semi-Final
QUEEN'S PK, GLASGOW v Nott'm Forest 1–1, 3–0; BLACKBURN R v Old Carthusians 5–1

BLACKBURN ROVERS **2**
QUEEN'S PARK **0**

Although Rovers were the Cup holders, Queen's Park again took the field in the Final as favourites, but once more their long journey was doomed to end in failure.

Rovers' superiority this time soon became apparent, and after Forrest's early strike they were never in danger of losing the match. Twenty minutes from the end Brown, who had played throughout like a man inspired, added a second goal.

Gillespie in the Queen's Park goal was always busy, and, but for his smartness, the defeat would have been much greater. Arthur, on the other hand, only had recourse to handle the ball five times in the whole match, and not at all in the first half.

The match finally got under way after the over-anxious Queen's Park forwards had produced two false starts, and Rovers were the first to threaten when Lofthouse's shot skimmed the bar. They went ahead after sixteen minutes when Brown dodged past Arnott and sent in a good shot that was blocked. Forrest instantly hit a left-foot piledriver into the goal.

Very soon after Arthur had been forced to use his hands for the first time in the match, Rovers' Fecitt ran the ball down the left side and squared it for Brown, coming up in the nick of time, to make it 2–0.

Blackburn Rovers: H. J. Arthur; R. G. Turner, F. Suter; H. M'Intyre, G. Haworth, J. H. Forrest; J. M. Lofthouse, J. Douglas, J. Brown, H. E. Fecitt, J. Sowerbutts
Queen's Park: G. Gillespie; W. Arnott, W. Macleod; C. Campbell, J. MacDonald, A. Hamilton; W. Anderson, W. Sellar, W. Gray, N. McWhannel, D. S. Allan.
Referee: Major Marindin (Royal Engineers)

1885-6

First Round
PNE v Gt Lever wo; Queen's Pk, Glasgow v Partick Thistle 5–1; South Shore v Higher Walton 4–3; Hurst v Bradshaw 3–1; Rawtenstall v Glasgow Rangers wo; Halliwell v Fishwick Ramblers 2–1; Astley Bridge v Southport 3–2; Bolton Wand v Eagley 6–0; BLACKBURN R v Clitheroe 2–0; Church v Blackburn Olympic 3–1; Accrington S v Witton 5–4; 3rd Lanark RV v Blackburn Park Road 4–2; Rossendale v Low Moor 6–2; Padiham v Heart of Midlothian wo; Darwen Old Wand v Burnley 11–0; Oswaldtwistle R v Lower Darwen 3–1; Derby Midland v Birmingham Excelsior 2–1; Wolves v Derby St Luke's 7–0; Aston Villa v Walsall T 5–0; WBA v Aston Unity 4–1; Stafford Road v Matlock 7–0; Derby Co v St George's, Birmingham 3–0; Small Heath Alliance v Burton Wand 9–2; Wednesbury Old Ath v Burton Swifts 5–1; Darwen v Junction Street School, Derby 2–2, 4–0; Walsall Swifts bye; Sheffield v Newark 3–0; Notts Olympic v Notts Wand 2–2, 4–1; Nott'm Forest v Mellors 6–2; Notts Rangers v Lockwood Brothers 2–2, 4–0; Sheffield Heeley v Eckington Works 2–1; Staveley v Mexborough wo; Long Eaton Rangers v Sheff Wed 2–0; Notts Co v Rotherham 15–0; Burslem Port Vale v Chirk 3–1; Oswestry v Bollington 5–0; Macclesfield v Northwich Vic 4–1; Crewe Alex v Stoke-on-Trent 2–2, 1–0; Leek v Wrexham Olympic 6–3; Davenhill v Goldenhill 2–1; Newtown v Hartford St John's 3–1; Druids v Stafford Rangers 4–1; Middlesbro v Horncastle wo; Grimsby v Lincoln C 2–0; Redcar v Sunderland 3–0; Lincoln Lindum v Grimsby and District 4–0; Gainsborough Trinity v Grantham 4–1; Darlington bye; Luton Wand v Chesham 3–2; Gt Marlow v Luton T 3–0; Upton Pk v United London Scottish 4–2; Old Westminsters v Hotspur 3–1; Romford v Hanover Utd 1–1, 3–0; Old Brightonians v Acton 2–1; Old Wykehamists v Uxbridge 5–0; Old Carthusians v Chatham 2–0; Old Etonians v Bournemouth R wo; Rochester v Reading 6–1; Brentwood v Maidenhead 3–0; Lancing Old Boys v Barnes 7–1; Clapton v Hendon 4–0; Old Harrovians v St James's, Forest Gate wo; Swifts v Casuals 7–1; Clapham R v 1st Surrey Rifles 12–0; South Reading v Dulwich 2–1; Old Foresters v Royal Engineers 5–1

Second Round
Bolton Wand v Rawtenstall wo; PNE v Astley Bridge 11–3; Halliwell v Hurst wo; South Shore v Queen's Pk, Glasgow wo; Rossendale v Padiham 9–1; BLACKBURN R v Oswaldtwistle R 1–0; Darwen Old Wand v Accrington S 2–1; Church v 3rd Lanark RV wo; Walsall Swifts v Derby Midland 3–1; WBA v Wednesbury Old Ath 3–2; Derby Co v Aston Villa 2–0; Wolves v Stafford Road 4–2; Small Heath Alliance v Darwen 3–1; Staveley v Long Eaton Rangers 4–1; Notts Rangers v Sheffield Heeley 6–1; Nott'm Forest v Notts Olympic 4–1; Notts Co v Sheffield Club 8–0; Leek v Newton wo; Burslem Port Vale v Druids 2–2, 5–1; Davenham v Macclesfield 8–1; Crewe Alex v Oswestry wo; Grimsby T v Darlington 8–0; Redcar v Lincoln Lindum 2–0; Middlesbro v Gainsboro Tr 2–1; Old Wykehamists v Luton Wand 10–0; Old Westminsters v Old Brightonians 3–0; Gt Marlow v Old Etonians 8–0; Old Carthusians v Upton Pk 8–0; Romford bye; South Reading v Clapton wo; Brentwood v Lancing Old Boys 6–1; Swifts v Rochester 5–1; Old Harrovians v Old Foresters 2–1; Clapham R bye

Third Round
South Shore v Halliwell 6–1; PNE v Bolton Wand 3–2; Church v Rossendale 5–1; BLACKBURN R v Darwen Old Wand 6–1; Wolves v Walsall Swifts 2–1; Small Heath Alliance v Derby Co 4–2; WBA bye; Staveley v Nott'm Forest 2–1; Notts Co v Notts Rangers 3–0; Davenham v Crewe Alex 2–1; Burslem Port Vale v Leek wo; Middlesbro v Grimsby T 2–1; Redcar bye; Old Westminsters v Romford 5–1; Old Wykehamists v Gt Marlow wo; Old Carthusians bye; South Reading v Clapham R wo; Swifts v Old Harrovians wo; Brentwood bye

Fourth Round
Bolton Wand bye; South Shore bye; Church bye; BLACKBURN R bye; WBA v Wolves 3–1; Small Heath Alliance bye; Staveley bye; Notts Co bye; Davenham bye; Burslem Port Vale bye; Middlesbro bye; Redcar bye; Old Carthusians bye; Old Westminsters bye; Brentwood v South Reading 3–0; Swifts bye

Fifth Round
South Shore v Notts Co 2–1; Swifts v Church 6–2; WBA v Old Carthusians 1–0; Redcar v Middlesbro 2–1; BLACKBURN R v Staveley 7–1; Small Heath Alliance v Davenham 2–1; Brentwood v Burslem Port Vale wo; Old Westminsters v Bolton Wand wo

Sixth Round
Small Heath Alliance v Redcar 2–0; WBA v Old Westminsters 6–0; Swifts v South Shore 2–1; BLACKBURN R v Brentwood 3–1

Semi-Final
BLACKBURN R v Swifts 2–1; WBA v Small Heath Alliance 4–0

BLACKBURN ROVERS **2**
WEST BROMWICH ALBION **0** (after a 0–0 draw)

Blackburn had reached the Final for a third time by virtue of a narrow 2–1 victory against Swifts in the semi-final. Their opponents this time were West Bromwich, who showed their mettle as cup fighters from the moment they set foot on the Oval pitch.

Few gave Albion a chance that day, but there was a shock in store for everyone, the Rovers included, for the match finished goalless. In fact, had it not been for some great defensive work by Suter, Turner and Arthur in Rovers' goal, Albion would certainly have won.

Rovers' excuse for a below-par display was that the team had got cold watching the Boat Race in the morning, had had to miss lunch, and left themselves barely enough time to drive to Kennington and get changed before the Final kicked-off. Rovers, in fact, very nearly won in the closing minutes when Fecitt's shot glanced a fraction the wrong side of a post.

The replay took place at the Derby County cricket ground, and for the first time the Cup was fought for and won outside London. Snow had fallen all through the morning of the match, only ceasing shortly before the kick-off, and yet a 12,000 crowd gathered to see the game.

Rovers, now with Walton in for Heyes, led at half-time with a goal by Sowerbutts, scored after twenty-six minutes as a result of a raid in which Walton and Fecitt were prominent. The same player again beat Roberts, but the Rovers players made no appeal for a goal, thinking him offside. Later it transpired that the referee would have been willing to allow the goal to stand, as Sowerbutts had been played on by an Albion defender.

Albion, with their famous rushing tactics, fought like demons, and constantly harried Arthur in the Rovers goal. At a time when Albion were striving hard for an equalizer, a memorable goal by centre-forward Jimmy Brown clinched victory for Rovers with seventeen minutes to go. An Albion attack broke down and Brown collected a pass from M'Intyre well inside his own half, and suddenly set off on a run for goal. He dribbled past man after man and at last slipped the ball between the Albion posts for a wonderful individualist goal.

Rovers were presented by the Football Association with a handsome silver shield to commemorate their achievement in winning the Cup three years in succession, surely now unrepeatable.

Blackburn Rovers: H. J. Arthur; Turner, Suter; Douglas, Forrest, M'Intyre; Walton, Strachan, Brown, Fecitt, J. Sowerbutts. (Heyes played in the first match at the Oval, but Walton took his place in the replay)
West Bromwich Albion: Roberts; H. Green, H. Bell; Horton, Perry, Timmins; Woodhall, T. Green, Bayliss, Loach, G. Bell
Referee: Major Marindin (Royal Engineers)

1886-7

First Round
Blackburn R v Halliwell wo; Astley Bridge v Burnley 3–3, 2–2 (both disqualified); Bolton Wand v South Shore 5–3; Witton v Oswaldtwistle R 3–2; 3rd Lanark RV v Higher Walton 5–0; Darwen v Heart of Midlothian 7–1; Renton v Accrington S 1–0; PNE v Queen's Pk, Glasgow 3–0; Glasgow Rangers v Everton wo; Cowlairs v Darwen Old Wand 4–1; Fleetwood Rangers v Newton Heath wo; Cliftonville, Belfast v Blackburn Park Road 2–2, 7–2; Partick Thistle v Blackburn Olympic 3–1; Church v Rawtenstall 1–1, 7–1; Gt Lever v Bootle 4–2; Rossendale bye; Crosswell's Brewery, Oldbury v Burton Swifts 1–0; Wolves v Matlock 6–0; Derby Junction v St George's Wellington 1–0; WBA v Burton Wand 6–0; Mitchell's St George's v Small Heath Alliance 3–1; ASTON VILLA v Wednesbury Old Ath 13–0; Derby Co v Aston Unity 4–1; Derby Midland v Birmingham Excelsior 3–3, 2–1; Walsall T v Derby St Luke's 3–3, 6–1; Lockwood Brothers v Long Eaton Rangers 1–0; Notts Rangers v Sheffield Club 3–0; Cleethorpe T v Mellors Limited 2–1; Notts Co v Basford R 13–0; Grimsby T v Sheffield Heeley 4–1; Staveley v Attercliffe 7–0; Nott'm Forest v Notts Olympic 3–0; Rotherham bye; Crewe Alex v Wrexham Olympic 4–1; Leek v Druids 2–1; Goldenhill v Macclesfield 4–2; Chirk v Hartford St John's 8–1; Burslem Port Vale v Davenham 1–1, 3–0; Oswestry v Bollington 8–2; Northwich Vic v Furness Vale R 10–0; Stoke-on-Trent v Carnarvon Wand 10–1; Chester bye; Gainsboro Tr v South Bank 4–1; West End, Newcastle v Sunderland 1–0; Redcar v Tyne 4–0; Grantham v Lincoln Lindum 1–0; Middlesbro v Bishop Auckland Church Institute 1–0; Horncastle v Darlington 2–1; Lincoln C bye; Chatham v Bournemouth R wo; Brentwood v Clapton 5–0; Old Wykehamists v Hanover Utd 3–0; Hotspur v Luton T 3–1; Caledonians v Hendon 2–1; Old Carthusians v Reading 2–1; Swifts v Luton Wand 13–0; Old Foresters v Cannon wo; Swindon T v Watford R 1–0; Maidenhead v South Reading 2–0; Chesham v Lyndhurst 4–2; Gt Marlow v Rochester 2–0; Upton Pk v 1st Surrey Rifles 9–0; Dulwich v Casuals 4–2; Old Brightonians v Clapham R 6–0; Old Etonians v Royal Engineers 1–0; Old Westminsters v Old Harrovians 4–1

Second Round
Darwen v Astley Bridge or Burnley wo; Bolton Wand v 3rd Lanark RV 3–2; Renton v Blackburn R 2–2, 2–0; PNE v Witton 6–0; Cowlairs v Rossendale 10–2; Cliftonville v Gt Lever 3–1; Partick Thistle v Fleetwood Rangers 7–0; Glasgow Rangers v Church 2–1; WBA v Derby Junction 2–1; Wolves v Crosswell's Brewery 14–0; ASTON VILLA v Derby Midland 14–0; Mitchell's St George's v Derby Co 2–1; Walsall T bye; Staveley v Rotherham 4–0; Notts Co v Notts Rangers 3–3, 5–0; Lockwood Brothers v Cleethorpes T 4–1; Nott'm Forest v Grimsby T 2–2, 1–0; Goldenhill v Chester 3–2; Leek v Oswestry 4–2; Crewe Alex v Stoke-on-Trent 6–4; Chirk v Northwich Vic 3–0; Burslem Port Vale bye; Lincoln C v Middlesbro 1–1, 2–0; Grantham v Redcar 3–2; Gainsboro Tr v West End 5–2; Horncastle bye; Old Carthusians v Crusaders 4–2; Caledonians v Old Wykehamists 1–0; Swifts v Swindon T 7–1; Chatham v Hotspur 1–0; Old Foresters bye; Old Westminsters v Old Brightonians 1–1, 3–1; Dulwich v Maidenhead 3–2; Gt Marlow v Upton Pk 4–0; Old Etonians v Chesham 7–1

Third Round
PNE v Renton 2–0; Darwen v Bolton Wand 4–3; Partick Thistle v Cliftonville 11–1; Glasgow Rangers v Cowlairs 3–2; Mitchell's St George's v Walsall T 7–2; WBA bye; ASTON VILLA v Wolves 2–2, 3–3, 2–0; Lockwood Brothers v Nott'm Forest 2–1; Notts Co v Staveley 3–0; Chirk v Goldenhill wo; Crewe Alex bye; Leek v Burslem Port Vale 2–2, 3–1; Lincoln C v Gainsboro Tr 2–2, 1–0; Horncastle v Grantham 2–0; Old Foresters v Chatham 4–1; Old Carthusians v Caledonians wo; Swifts bye; Old Westminsters v Old Etonians 3–0; Gt Marlow v Dulwich 2–0

Fourth Round
PNE bye; Darwen bye; Partick Thistle bye; Glasgow Rangers bye; WBA v Mitchell's St George's 1–0; ASTON VILLA bye; Lockwood Brothers bye; Notts Co bye; Chirk bye; Leek v Crewe Alex 1–0; Lincoln C bye; Horncastle bye; Old Foresters v Swifts 2–0; Old Carthusians bye; Old Westminsters bye; Gt Marlow bye

Fifth Round
PNE v Old Foresters 3–0; Notts Co v Gt Marlow 5–2; Darwen v Chirk 3–1; Old Westminsters v Partick Thistle 1–0; Glasgow Rangers v Lincoln C 3–0; Old Carthusians v Leek 2–0; ASTON VILLA v Horncastle 5–0; WBA v Lockwood Brothers 2–1

ASTON VILLA **2**
WEST BROMWICH ALBION **0**

For the first time, but by no means the last, the Final was fought out by two sides from the Birmingham area. Albion, after their splendid 3–1 win against the Scottish imports of Preston North End in the semi-final, were expected to win, and they certainly began the match as if they had the world at their feet.

Villa could thank their defence for not cracking before the Albion onslaught in the first twenty minutes. Warner played a brave game in goal, repeatedly foiling Albion's attempts to charge him, ball in hand, over his own goal-line.

Albion's forwards had tried so hard in the first half without the reward of a goal, that they began, perhaps understandably, to lose heart in the battle against the rugged Villa defenders. After half-time the play very definitely swung Villa's way, and they took the lead on the hour as a result of a ghastly error of judgement on the part of Albion goalkeeper Roberts. Assuming wrongly that Hodgetts was offside, Roberts made no attempt to save the winger's shot.

In the last minute, Hunter, Villa's centre-forward and captain, intercepted a back-pass, and, after colliding with Roberts, succeeded in stabbing the ball over the line while lying on the ground.

Aston Villa: Warner; Coulton, Simmonds; Yates, Dawson, Burton; Davis, Brown, Hunter, Vaughton, Hodgetts
West Bromwich Albion: Roberts; H. Green, Aldridge; Horton, Perry, Timmins; Woodhall, T. Green, Bayliss, Paddock, Pearson
Referee: Major Marindin (Royal Engineers)

Sixth Round
WBA v Notts Co 4–1; PNE v Old Carthusians 2–1; ASTON VILLA v Darwen 3–2; Glasgow Rangers v Old Westminsters 5–1

Semi-Final
ASTON VILLA v Glasgow Rangers 3–1; WBA v PNE 3–1

1887-8

First Round

Scarborough v Shankhouse *; South Bank v East End, Newcastle 3–2; Elswick Rangers v Church Institute 2–0; Whitburn v Middlesbro 0–4; Sunderland v Morpeth Harriers 3–2; West End, Newcastle v Redcar 5–1; Gateshead v Darlington 0–3; Church v Cliftonville, Belfast *; Oswaldtwistle R v Witton 3–4; Rawtenstall v Darwen 1–3; Blackburn R v Bury wo; Accrington S v Rossendale 11–0; Blackburn Park Road v Belfast Distillery 3–6; Burnley v Darwen Old Wand 4–0; Blackburn Olympic bye; Liverpool Stanley v Halliwell 1–4; Higher Walton v Heywood Central 8–1; Bootle v Workington 6–0; Hurst v Astley Bridge 5–3 (Hurst disqualified); PNE v Hyde 26–0; South Shore v Denton 2–0; Bolton Wand v Everton 2–2, 1–1, 2–1; Fleetwood Rangers v West Manchester 4–1; Stoke v Burslem Port Vale 1–0; Leek v Northwich Vic 2–4; Chirk v St Oswald's, Chester 4–1; Crewe Alex v Druids 5–0; Vale of Llangollen v Oswestry 0–2; Chester v Davenham 2–3; Macclesfield v Shrewsbury T 1–3; Over Wand v Wellington St George's 3–1; Wrexham Olympic bye; Aston Shakespeare v Burton Wand 2–3 (Burton disqualified); Walsall Swifts v Wolves 1–2; Walsall T v Mitchell's St George's 1–2; Warwick Co v Excelsior 0–5; Small Heath Alliance v Aston Unity 6–1; Stafford Road v Gt Bridge Unity 2–1; WBA v Wednesbury Old Ath 7–1; Burton Swifts v Birmingham Southfield 7–0; Oldbury T v Aston Villa 0–4; Staveley v Derby Co 1–2; Ecclesfield v Derby Midland 4–1; Sheffield v Lockwood Brothers 1–3; Long Eaton Rangers v Park Grange 6–3; Belper T v Sheff Wed 2–3; Owlerton v Eckington Works 2–1; Derby St Luke's v Derby Junction 2–3; Heeley v Attercliffe 9–0; Matlock v Rotherham 2–3; Basford R v Lincoln Albion 3–2; Notts Rangers v Jardines 10–1; Lincoln Lindum v Grantham 0–4; Notts Swifts v Nott'm Forest 1–2; Gainsboro Tr v Boston 7–0; Mellor's Limited v Notts Olympic 1–2; Lincoln C v Horncastle 4–1; Cleethorpes v Grimsby T 0–4; Lincoln Ramblers v Notts Co 0–9; Chatham v Luton T 5–1; Rochester v Royal Engineers 0–3; Hitchin v Old Wykehamists 2–9; Millwall R v Casuals *; Crusaders, Belfast v Lyndhurst 9–0; Lancing Old Boys v Old Etonians 2–4; Clapton v Old Westminsters 1–4; Old St Mark's v East Sheen 7–2; Reading v Dulwich 0–2; Gt Marlow v South Reading 4–1; Old Brightonians v Swindon T 1–0; Old Carthusians v Hanover Utd 5–0; Chesham v Watford R 1–3; Swifts v Maidenhead 3–1; London Caledonians v Old Foresters 1–6; Hendon v Old Harrovians 2–4; Hotspur bye

Second Round

Darlington v Elswick Rangers 4–3; Sunderland v Belfast Distillery 3–1; Middlesbro v South Bank 4–1; Shankhouse bye; Blackburn Olympic v Blackburn R 1–5; West End, Newcastle v Witton 2–4; Accrington S v Darwen Old Wand 3–2; Darwen v Church 2–0; Astley Bridge v Halliwell 0–4; Fleetwood Rangers v Higher Walton 1–3; Bootle v South Shore 1–1 (Bootle claimed match); PNE v Bolton Wand 9–1; Wrexham Olympic v Davenham 1–2; Chirk v Shrewsbury T 10–2; Northwich Vic v Crewe Alex 1–0; Over Wand v Stoke-on-Trent 0–3; Oswestry bye; Burton Swifts v Gt Bridge Unity 2–5; Lockwood Brothers bye; Small Heath Alliance v Aston Villa 0–4; Wolves v Aston Shakespeare 3–0; Mitchell's St George's v WBA 0–1; Birmingham Excelsior bye; Owlerton v Sheffield Heeley 1–2; Derby Junction v Rotherham 3–0; Long Eaton Rangers v Sheff Wed 1–2; Derby Co v Ecclesfield 6–0; Lincoln C v Gainsboro Tr 2–1; Grantham v Notts Rangers 0–4; Notts Co v Basford R wo; Nott'm Forest v Mellors Limited 2–0; Grimsby T bye; Old Etonians v Old St Mark's 3–2; Chatham v Royal Engineers 3–1; Old Wykehamists v Crusaders, Belfast 2–3; Old Westminsters v Millwall R 8–1; Dulwich v Hotspur 2–0; Gt Marlow v Old Foresters 2–3; Old Harrovians v Old Brightonians 0–4; Watford R v Old Carthusians 1–3; Swifts bye

Third Round

Darlington v Shankhouse 0–2; Middlesbro v Sunderland 2–2, 2–4; Accrington S v Blackburn R 1–3; Darwen v Witton 1–1, 2–0; Higher Walton v Bootle 1–6; PNE v Halliwell 6–0; Stoke-on-Trent v Oswestry 3–0; Davenham v Chirk 1–6; Crewe Alex bye; Birmingham Excelsior v Gt Bridge Unity 1–2; WBA v Wolves 2–0; Aston Villa bye; Derby Junction v Lockwood Brothers 2–1; Derby Co v Owlerton 6–2; Sheff Wed bye; Grimsby T v Lincoln C 2–0; Nott'm Forest v Notts Co 2–1; Notts Rangers bye; Crusaders, Belfast v Chatham 4–0; Old Etonians v Old Westminsters 7–2; Dulwich v Swifts 1–3; Old Brightonians v Old Carthusians 0–5; Old Foresters bye

* Score unknown

WEST BROMWICH ALBION **2**
PRESTON NORTH END **1**

After two Final defeats in successive years, Albion won at the third attempt. Preston, their opponents, had annihilated Hyde 26–0 in an earlier round, to this day a record score in the Cup competition, and had forty-three consecutive victories to their credit and a Cup goal-tally of fifty for and only two against.

They were so supremely confident of winning the Final, so the story goes, that their captain actually asked if the team could be photographed with the trophy before the match.

For the first time a ground was closed for a football match – on a 17,000 crowd inside the Oval – and unfancied Albion gained a popular, if surprising, victory. A side of purely local Staffordshire extraction, with a weekly wage bill of £10, took on 'Proud Preston', a team of highly paid artists, and won by two goals (Bayliss and Woodhall) to one, after Dewhurst's equalizer for Preston had been hotly disputed.

The open, long-passing game of West Bromwich, backed by their tremendous enthusiasm, swept aside Preston's artistry and achieved a victory largely inspired by their diminutive outside-right Bassett, essentially a man for the big occasion.

West Bromwich Albion: Roberts; Aldridge, Green; Horton, Perry, Timmins; Bassett, Woodhall, Bayliss, Wilson, Pearson
Preston North End: Dr R. H. Mills-Roberts; Howarth, N. J. Ross; Holmes, Russell, Graham; Gordon, J. Ross, J. Goodall, F. Dewhurst, Drummond
Referee: Major Marindin (Royal Engineers)

Fourth Round
Gt Bridge Unity v Bootle 2–1; Nott'm Forest v Old Etonians 6–0; Old Foresters v Grimsby T 4–2; Crewe Alex v Swifts 2–2 (Swifts disqualified); Crusaders, Belfast v Sheff Wed 0–1; Shankhouse v Aston Villa 0–9; Darwen v Notts Rangers 3–1; Chirk bye; Derby Junction bye; Derby Co bye; WBA bye; Middlesbro bye; Blackburn R bye; Old Carthusians bye; PNE bye; Stoke-on-Trent bye

Fifth Round
Old Carthusians v Gt Bridge Unity 2–0; Darwen v Blackburn R 0–3; WBA v Stoke-on-Trent 4–1; Crewe Alex v Derby Co 1–0; Aston Villa v PNE 1–3; Middlesbro v Old Foresters 4–0; Derby Junction v Chirk 1–0; Nott'm Forest v Sheff Wed 2–4

Sixth Round
WBA v Old Carthusians 4–2; Middlesbro v Crewe Alex 0–2; Derby Junction v Blackburn R 2–1; Sheff Wed v PNE 1–3
Semi-Final
WBA v Derby Junction 3–0; PNE v Crewe Alex 4–0

1888–9

First Round
Grimsby T v Sunderland Alb 3–1; Bootle v PNE 0–3; Halliwell v Crewe Alex 2–2, 5–1;
Birmingham St George's v Long Eaton Rangers 3–2; Chatham v South Shore 2–1;
Nott'm Forest v Linfield A wo; Small Heath v WBA 2–3; Burnley v Old Westminsters 4–3;
WOLVES v Old Carthusians 4–3; Walsall T Swifts v Sheffield Heeley 5–1; Sheff Wed v
Notts Rangers 1–1, 3–0; Notts Co v Old Brightonians 2–0; Blackburn R v Accrington S 1–1, 5–0;
Swifts v Wrexham 3–1; Aston Villa v Witton 3–2; Derby Co v Derby Junction 1–0

Second Round
Grimsby T v PNE 0–2; Halliwell v Birmingham St George's 2–3; Chatham v Nott'm Forest
1–1, 2–2, 3–2; WBA v Burnley 5–1; WOLVES v Walsall T Swifts 6–1; Sheff Wed v Notts Co
3–2; Blackburn R v Swifts wo; Aston Villa v Derby Co 5–3

Third Round
PNE v Birmingham St George's 2–0; Chatham v WBA 1–10; WOLVES v Sheff Wed 5–0;
Blackburn R v Aston Villa 8–1

Semi-Final
PNE v WBA 1–0; WOLVES v Blackburn R 1–1, 3–1

Preston North End: Dr R. H. Mills-Roberts; Howarth, Homes; Drummond, Russell, Graham;
Gordon, Ross, J. Goodall, F. Dewhurst, Thompson
Wolverhampton Wanderers: Baynton; Baugh, Mason; Fletcher, Allen, Lowder; Hunter,
Wykes, Broodie, Woods, Knight
Referee: Major Marindin (Royal Engineers)

PRESTON NORTH END **3**
WOLVERHAMPTON WANDERERS **0**

In 1888, the year of the formation of the Football League, the scheme put forward by Gregson (Secretary of the Lancashire Association) to divide the Cup competition into two sections – a Qualifying Competition and a Competition Proper – was accepted. Many of the 149 clubs entering the competition of the 1888–9 season employed professional players, and the new system was introduced so that the best clubs would not have to waste their time against weak opponents in meaningless games.

Against this background, Preston, sweeping away their previous disappointments, had an incredibly successful season. They won the League Championship without losing a match and the Cup without conceding a goal – figures which have never since been equalled.

Preston were the dominant team of the day. The side was chosen with marvellous precision, each man being an expert in his position. The training was thorough, and individual players were encouraged to subordinate their own interests to those of the team as a whole.

Although no southern team was involved, Preston's reputation was such that a record crowd of 23,000 was attracted to the Oval for the Final. The gates were closed an hour before the start, and one of the umpires had great difficulty getting into the ground.

The match began with a lot of wild rushing and reckless kicking, as the early excitement seemed to get the better of both teams. But they soon settled down, and Knight and Wood missed good early chances for the Wolves. Preston's game of short passes to feet gave them the edge over Wolves' long passes in the air, and they went into the lead in less than fifteen minutes. Baynton punched out Ross's shot and Dewhurst thumped the ball back between the posts to the accompaniment of loud cheers.

Ten minutes later Ross dodged Allen and Mason and hit a shot straight at Baynton. The ball slipped through the goalkeeper's fingers and behind the goal-line: 2–0 to Preston.

Wolves directed several long shots at Mills-Roberts during the early part of the second half, but these would have been more dangerous if the Wolves men had dribbled or passed when nearer to the Preston goal. In fact, only two or three shots had been even moderately difficult to stop.

Twenty minutes from time a neat interchange of passes between Gordon and Ross allowed the latter finally to dribble to the by-line and cross the ball over. Mason miscued his attempted clearance, Dewhurst crashed into Baynton, and Thompson, running in, scored Preston's third.

1889–90

First Round
PNE v Newton Heath 6–1; Lincoln C v Chester 2–0; Bolton Wand v Belfast Distillery 10–1;
Sheff Utd v Burnley 2–1; SHEFF WED v Swifts 6–1; Accrington S v WBA 3–1; Notts Co v
Birmingham St George's 4–4, 6–2; South Shore v Aston Villa 2–4; Bootle v Sunderland Alb 1–3;
Derby Midland v Nott'm Forest 3–0; BLACKBURN R v Sunderland 4–2; Newcastle West End v
Grimsby T 1–2; Wolves v Old Carthusians 2–0; Small Heath v Clapton 3–1; Stoke v
Old Westminsters 3–0; Everton v Derby Co 11–2

Second Round
PNE v Lincoln C 4–0; Bolton Wand v Sheff Utd 13–0; SHEFF WED v Accrington S 2–1;
Notts Co v Aston Villa 4–1; Bootle v Derby Midland 2–1; BLACKBURN R v Grimsby T 3–0;
Wolves v Small Heath 2–1; Stoke v Everton 4–2

Third Round
PNE v Bolton Wand 2–3; SHEFF WED v Notts Co 2–1; Bootle v BLACKBURN R 0–7;
Wolves v Stoke 3–2

Semi-Final
Bolton Wand v SHEFF WED 1–2; BLACKBURN R v Wolves 1–0

BLACKBURN ROVERS **6**
SHEFFIELD WEDNESDAY **1**

The 1890 Final produced a first-ever 'Battle of the Roses'. Yorkshire were represented by Sheffield Wednesday, making their first appearance at the Oval, and Lancashire by Blackburn Rovers, winners of three successive Finals there in the middle eighties.

Blackburn included only three survivors from their Cup-winning sides — Forrest, Lofthouse and Walton — but, with no fewer than nine internationals now in their ranks, they were considered to be even more powerful than before.

Wednesday's players were all English, in fact all local products, and they came down to London hoping to emulate the purely local West Bromwich team that had put paid to Preston's hopes three years earlier.

For poor Wednesday, however, the Final was nothing less than traumatic. Instead of being inspired by the occasion, they found it altogether too much for them and were nervous from the start. Rovers romped away with the Cup and notched six goals into the bargain. No Final team has scored more.

The Blackburn forwards were in great form, outside-left Townley scoring three times to set another record that has never been beaten in a Final. Walton, Southworth and Lofthouse got the other Blackburn goals and Mumford was on target for Wednesday.

Blackburn Rovers: J. K. Horne; Southworth (Jas.), Forbes; Barton, Dewar, Forrest; Lofthouse, Campbell, Southworth (John), Walton, Townley
Sheffield Wednesday: Smith (J.); Brayshaw, H. Morley; Dungworth, Betts, Waller; Ingram, Woodhouse, Bennett, Mumford, Cawley
Referee: Major Marindin (Royal Engineers)

1890–1

First Round
Middlesbro Ir v BLACKBURN R 0–3; Chester v Lincoln C 1–0; Accrington S v Bolton Wand 2–2, 5–1; Long Eaton Rangers v Wolves 1–2; Royal Arsenal v Derby Co 1–2; Sheff Wed v Halliwell 12–0; Crusaders, Belfast v Birmingham St George's 0–2; WBA v Old Westminsters wo; Darwen v Kidderminster 13–0; Sunderland v Everton 1–0; Clapton v Nott'm Forest 0–14; Sunderland Alb v 93rd Highlanders 2–0; Sheff Utd v NOTTS CO 1–9; Burnley v Crewe Alex 4–2; Stoke v PNE 3–0; Aston Villa v Casuals 13–1

Second Round
BLACKBURN R v Chester 7–0; Accrington S v Wolves 2–3; Derby Co v Sheff Wed 2–3; Birmingham St George's v WBA 0–3; Darwen v Sunderland 0–2; Nott'm Forest v Sunderland Alb 1–1, 0–0, 5–0; NOTTS CO v Burnley 2–1; Stoke v Aston Villa 3–0

Third Round
BLACKBURN R v Wolves 2–0; Sheff Wed v WBA 0–2; Sunderland v Nott'm Forest 4–0; NOTTS CO v Stoke 1–0

Semi-Final
BLACKBURN R v WBA 3–2; Sunderland v NOTTS CO 3–3, 0–2

BLACKBURN ROVERS **3**
NOTTS COUNTY **1**

Strange though it may seem for all the tremendous feats performed by the Rovers in the competition, it was Notts County who most people thought would win the 1891 Final. Only a week before the Final, for example, County had beaten the holders 7–1 in a League match at Blackburn. The writing was surely on the wall.

Rovers, however, proved to be quicker on the ball, played better as a team, and their shooting was much more dangerous than County's. The defence seldom put a foot wrong, and Dewar at centre-half played the game of his life.

Nine minutes after the start Lofthouse's throw-in from near the corner-flag led to Rovers' opening goal, probably scored by Dewar in a terrific scramble for the ball. Thirteen minutes later Southworth put Rovers further ahead, and Townley headed a third four minutes after that.

The supremacy of the 'Blue and Whites' was not seriously challenged after they had changed round, three goals to the good, though Oswald succeeded in reducing the deficit with a goal for County in the seventy-first minute.

By their success, Blackburn equalled the record of the Wanderers team which had won the Cup five times during the first seven years of its existence.

Blackburn Rovers: Pennington; Brandon, J. Forbes; Barton, Dewar, Forrest; Lofthouse, Walton, Southworth (John), Hall, Townley
Notts County: Thraves; Ferguson, Hendry; H. Osborne, Calderhead, Shelton; A. McGregor, McInnes, Oswald, Locker, H. B. Daft
Referee: C. J. Hughes (Northwich)

1891–2

First Round
Old Westminsters v WBA 2–3; Blackburn R v Derby Co 4–1; Sheff Wed v Bolton Wand 4–1;
Small Heath v Royal Arsenal 5–1; Sunderland Alb v Birmingham St George's 4–0;
Nott'm Forest v Newcastle East End 2–1; Luton T v Middlesbro 0–3; PNE v Middlesbro Ir 6–0;
Crewe Alex v Wolves 2–2, 1–4; Blackpool v Sheff Utd 0–3; ASTON VILLA v Heanor T 4–1;
Bootle v Darwen 0–3; Crusaders, Belfast v Accrington S 1–4; Sunderland v Notts Co 4–0; Everton v
Burnley 1–3; Stoke v Casuals 3–0

Second Round
WBA v Blackburn R 3–1; Sheff Wed v Small Heath 2–0; Sunderland Alb v Nott'm Forest 0–1;
Middlesbro v PNE 1–2; Wolves v Sheff Utd 3–1; ASTON VILLA v Darwen 2–0; Accrington S v
Sunderland 1–3; Burnley v Stoke 1–3

Third Round
WBA v Sheff Wed 2–1; Nott'm Forest v PNE 2–1; Wolves v Aston Villa 1–3; Sunderland v Stoke
2–2, 4–0

Semi-Final
WBA v Nott'm Forest 1–1, 1–1, 6–2; ASTON VILLA v Sunderland 4–1

WEST BROMWICH ALBION **3**
ASTON VILLA **0**

The 1892 Final was the last to be played at Kennington Oval and the first in which goal-nets were used.

Five years earlier the two Midland rivals, Albion and Villa, had staged the first Final with a provincial 'local derby' atmosphere, and here they were together again.

Albion's form throughout the season had been inconsistent, and when Villa, semi-final conquerors of the great Sunderland team of 'all the talents', began the match in such good attacking form, it looked odds-on that Villa would win the Cup for the second time.

But there was a surprise in store for them. A sudden break and Bassett was sprinting down the right wing to centre perfectly for Geddes to shoot home. Albion, improbably, were in the lead.

In a subtle way the Albion half-backs, Groves, Perry and Reynolds, had been taking a grip on affairs in midfield. Before half-time another brilliant run by Bassett and another perfect centre gave Nicholls the chance to send Albion in with a comfortable 2–0 lead at the interval.

The match was virtually over. Villa's forwards continued to be frustrated in the second half, and Reynolds completed the rout near the end with a third Albion goal from a long shot.

West Bromwich Albion: Reader; Nicholson, M'Culloch; Reynolds, Perry, Groves; Bassett, M'Leod, Nicholls, Pearson, Geddes
Aston Villa: Warner; Evans, Cox; Devey (H.), Cowan, Baird; Athersmith, Devey (J.), Dickson, Campbell, Hodgetts
Referee: J. C. Clegg (Sheffield)

1892–3

First Round
EVERTON v WBA 4–1; Nott'm Forest v Casuals 4–0; Sheff Wed v Derby Co 3–2; Burnley v Small Heath 2–0; Accrington S v Stoke 2–1; PNE v Burton Swifts 9–2; Marlow v Middlesbro Ir 1–3; Notts Co v Shankhouse 4–0; WOLVES v Bolton Wand 1–1, 2–1; Newcastle Utd v Middlesbro 2–3; Darwen v Aston Villa 5–4; Grimsby T v Stockton 5–0; Blackburn R v Newton Heath 4–0; Loughborough v Northwich Vic 1–2; Blackpool v Sheff Utd 1–3; Sunderland v Royal Arsenal 6–0

Second Round
EVERTON v Nott'm Forest 4–2; Sheff Wed v Burnley 1–0; Accrington S v PNE 1–4; Middlesbro Ir v Notts Co 3–2; WOLVES v Middlesbro 2–1; Darwen v Grimsby T 2–0; Blackburn R v Northwich Vic 4–1; Sheff Utd v Sunderland 1–3

Third Round
EVERTON v Sheff Wed 3–0; PNE v Middlesbro Ir 2–2, 7–0; WOLVES v Darwen 5–0; Blackburn R v Sunderland 3–0

Semi-Final
EVERTON v PNE 2–2, 0–0, 2–1; WOLVES v Blackburn R 2–1

WOLVERHAMPTON WANDERERS **1**
EVERTON **0**

The Final was never again to be played at the Oval, the cricket authorities fearing that the huge crowds now gathering to watch the big match would damage their world-famous pitch, so the Cup celebrated its twenty-first birthday at the Manchester Athletic Club ground at Fallowfield.

Part of the 45,000 crowd – about double the previous record – overflowed along the touch-lines, and it was a wonder that the game ever started.

Everton took the field as strong favourites, not only because they had defeated Preston in a semi-final tie which had gone to three games, but because they were regarded as a genuinely talented side. A week before the Final, Everton sent their reserve side to Wolverhampton for a League fixture, and the 'stiffs', embarrassingly for the Wolves, won 4–2.

However, once again the Final favourites crashed. Wolves' bustling tactics threw Everton completely out of their stride, the latter's close passing game proving totally ineffective. It was a triumph of teamwork on the part of Wolves' all-English team, though they did have an outstanding individual in outside-right Topham. He had fired several powerful shots at goal, and one of them sent a policeman in the crowd flying. Harry Allen, a splendid centre-half, played a captain's part by scoring the second-half goal that won the Cup.

Wolverhampton Wanderers: Rose; Baugh, Swift; Malpass, Allen, Kinsey; R. Topham, Wykes, Butcher, Wood, Griffin
Everton: Williams; Howarth, Kelso; Stewart, Holt, Boyle; Latta, Gordon, Maxwell, Chadwick, Milward
Referee: C. J. Hughes (Northwich)

1893–4

First Round
Middlesbro Ir v Luton T 2–1; Nott'm Forest v Heanor T 1–0; NOTTS CO v Burnley 1–0; Stockport Co v Burton Wand 0–1; Leicester Fosse v South Shore 2–1; Derby Co v Darwen 2–0; Newton Heath v Middlesbro 4–0; WBA v Blackburn R 2–3; Newcastle Utd v Sheff Utd 2–0; Small Heath v BOLTON WAND 3–4; Liverpool v Grimsby T 3–0; PNE v Reading 18–0; Woolwich Arsenal v Sheff Wed 1–2; Stoke v Everton 1–0; Sunderland v Accrington S 3–0; Aston Villa v Wolves 4–2

Second Round
Middlesbro Ir v Nott'm Forest 0–2; NOTTS CO v Burton Wand 2–0; Leicester Fosse v Derby Co 0–0, 0–3; Newton Heath v Blackburn R 0–0, 1–5; Newcastle Utd v BOLTON WAND 1–2; Liverpool v PNE 3–2; Sheff Wed v Stoke 1–0; Sunderland v Aston Villa 2–2, 1–3

Third Round
Nott'm Forest v NOTTS CO 1–1, 1–4; Derby Co v Blackburn R 1–4; BOLTON WAND v Liverpool 3–0; Sheff Wed v Aston Villa 3–2

Semi-Final
NOTTS CO v Blackburn R 1–0; BOLTON WAND v Sheff Wed 2–1

NOTTS COUNTY **4**
BOLTON WANDERERS **1**

The Football Association chose Goodison Park, Liverpool as the venue for the 1894 Final, and every precaution was taken to avoid a repetition of the previous year's fiasco at Fallowfield. The 37,000 crowd was smaller than anticipated, many people obviously fearful of being hurt in a crush.

County ran away with the Cup, scoring four goals, and becoming the first Second Division club to triumph in a Final. What the score might have been but for Sutcliffe, the Bolton goalkeeper, whom the County forwards pounded the whole afternoon, can only be imagined.

Logan, playing a superb game at centre-forward, was still able to register a hat-trick and thereby equal Townley's feat for Blackburn in 1890. Watson was County's other scorer, and Cassidy replied for Bolton.

Bolton tried their best, but were labouring under severe disadvantages. Paton was swathed in bandages, Gardiner wasn't fit, Bentley was ill, Somerville was troubled with a facial injury and shouldn't have played, and Hughes got hurt only five minutes after the start.

County, though in the Second Division, were the best side in the country for a period of about six weeks, which, fortunately for them, coincided with the Final.

Notts County: Toone; Harper, Hendry; Bramley, Calderhead, A. Shelton; Watson, Donnelly, Logan, Bruce, H. B. Daft
Bolton Wanderers: Sutcliffe; Somerville, Jones; Gardiner, Paton, Hughes; Dickinson, Wilson, Tannahill, Bentley, Cassidy
Referee: C. J. Hughes (Northwich)

1894–5

First Round
ASTON VILLA v Derby Co 2–1; Newcastle Utd v Burnley 2–1; Barnsley St Peter's v Liverpool 1–2; Southampton St Mary's v Nott'm Forest 1–4; Sunderland v Fairfield 11–1; Luton T v PNE 0–2; Bolton Wand v Woolwich Arsenal 1–0; Bury v Leicester Fosse 4–1; Sheff Utd v Millwall A 3–1; Small Heath v WBA 1–2; Darwen v Wolves 0–0, 0–2; Newton Heath v Stoke 2–3; Sheff Wed v Notts Co 5–1; Middlesbro v Chesterfield 4–0; Southport Central v Everton 0–3; Burton Wand v Blackburn R 1–2

Second Round
ASTON VILLA v Newcastle Utd 7–1; Liverpool v Nott'm Forest 0–2; Sunderland v PNE 2–0; Bolton Wand v Bury 1–0; Sheff Utd v WBA 1–1, 1–2; Wolves v Stoke 2–0; Sheff Wed v Middlesbro 6–1; Everton v Blackburn R 1–1, 3–2

Third Round
ASTON VILLA v Nott'm Forest 6–2; Sunderland v Bolton Wand 2–1; WBA v Wolves 1–0; Sheff Wed v Everton 2–0

Semi-Final
ASTON VILLA v Sunderland 2–1; WBA v Sheff Wed 2–0

ASTON VILLA **1**
WEST BROMWICH ALBION **0**

Villa and Albion had played the last Final at the Oval, and these same two famous clubs were now contesting the first to be held at the Crystal Palace. They had faced each other twice in Finals – in 1887 and 1892 – and, with honours even, this was to be the decider.

Most of the 42,000 crowd missed the goal that won the match for Villa. It came, dramatically, after only thirty seconds, though there was some doubt about who scored it.

Devey, the Villa centre-forward, swung the ball out to his inside-left, Hodgetts. Hodgetts' long cross-pass found Athersmith on the right, and he centred for Chatt to shoot on the half-volley. The ball looked destined for the net but was diverted, either by goalkeeper Reader or by a defender on the line, to Devey who scored.

Most people in the ground had been prepared to credit Chatt with the goal, but Devey is now thought to have got the final, perhaps involuntary touch. The goal has been known ever since as Villa's 'Crystal Palace thunderbolt'.

Villa were the favourites and, for once, the favourites not only won but deserved to win. Only some great goalkeeping by 'Kicker' Reader and courageous defence, especially by right-back Williams, prevented the Villa forwards from adding to their score. Albion were unlucky, also, to lose centre-half Higgins for a while with a cut head. He later returned to the fray but with his head heavily bandaged.

McLeod and Bassett, the latter once again playing brilliantly on the right wing, were still trying desperately to the end to save the day for Albion. It was Bassett's last Final and probably his finest, though he often found himself crowded off the ball by the big Villa defenders. He appeared in three Finals and earned two winners' medals.

In September 1895 the Cup was stolen from the shop window of William Shillcock, football and football boot manufacturer, of Newtown Row, Birmingham. Police investigation and the offer of a £10 reward failed to produce any result. The original Cup has never been seen or heard of since, and Villa were fined £25 – a sum which paid for the new trophy provided by Messrs Vaughton's Ltd of Birmingham.

Aston Villa: Wilkes; Spencer, Welford; Reynolds, Cowan (Jas.), Russell; Athersmith, Chatt, Devey (J.), Hodgetts, Smith (S.)
West Bromwich Albion: Reader; Williams, Horton; Taggart, Higgins, T. Perry; Bassett, McLeod, Richards, Hutchinson, Banks
Referee: J. Lewis (Blackburn)

1895–6

First Round
Notts Co v WOLVES 2–2, 3–4; Liverpool v Millwall A 4–1; Burnley v Woolwich Arsenal 6–1; Stoke v Spurs 5–0; Derby Co v Aston Villa 4–2; Newton Heath v Kettering 2–1; Darwen v Grimsby T 0–2; Blackburn R v WBA 1–2; Southampton St Mary's v SHEFF WED 2–3; Sunderland v PNE 4–1; Nott'm Forest v Everton 0–2; Burton Wand v Sheff Utd 1–1, 0–1; Blackpool v Burton Swifts 4–1; Crewe Alex v Bolton Wand 0–4; Chesterfield v Newcastle Utd 0–4; Small Heath v Bury 1–4

Second Round
WOLVES V Liverpool 2–0; Burnley v Stoke 1–1, 1–7; Derby Co v Newton Heath 1–1, 5–1; Grimsby T v WBA 1–1, 0–3; SHEFF WED v Sunderland 2–1; Everton v Sheff Utd 3–0; Blackpool v Bolton Wand 0–2; Newcastle Utd v Bury 1–3

Third Round
WOLVES v Stoke 3–0; Derby Co v WBA 1–0; SHEFF WED v Everton 4–0; Bolton Wand v Bury 2–0

Semi-Final
WOLVES v Derby Co 2–1; SHEFF WED v Bolton Wand 1–1, 3–1

SHEFFIELD WEDNESDAY **2**
WOLVERHAMPTON WANDERERS **1**

After Wolves had won the Cup in 1893, the club's chairman had obtained permission from the Football Association to present each player with a ten-inch high silver replica of the trophy. One of these models was used as a copy for the new Cup.

The first club to win the new trophy were Sheffield Wednesday, semi-finalists in the previous two seasons, and their opponents were Wolves, now disputing their third Final in eight seasons.

The hero of a fierce match was Wednesday's outside-left Spiksley, and once again the Crystal Palace crowd saw a very early goal. In just over a minute a brilliant run by Davis and Spiksley ended with the latter giving Wednesday the lead, but Black quickly hooked in an equalizer for Wolves from close to the post.

Wednesday, however, were not to be subdued, and before half-time Spiksley put them ahead again with a terrific shot that hit an upright on its way into the net. The ball had in fact been hit with such force that it rebounded into the field of play before Tennant realized where the shot had gone. It was only after the final whistle had been blown, and he had asked the Wednesday captain where the replay was going to be, that the Wolves goalkeeper learnt that two shots had beaten him that afternoon.

Wednesday were never really expected to reach the Final, not being exceptionally strong in the League, yet they always managed to rise to the occasion in the Cup. At their Olive Grove ground they were reckoned invincible in a cup-tie. In the Final they had the advantage of Spiksley's early goal. However, with a few minutes remaining of one of the best Finals for several years and Wednesday 2–1 in the lead, Wolves came back into the game and forced Wednesday on to the defensive, bombarding Massey with shot after shot.

Wednesday's play deteriorated in the last quarter of an hour, excitement getting the better of some of their players, but they were still able to make two breakaways, and Brady hit the crossbar in one of them.

Sheffield Wednesday: Massey; Earp, Langley; H. Brandon, Crawshaw, Petrie; Brash, Brady, L. Bell, Davis, Spiksley
Wolverhampton Wanderers: Tennant; Baugh, Dunn; Owen, Malpass, Griffiths; Tonks, Henderson, Beats, Wood, Black
Referee: Captain W. Simpson

1896–7

First Round
ASTON VILLA v Newcastle Utd 5–1; Small Heath v Notts Co 1–2; PNE v Man C 6–0; Stoke v Glossop NE 5–0; Burnley v Sunderland 0–1; Nott'm Forest v Sheff Wed 1–0; Luton T v WBA 0–1; Liverpool v Burton Swifts 4–3; EVERTON v Burton Wand 5–2; Bury v Stockton 0–0, 12–1; Blackburn R v Sheff Utd 2–1; Millwall A v Wolves 1–2; Derby Co v Barnsley St Peter's 8–1; Bolton Wand v Grimsby T 0–0, 3–3, 3–2; Heanor T v Southampton St Mary's 1–1, 0–1; Newton Heath v Kettering 5–1

Second Round
ASTON VILLA v Notts Co 2–1; PNE v Stoke 2–1; Sunderland v Nott'm Forest 1–3; WBA v Liverpool 1–2; EVERTON v Bury 3–0; Blackburn R v Wolves 2–1; Derby Co v Bolton Wand 4–1; Southampton St Mary's v Newton Heath 1–1, 1–3

Third Round
ASTON VILLA v PNE 1–1, 0–0, 3–2; Nott'm Forest v Liverpool 1–1, 0–1; EVERTON v Blackburn R 2–0; Derby Co v Newton Heath 2–0

Semi-Final
ASTON VILLA v Liverpool 3–0; EVERTON v Derby Co 3–2

Aston Villa: Whitehouse; Spencer, Evans; Reynolds, Cowan (Jas.), Crabtree; Athersmith, Devey (J.), Campbell, Wheldon, Cowan (John)
Everton: Menham; Meecham, Storrier; Boyle, Holt, Stewart; Taylor, Bell, Hartley, Chadwick, Milward
Referee: J. Lewis (Blackburn)

ASTON VILLA **3**
EVERTON **2**

If the first two matches at the Crystal Palace had produced sensational openings, the third was perhaps the greatest Final ever played. Villa that year had taken the League championship by eleven points, and, by also winning the Final 3–2 against Everton, equalled Preston's 'double' feat of 1889.

All five goals came within the space of twenty-five minutes before half-time, and the lead changed hands three times. The more consistent Villa played the better football and deserved their victory. Bell played an inspired game for Everton at inside-right, but fate and a wonderful line of half-backs were against them, and Villa took the Cup back to Birmingham for the third time.

Villa seemed to settle down at once, the half-backs looking far too clever for their opponents. Many times the ball was played up to the front men with tremendous accuracy, and time after time the Villa half-backs broke up an Everton attack. It was all that the stout Everton defence could do to keep the eager Villa forwards at bay. Athersmith twice got into dangerous positions but was forced to shoot from difficult angles and both times the ball went behind.

Villa could not be denied for long, and they scored their first after eighteen minutes. Athersmith and Devey worked their way down the right, and Devey sent Campbell through to fire in a long shot which swerved in the wind and flew into the net giving Menham no chance. Villa kept the advantage for only five minutes. After that a brilliant, high-speed move between Hartley and Bell ended with Bell crashing the ball past Whitehouse from close range.

The game was still less than half an hour old when Everton went 2–1 up. James Cowan gave away a free-kick, and the taker, Boyle, hit it straight into the net.

For ten minutes Everton attacked strongly and looked certain to score a third. Yet, in a match which continued to be played at a dazzling pace, Villa grabbed two goals in the course of five minutes. First Wheldon put the score level from Crabtree's free-kick, and then Villa took the lead for a second time when Athersmith and Reynolds between them won a corner on the right. Reynolds lofted the ball across goal and Crabtree dashed forward, unmarked, to head in.

Whitehouse made two good saves for Villa in the three minutes remaining to the interval. The cut and thrust continued throughout the second half, but no further goals were added.

1897–8

First Round
Southampton St Mary's v Leicester Fosse 2–1; PNE v Newcastle Utd 1–2; Luton T v Bolton Wand 0–1; Man C v Wigan C 1–0; WBA v New Brighton Tower 2–0; Sunderland v Sheff Wed 0–1; NOTT'M FOREST v Grimsby T 4–0; Long Eaton Rangers v Gainsboro Tr 0–1; Liverpool v Hucknall St John's 2–0; Newton Heath v Walsall 1–0; Notts Co v Wolves 0–1; DERBY CO v Aston Villa 1–0; Burnley v Woolwich Arsenal 3–1; Burslem Port Vale v Sheff Utd 1–1, 2–1; Everton v Blackburn R 1–0; Bury v Stoke 1–2

Second Round
Southampton St Mary's v Newcastle Utd 1–0; Bolton Wand v Man C 1–0; WBA v Sheff Wed 1–0; NOTT'M FOREST v Gainsboro Tr 4–0; Liverpool v Newton Heath 0–0, 2–1; Wolves v DERBY CO 0–1; Burnley v Burslem Port Vale 3–0; Everton v Stoke 0–0, 5–1

Third Round
Southampton St Mary's v Bolton Wand 0–0, 4–0; WBA v NOTT'M FOREST 2–3; Liverpool v DERBY CO 1–1, 1–5; Burnley v Everton 1–3

Semi-Final
Southampton St Mary's v NOTT'M FOREST 1–1, 0–2; DERBY CO v Everton 3–1

NOTTINGHAM FOREST **3**
DERBY COUNTY **1**

Derby, the favourites, had knocked out both the previous year's finalists earlier in the competition and had beaten Forest 5–0 in a League match only one week before the Final.

Nevertheless from the very beginning it was Forest most of the way, although the standard of play generally fell a long way behind the superb exhibition provided by Villa and Everton the previous year. In an early attack, Methven was lucky to get in the way of Capes's shot, after McInnes and Richards had dallied unnecessarily.

One of the Forest team, Spouncer, had missed most of the pre-Final training sessions, being unable to obtain leave of absence from his work, but it was Spouncer who featured in the build-up to the first goal after nineteen minutes. Benbow raced down the middle and clipped a fine pass out to Spouncer on the left. The winger was fouled by Cox near the by-line, and Wragg's free-kick went to Capes whose low shot went through the defensive wall and beat Fryer in goal.

Derby began to have slightly the better of things after the goal, and in the thirty-first minute the legendary Steve Bloomer headed a good goal from Leiper's expertly placed free-kick, the ball striking the crossbar and bouncing down behind Allsop. Forest made a concerted effort as the interval approached and scored the goal that effectively won the Cup when Fryer parried Richards' shot and Capes closed in to shoot steadily along the ground and into the net.

Wragg, injured in the first half, wrenched his leg again and had to move out to the wing. Capes retreated into midfield and Spouncer had to go inside. Though handicapped, Forest came back with a third goal four minutes from time. Boag headed out from a corner-kick but McPherson slipped in to drive in a ground shot.

Play had almost all been in Derby's favour in the second half, but the rock-like Forest defence held out. Allsop leapt to turn away Cox's drive and McPherson saved a certain goal by charging down Bloomer's shot.

Victory undoubtedly went to the better team. Indeed, their marked superiority must have come as a surprise to those who had expected a Derby walk-over.

Nottingham Forest: Allsop; Richie, Scott; Forman (Frank), McPherson, Wragg; McInnes, Richards, Benbow, Capes, Spouncer
Derby County: Fryer; Methven, Leiper; Cox, Goodall (A.), Turner; Goodall (J.), Bloomer, Boag, Stevenson, McQueen
Referee: J. Lewis (Blackburn)

1898-9

First Round
Everton v Jarrow 3−1; Nott'm Forest v Aston Villa 2−1; SHEFF UTD v Burnley 2−2, 2−1; PNE v Grimsby T 7−0; WBA v South Shore 8−0; Heanor T v Bury 0−3; Liverpool v Blackburn R 2−0; Glossop v Newcastle Utd 0−1; Notts Co v Kettering 2−0; New Brompton v Southampton 0−1; Woolwich Arsenal v DERBY CO 0−6; Bolton Wand v Wolves 0−0, 0−1; Small Heath v Man C 3−2; Stoke v Sheff Wed 2−2, 2−0; Newton Heath v Spurs 1−1, 3−5; Bristol C v Sunderland 2−4

Second Round
Everton v Nott'm Forest 0−1; SHEFF UTD v PNE 2−2, 2−1; WBA v Bury 2−1; Liverpool v Newcastle Utd 3−1; Notts Co v Southampton 0−1; DERBY CO v Wolves 2−1; Small Heath v Stoke 2−2, 1−2; Spurs v Sunderland 2−1

Third Round
Nott'm Forest v SHEFF UTD 0−1; WBA v Liverpool 0−2; Southampton v DERBY CO 1−2; Stoke v Spurs 4−1

Semi-Final
SHEFF UTD v Liverpool 2−2, 4−4, 0−0, 1−0; DERBY CO v Stoke 3−1

SHEFFIELD UNITED **4**
DERBY COUNTY **1**

Sheffield United, after four tremendous semi-final matches with Liverpool which included a 4–4 draw in the first replay, had fought their way to the Final for the first time in their history.

Their opponents were Derby County, and the prospects of it being a case of first time lucky for Sheffield didn't look bright at half-time. Centre-forward Boag had given Derby a first-half lead, and there should have been other goals. The great Steve Bloomer in particular was guilty of missing some good chances.

Sheffield always showed themselves as dangerous Cup fighters, and they came back with a vengeance in the second half, storming their way to a 4–1 victory with goals from Bennett, Beers, Almond and Priest. Derby could find no answer to that.

The quality of the football in an excellent Final was always high, and the most interesting feature was the duel between 'Nudger' Needham, Sheffield's left-half, and Derby's free-scoring inside-right Bloomer. By his hard tackling and never-say-die attitude, Needham was the clear winner of that particular argument.

Sheffield in the end deserved their victory, not only for their wonderful second-half rally, but also because they had had such a difficult path to the Final.

Sheffield United: Foulke; Thickett, Boyle; Johnson, Morren, Needham; Bennett, Beers, Hedley, Almond, Priest
Derby County: Fryer; Methven, Staley; Cox, Paterson, May; Arkesden, Bloomer, Boag, McDonald, Allen
Referee: A. Scragg (Crewe)

1899–1900

First Round
PNE v Spurs 1–0; Blackburn R v Portsmouth 0–0, 1–1, 5–0; Nott'm Forest v Grimsby T 3–0;
Sunderland v Derby Co 2–2, 3–0; Sheff Wed v Bolton Wand 1–0; Sheff Utd v Leicester Fosse 1–0;
Notts Co v Chorley 6–0; Burnley v BURY 0–1; SOUTHAMPTON v Everton 3–0; Newcastle Utd v
Reading 2–1; WBA v Walsall 1–1, 6–0; Liverpool v Stoke 0–0, 1–0; Wolves v QPR 1–1, 0–1;
Jarrow v Millwall A 0–2; Aston Villa v Man C 1–1, 3–1; Bristol C v Stalybridge R 2–1

Second Round
PNE v Blackburn R 1–0; Nott'm Forest v Sunderland 3–0; Sheff Wed v Sheff Utd 1–1, 0–2;
Notts Co v BURY 0–0, 0–2; SOUTHAMPTON v Newcastle Utd 4–1; WBA v Liverpool 1–1, 2–1;
QPR v Millwall A 0–2; Aston Villa v Bristol C 5–1

Third Round
PNE v Nott'm Forest 0–0, 0–1; Sheff Utd v BURY 2–2, 0–2; SOUTHAMPTON v WBA 2–1;
Millwall A v Aston Villa 1–1, 0–0, 2–1

Semi-Final
Nott'm Forest v BURY 1–1, 2–3; SOUTHAMPTON v Millwall A 0–0, 3–0

BURY **4**
SOUTHAMPTON **0**

Keeping up its reputation for surprises, the Cup competition in this season saw most of the 'crack' clubs dismissed in the early rounds, the Final being left to Bury and Southampton, neither of whom were expected to get this far.

Southampton's progress through to the Final had included victories against Newcastle and West Bromwich, the latter certainly no mean feat, but their success was not complete. They failed to hold the Bury side for whom McLuckie (twice), Wood and Plant scored in an emphatic 4–0 win.

Bury had a much easier passage against Southampton than they had had in the semi-final tie with Nottingham Forest. Then they were within a minute of defeat before a last desperate effort from Pray and McLuckie altered the score from 1–2 to 3–2.

As this was the first time since 1883 that a southern club had competed in the Final, a record attendance at the Crystal Palace was expected. In fact, the crowd of 69,000 was 5,000 down on the previous year.

Southampton were a southern club in name only, for there were only two southerners in the team, and neither of those were from Southampton. Bury themselves had six Scots in their line-up.

Bury: Thompson; Darrock, Davidson; Pray, Leeming, Ross; Richards, Wood, McLuckie, Sagar, Plant
Southampton: Robinson; Meehan, Durber; Meston, Chadwick, Petrie; Turner, Yates, Farrell, Wood, Milward
Referee: A. G. Kingscott (Derby)

1900-1

First Round
Bolton Wand v Derby Co 1−0; Reading v Bristol R 2−0; SPURS v PNE 1−1, 4−1; Sheff Wed v Bury 0−1; Middlesbro v Newcastle Utd 3−1; Kettering v Chesterfield 1−1, 2−1; Woolwich Arsenal v Blackburn R 2−0; WBA v Man C 1−0; Notts Co v Liverpool 2−0; Wolves v New Brighton Tower 5−1; Sunderland v SHEFF UTD 1−2; Southampton v Everton 1−3; Stoke v Small Heath 1−1, 1−2; Newton Heath v Burnley 0−0, 1−7; Aston Villa v Millwall A 5−0; Nott'm Forest v Leicester Fosse 5−1

Second Round
Bolton Wand v Reading 0−1; SPURS v Bury 2−1; Middlesbro v Kettering 5−0; Woolwich Arsenal v WBA 0−1; Notts Co v Wolves 2−3; SHEFF UTD v Everton 2−0; Small Heath v Burnley 1−0; Aston Villa v Nott'm Forest 0−0, 3−1

Third Round
Reading v SPURS 1−1, 0−3; Middlesbro v WBA 0−1; Wolves v SHEFF UTD 0−4; Small Heath v Aston Villa 0−0, 0−1

Semi-Final
SPURS v WBA 4−0; SHEFF UTD v Aston Villa 2−2, 3−0

Brown scores for Tottenham

TOTTENHAM HOTSPUR 3
SHEFFIELD UNITED 1 (after a 2–2 draw)

Tottenham kicked off with a Crystal Palace crowd of 110,000 filling every available inch of space on the great banks and in the stands. Sheffield, prompted by Needham's brilliance, were soon into their stride, and took an eleventh-minute lead when Priest shot home from twenty yards. Inside a quarter of an hour Brown had headed past the giant goalkeeper Foulke and Tottenham were level.

The Bramall Lane team were finding their opponents to be a side with greater speed, agility and dash than the Aston Villa combination whom they had overcome in the semi-final. The Final teams were very evenly matched, but with Sheffield marginally the better outfit in the first half.

When Brown was put through by Cameron to beat Foulke again with a rising shot for Tottenham five minutes after the interval, the predominantly southern crowd went wild. Hats went into the air, handkerchiefs were waved, and spectators daringly perched in the trees around the ground almost fell out of the branches. But the match was far from settled, for within a minute a strange incident changed the face of the match.

A linesman flagged for a corner-kick after Bennett had charged Tottenham goalkeeper Clawley near the goal-line and the ball had gone behind. The referee then surprised everyone by awarding a goal to Sheffield, on the grounds that the ball had crossed the goal-line as Clawley had attempted to field Lipsham's shot from the left seconds before Bennett had moved in to charge him. The general opinion was that referee Kingscott had made a sad error of judgement. He was too far up the field to be able to decide the point, yet he refused to consult with a linesman much nearer to the incident.

A week later the sides met again, this time at Burnden Park, Bolton, and the crowd now was a mere 22,000. Tottenham triumphed on a wet and windy afternoon, and brought the Cup back to the south at last after eighteen years. Sheffield had led at half-time in the replay, Priest shooting just inside a post from Lipsham's pass into the centre, but Tottenham came through to victory with goals by Cameron, Smith and Brown. The third, Brown's glancing header from Smith's corner-kick in the eighty-second minute, was the best goal of the day.

Southern League Tottenham became the first (and, since then, the only) non-League team to win the Cup. They didn't become members of the Second Division of the Football League until 1908.

Tottenham Hotspur: Clawley; Erentz, Tait; Norris, Hughes, Jones; Smith, Cameron, Brown, Copeland, Kirwan
Sheffield United: Foulke; Thickett, Boyle; Johnson, Morren, Needham; Bennett, Field, Hedley, Priest, Lipsham
Referee: A. G. Kingscott (Derby)

1901–2

First Round
Spurs v SOUTHAMPTON 1–1, 2–2, 1–2; Liverpool v Everton 2–2, 2–0; Bury v WBA 5–1; Walsall v Burnley 1–0; Glossop v Nott'm Forest 1–3; PNE v Man C 1–1, 0–0, 2–4; Aston Villa v Stoke 2–2, 1–2; Bristol R v Middlesbro 1–1, 1–0; Northampton v SHEFF UTD 0–2; Wolves v Bolton Wand 0–2; Woolwich Arsenal v Newcastle Utd 0–2; Sheff Wed v Sunderland 0–1; Blackburn R v Derby Co 0–2; Lincoln C v Oxford C 0–0, 4–0; Portsmouth v Grimsby T 1–1, 2–0; Notts Co v Reading 1–2

Second Round
SOUTHAMPTON v Liverpool 4–1; Walsall v Bury 0–5; Man C v Nott'm Forest 0–2; Bristol R v Stoke 0–1; SHEFF UTD v Bolton Wand 2–1; Newcastle Utd v Sunderland 1–0; Lincoln C v Derby Co 1–3; Reading v Portsmouth 0–1

Third Round
Bury v SOUTHAMPTON 2–3; Nott'm Forest v Stoke 2–0; SHEFF UTD v Newcastle Utd 1–1, 2–1; Derby Co v Portsmouth 0–0, 6–3

Semi-Final
SOUTHAMPTON v Nott'm Forest 3–1; SHEFF UTD v Derby Co 1–1, 1–1, 1–0

SHEFFIELD UNITED **2**
SOUTHAMPTON **1** (after a 1–1 draw)

The Cup holders went out in the first round of this season, and their conquerors, Southampton, reached the Final and faced Sheffield United, on their third visit to the Crystal Palace in four years.

The Final for the third year in succession was a battle between North and South. Sheffield, a well-balanced and capable team, were captained by Ernest 'Nudger' Needham, a tireless and skilful player. In goal they had Foulke, amazingly agile for a man of his weight (22 stone), and the pick of the forwards was probably Bennett, their international outside-right.

Unfortunately, United had to take the field without Bennett in the replay. Inside-right Common, whose goal had earned them a draw in the first match, moved outside, and Barnes, a reserve, filled the inside position. Common adapted himself well, and to Barnes fell the distinction of notching the goal which decided the game, after Hedley's fifth-minute opener, and won the Cup for the North.

C. B. Fry, a man whose combined intellectual and athletic qualities made him one of the outstanding personalities of the day, was Southampton's star at right-back. Wood scored the late, disputed goal in the first match, and Brown kept the result close in the replay, but poor Southampton's second Final ended in failure.

Sheffield United: Foulke; Thickett, Boyle; Needham, Wilkinson, Johnson; Barnes, Common, Hedley, Priest, Lipsham. (Bennett was injured in the first match and Barnes took his place in the replay)
Southampton: Robinson; C. B. Fry, Molyneux; Meston, Bowman, Lee; A. Turner, Wood, Brown, Chadwick, J. Turner
Referee: T. Kirkham (Burslem)

1902–3

First Round
Spurs v WBA 0–0, 2–0; Bolton Wand v Bristol C 0–5; Aston Villa v Sunderland 3–1; Barnsley v Lincoln C 2–0; Woolwich Arsenal v Sheff Utd 1–3; BURY v Wolves 1–0; Grimsby T v Newcastle Utd 2–1; Notts Co v Southampton 0–0, 2–2, 2–1; DERBY CO v Small Heath 2–1; Blackburn R v Sheff Wed 0–0, 1–0; Nott'm Forest v Reading 0–0, 6–3; Glossop v Stoke 2–3; Millwall A v Luton T 3–0; PNE v Man C 3–1; Everton v Portsmouth 5–0; Man Utd v Liverpool 2–1

Second Round
Spurs v Bristol C 1–0; Barnsley v Aston Villa 1–4; Sheff Utd v BURY 0–1; Grimsby T v Notts Co 0–2; DERBY CO v Blackburn R 2–0; Stoke v Nott'm Forest 0–0, 2–0; Millwall A v PNE 4–1; Everton v Man Utd 3–1

Third Round
Spurs v Aston Villa 2–3; BURY v Notts Co 1–0; DERBY CO v Stoke 3–0; Millwall A v Everton 1–0

Semi-Final
Aston Villa v BURY 0–3; DERBY CO v Millwall A 3–0

BURY **6**
DERBY COUNTY **0**

Derby were without the injured Bloomer for the Final, but even so they had a strong side on paper. Yet the match turned out to be one of the most one-sided ever played, and Bury's 6–0 victory still stands as the record Final win. Bury also equalled another record, winning the Cup without conceding a goal in any round.

Derby's play was so inept that Bury were never fully extended. Monteith, the Bury goalkeeper, had nothing to do, though the ex-West Ham and Bristol City man had certainly had his capabilities thoroughly stretched at Sheffield in the second round. Defenders McEwen and Ross, the latter captain, contributed much to Bury's crushing victory. Richards was brilliant in attack, though he didn't score, and Leeming, who got a couple, showed himself to be a more than useful player, if a little slow.

Ross, Sagar, Wood and Plant scored Bury's other goals. For Derby, who could do nothing right, matters were made worse when their goalkeeper, Fryer, as he tried to save a goal, collided with Sagar, and, after sticking gallantly to his post for a while, was forced to retire in the sixty-fifth minute after Bury had completed a murderous four-goals-in-twenty-minutes.

Bury: Monteith; Lindsey, McEwen; Johnson, Thorpe, Ross; Richards, Wood, Sagar, Leeming, Plant
Derby County: Fryer; Methven, Morris; Warren, Goodall (A.), May; Warrington, York, Boag, Richards, Davis
Referee: J. Adams (Birmingham)

1903–4

First Round
MAN C v Sunderland 3–2; Woolwich Arsenal v Fulham 1–0; Millwall v Middlesbro 0–2; PNE v Grimsby T 1–0; Plymouth Arg v Sheff Wed 2–2, 0–2; Notts Co v Man Utd 3–3, 1–2; Everton v Spurs 1–2; Stoke v Aston Villa 2–3; Reading v BOLTON WAND 1–1, 2–3; Southampton v Burslem Port Vale 3–0; Bristol C v Sheff Utd 1–3; Bury v Newcastle Utd 2–1; Portsmouth v Derby Co 2–5; Wolves v Stockton 4–1; Blackburn R v Liverpool 3–1; WBA v Nott'm Forest 1–1, 1–3

Second Round
Woolwich Arsenal v MAN C 0–2; PNE v Middlesbro 0–3; Sheff Wed v Man Utd 6–0; Spurs v Aston Villa 1–0; BOLTON WAND v Southampton 4–1; Bury v Sheff Utd 1–2; Derby Co v Wolves 2–2, 2–2, 1–0; Blackburn R v Nott'm Forest 3–1

Third Round
MAN C v Middlesbro 0–0, 3–1; Spurs v Sheff Wed 1–1, 0–2; Sheff Utd v BOLTON WAND 0–2; Derby Co v Blackburn R 2–1

Semi-Final
MAN C v Sheff Wed 3–0; BOLTON WAND v Derby Co 1–0

MANCHESTER CITY **1**
BOLTON WANDERERS **0**

The first all-Lancashire final of 1904 drew a 62,000 crowd to the Crystal Palace. Bolton were admittedly the more experienced Cup fighters, having appeared in one final and two semi-finals, but it was City's consistency throughout the season that made them slight favourites.

The Final was expected to be a close affair, and so it proved. The single goal that decided the issue came after twenty minutes, when Billy Meredith, the finest right-winger of his generation, took a pass from Livingstone and dribbled in to score. In this first half City had much more of the play than Bolton, and deserved to be in front at half-time. Meredith, waiting behind Struthers, may have been fractionally offside when the ball was played through to him. The referee, however, was quite adamant that the goal should stand.

Bolton tried hard to save themselves in the second half, and the result was in doubt to the end. City, the more scientific side, held on to take the Cup to Manchester for the first time. It had not been a classic game, with poor shooting from both sides. Meredith, a football genius eventually capped fifty-one times by Wales, did little for a player of his reputation, other than score.

Manchester City: Hillman; McMahon, Burgess; Frost, Hynds, S. B. Ashworth; Meredith, Livingstone, Gillespie, Turnbull (A.), Booth
Bolton Wanderers: D. Davies; Brown, Struthers; Clifford, Greenhaigh, Freebairn; Stokes, Marsh, Yenson, White, Taylor
Referee: A. J. Barker (Hanley)

1904–5

First Round
Lincoln C v Man C 1–2; Bolton Wand v Bristol R 1–1, 3–0; Middlesbro v Spurs 1–1, 0–1;
NEWCASTLE UTD v Plymouth Arg 1–1, 1–1, 2–0; Woolwich Arsenal v Bristol C 0–0, 0–1;
Derby Co v PNE 0–2; Blackburn R v Sheff Wed 1–2; Small Heath v Portsmouth 0–2; Stoke v
Grimsby T 2–0; Liverpool v Everton 1–1, 1–2; Sunderland v Wolves 1–1, 0–1; Southampton v
Millwall 3–1; ASTON VILLA v Leicester Fosse 5–1; Bury v Notts Co 1–0; Fulham v Reading
0–0, 0–0, 1–0; Nott'm Forest v Sheff Utd 2–0

Second Round
Man C v Bolton Wand 1–2; Spurs v NEWCASTLE UTD 1–1, 0–4; Bristol C v PNE 0–0, 0–1;
Sheff Wed v Portsmouth 2–1; Stoke v Everton 0–4; Wolves v Southampton 2–3; ASTON VILLA v
Bury 3–2; Fulham v Nott'm Forest 1–0

Third Round
Bolton Wand v NEWCASTLE UTD 0–2; PNE v Sheff Wed 1–1, 0–3; Everton v Southampton 4–0;
ASTON VILLA v Fulham 5–0

Semi-Final
NEWCASTLE UTD v Sheff Wed 1–0; Everton v ASTON VILLA 1–1, 1–2

ASTON VILLA **2**
NEWCASTLE UNITED **0**

This year saw the beginning of the great era for Newcastle United, during which they played their way through to the Final five times in seven years: The Crystal Palace ground seemed to exert some mysterious 'hoodoo' over them, however, and they were never to show their true form there.

Another six-figure crowd saw Newcastle, League champions and hailed as favourites for the Cup, do battle with famous Cup-fighters Aston Villa. Within three minutes of the start, centre-forward Hampton finished off a move started by Leake, his centre-half, to give Villa a surprise lead.

The play swayed from end to end, with Howie missing a golden chance to equalize for Newcastle before half-time, but for the most part Villa were on top, and near the end Hall's long shot rebounded from Newcastle goalkeeper Lawrence for the waiting Hampton to clinch matters for Villa.

Villa's tremendous pace had at times bewildered Newcastle. Unlike their opponents, Villa cast aside all the nice theories of the short-passing game. Instead, the half-backs swept the ball out to the wing men, and they followed with long dropping centres into the goalmouth. Nor did the thick Crystal Palace turf suit Newcastle's style of play, but slowed up their ground passes.

Aston Villa: George; Spencer, Miles; Pearson, Leake, Windmill; Brown, Garratty, Hampton, Bache, Hall
Newcastle United: Lawrence; McCombie, Carr; Gardner, Aitken, McWilliam; Rutherford, Howie, Appleyard, Veitch, Gosnell
Referee: P. R. Harrower (London)

1905–6

First Round

Woolwich Arsenal v W Ham 1–1, 3–2; Worcester C v Watford 0–6; Sunderland v Notts Co 1–0; Burslem Port Vale v Gainsboro Tr 0–3; Man Utd v Staple Hill 7–2; Norwich C v Tonbridge WR 1–1, 5–0; Aston Villa v King's Lynn 11–0; New Crusaders v Plymouth Arg 3–6; NEWCASTLE UTD v Grimsby T 6–0; Derby Co v Kettering 4–0; Blackpool v Crystal Palace 1–1, 1–1, 1–0; Sheff Utd v Man C 4–1; Spurs v Burnley 2–0; Hull C v Reading 0–1; Birmingham v PNE 1–0; Stoke v Blackburn R 1–0; EVERTON v WBA 3–1; Clapton O v Chesterfield 0–0, 0–3; Bradford C v Barrow 3–2; Bishop Auckland v Wolves 0–3; Sheff Wed v Bristol R 1–0; Millwall v Burton Wand 1–0; Bury v Nott'm Forest 1–1, 2–6; Fulham v QPR 1–0; Liverpool v Leicester Fosse 2–1; Crewe Alex v Barnsley 1–1, 0–4; Brentford v Bristol C 2–1; Lincoln C v Stockport Co 4–2; Southampton v Portsmouth 5–1; New Brompton v Northampton 2–1; Middlesbro v Bolton Wand 3–0; Brighton v Swindon 3–0

Second Round

Woolwich Arsenal v Watford 3–0; Sunderland v Gainsboro Tr 1–1, 3–0; Man Utd v Norwich C 3–0; Aston Villa v Plymouth Arg 0–0, 5–1; Derby Co v NEWCASTLE UTD 0–0, 1–2; Blackpool v Sheff Utd 2–1; Spurs v Reading 3–2; Stoke v Birmingham 0–1; Chesterfield v EVERTON 0–3; Bradford C v Wolves 5–0; Sheff Wed v Millwall 1–1, 3–0; Fulham v Nott'm Forest 1–3; Barnsley v Liverpool 0–1; Brentford v Lincoln C 3–0; New Brompton v Southampton 0–0, 0–1; Brighton v Middlesbro 1–1, 1–1, 1–3

Third Round

Woolwich Arsenal v Sunderland 5–0; Man Utd v Aston Villa 5–1; NEWCASTLE UTD v Blackpool 5–0; Spurs v Birmingham 1–1, 0–2; EVERTON v Bradford C 1–0; Sheff Wed v Nott'm Forest 4–1; Liverpool v Brentford 2–0; Southampton v Middlesbro 6–1

Fourth Round

Man Utd v Woolwich Arsenal 2–3; Birmingham v NEWCASTLE UTD 2–2, 0–3; EVERTON v Sheff Wed 4–3; Liverpool v Southampton 3–0

Semi-Final

Woolwich Arsenal v NEWCASTLE UTD 0–2; EVERTON v Liverpool 2–0

EVERTON **1**
NEWCASTLE UNITED **0**

Newcastle had been deprived of the League and Cup double in 1905 by Aston Villa, and in the following year they reached the Final again, only to fail once more, this time to Everton.

The second edition of the 'team of all the talents' had a quality about their football which didn't augur well for Everton's chances. But the match was a dull one. The one outstanding player on the field, Sharp on Everton's right wing, set up the only goal of the afternoon. Veteran Taylor passed the ball out to him with fifteen minutes to go, he dashed past Carr, Newcastle's left-back, and Young, Everton's Scottish international centre-forward, glided his neat, low centre past Lawrence.

It was third time lucky for Everton, and their good fortune was to catch Newcastle on their least favourite ground, at Crystal Palace. The football, in fact, was no more than a lottery, and the only satisfying feature of the game was that the worst side lost. It was disappointing enough for Newcastle, losing finalists for the second year running, but this was nothing compared to the shock of losing at home in the first round the next season – to Crystal Palace of all teams, lying near the foot of the Southern League.

Everton: Scott; Balmer (W.), Crelly; Makepeace, Taylor, Abbot; Sharp, Bolton, Young, Settle, H. P. Hardman
Newcastle United: Lawrence; McCombie, Carr; Gardner, Aitken, McWilliam; Rutherford, Howie, Veitch, Orr, Gosnell
Referee: F. Kirkham (Preston)

1906–7

First Round
Burslem Port Vale v Irthlingboro 7–1; Notts Co v PNE 1–0; Blackburn R v Man C 2–2, 1–0; Spurs v Hull C 0–0, 0–0, 1–0; WBA v Stoke 1–1, 2–2, 2–1; Hastings v Norwich C 1–3; Derby Co v Chesterfield 1–1, 4–0; Lincoln C v Chelsea 2–2, 1–0; Stockport v Fulham 0–0, 1–2; Newcastle Utd v Crystal Palace 0–1; Brentford v Glossop 2–1; Middlesbro v Northampton 4–2; Blackpool v W Ham 1–2; EVERTON v Sheff Utd 1–0; Burnley v Aston Villa 1–3; Bolton Wand v Brighton 3–1; Grimsby T v Woolwich Arsenal 1–1, 0–3; Bristol C v Leeds C 4–1; Bristol R v QPR 0–0, 1–0; Millwall v Plymouth Arg 2–0; Nott'm Forest v Barnsley 1–1, 1–2; Portsmouth v Man Utd 2–2, 2–1; Oxford C v Bury 0–3; Burton Utd v New Brompton 0–0, 0–2; Oldham Ath v Kidderminster H 5–0; Liverpool v Birmingham 2–1; Bradford C v Reading 2–0; Crewe Alex v Accrington S 1–1, 0–1; Southampton v Watford 2–1; SHEFF WED v Wolves 3–2; Gainsboro Tr v Luton T 0–0, 1–2; Sunderland v Leicester Fosse 4–1

Second Round
Burslem Port Vale v Notts Co 2–2, 0–5; Blackburn R v Spurs 1–1, 1–1, 1–2; WBA v Norwich C 1–0; Derby Co v Lincoln C 1–0; Fulham v Crystal Palace 0–0, 0–1; Brentford v Middlesbro 1–0; W Ham v EVERTON 1–2; Bolton Wand v Aston Villa 2–0; Woolwich Arsenal v Bristol C 2–1; Bristol R v Millwall 3–0; Barnsley v Portsmouth 1–0; Bury v New Brompton 1–0; Oldham Ath v Liverpool 0–1; Bradford C v Accrington S 1–0; Southampton v SHEFF WED 1–1, 1–3; Luton T v Sunderland 0–0, 0–1

Third Round
Notts Co v Spurs 4–0; WBA v Derby Co 2–0; Crystal Palace v Brentford 1–1, 1–0; EVERTON v Bolton Wand 0–0, 3–0; Woolwich Arsenal v Bristol R 1–0; Barnsley v Bury 1–0; Liverpool v Bradford C 1–0; SHEFF WED v Sunderland 0–0, 1–0

Fourth Round
WBA v Notts Co 3–1; Crystal Palace v EVERTON 1–1, 0–4; Barnsley v Woolwich Arsenal 1–2; SHEFF WED v Liverpool 1–0

Semi-Final
WBA v EVERTON 1–2; Woolwich Arsenal v SHEFF WED 1–3

SHEFFIELD WEDNESDAY **2**
EVERTON **1**

Everton, favourites to retain the trophy, were lying third in the League and had ten men in their side who had helped take the Cup to Lancashire the previous year. But, as so often happened, the fancied team in the Final lost.

It was an undistinguished match, with the ball too much in the air, and fouls rather plentiful. Neither side played as well as they were supposed to be capable of doing. From the start Everton seemed embarrassed by Wednesday's rushing and bustling tactics.

A mix-up in the Everton defence enabled Wednesday to take a twentieth minute lead. Chapman swung the ball into the goalmouth for Stewart to give it the final touch.

During the closing minutes of the first half Everton hit their best form of the match, and Jack Sharp, whose goal had won the Final in 1906, scored a picture goal to level the scores.

Only four minutes remained of the match when Wilson, the Wednesday centre-forward, received the ball from a throw-in and hooked it unexpectedly across the goalmouth for Simpson, his outside-left, to head home one of the softest goals imaginable.

Sheffield Wednesday: Lyall; Layton, Burton; Brittleton, Crawshaw, Bartlett; Chapman, Bradshaw, Wilson, Stewart, Simpson
Everton: Scott; Balmer (W.), Balmer (R.); Makepeace, Tallor, Abbott; Sharp, Bolton, Young, Settle, H. P. Hardman
Referee: N. Whittaker (London)

1907–8

First Round
Bradford C v WOLVES 1–1, 0–1; Bury v Millwall 2–1; Swindon T v Sheff Utd 0–0, 3–2; QPR v Reading 1–0; Stoke v Lincoln C 5–0; Gainsboro Tr v Watford 1–0; Hastings v Portsmouth 0–1; Leicester Fosse v Blackburn R 2–0; Notts Co v Middlesbro 2–0; Bolton Wand v Woking 5–0; Oldham Ath v Leeds C 2–1; Everton v Spurs 1–0; Burnley v Southampton 1–2; WBA v Birmingham 1–1, 2–1; Northampton v Bristol R 0–1; Chesterfield v Stockton 4–0; NEWCASTLE UTD v Nott'm Forest 2–0; W Ham v Rotherham T 1–0; Liverpool v Derby Co 4–2; Brighton v PNE 1–1, 1–0; Bristol C v Grimsby T 0–0, 1–2; Carlisle Utd v Brentford 2–2, 3–1; Coventry C v Crystal Palace 2–4; Plymouth Arg v Barnsley 1–0; Glossop v Man C 0–0, 0–6; New Brompton v Sunderland 3–1; Luton v Fulham 3–8; Norwich C v Sheff Wed 2–0; Man Utd v Blackpool 3–1; Chelsea v Worksop 9–1; Aston Villa v Stockport Co 3–0; Woolwich Arsenal v Hull C 0–0, 1–4

Second Round
WOLVES v Bury 2–0; Swindon T v QPR 2–1; Stoke v Gainsboro Tr 1–1, 2–2, 3–1; Portsmouth v Leicester Fosse 1–0; Notts Co v Bolton Wand 1–1, 1–2; Oldham Ath v Everton 0–0, 1–6; Southampton v WBA 1–0; Bristol R v Chesterfield 2–0; NEWCASTLE UTD v W Ham 2–0; Liverpool v Brighton 1–1, 3–0; Grimsby T v Carlisle Utd 6–2; Plymouth Arg v Crystal Palace 2–3; Man C v New Brompton 1–1, 2–1; Norwich C v Fulham 1–2; Man Utd v Chelsea 1–0; Aston Villa v Hull C 3–0

Third Round
WOLVES v Swindon T 2–0; Portsmouth v Stoke 0–1, Bolton Wand v Everton 3–3, 1–3; Southampton v Bristol R 2–0; NEWCASTLE UTD v Liverpool 3–1; Grimsby T v Crystal Palace 1–0; Man C v Fulham 1–1, 1–3; Aston Villa v Man Utd 0–2

Fourth Round
Stoke v WOLVES 0–1; Everton v Southampton 0–0, 2–3; NEWCASTLE UTD v Grimsby T 5–1; Fulham v Man Utd 2–1

Semi-Final
WOLVES v Southampton 2–0; NEWCASTLE UTD v Fulham 6–0

WOLVERHAMPTON WANDERERS **3**
NEWCASTLE UNITED **1**

Newcastle, reigning League champions, once again played their way through to a Crystal Palace Final. This time they met Wolverhampton, a robust and fast-moving side, but placed only in the middle of the Second Division. Surely now, after the disappointments of 1905 and 1906, Newcastle would carry off the prize.

Newcastle's 'pretty' game of tip-tap from one man to the other came woefully unstuck against the quick-tackling Wolves team. In fact, Wolves' one chance of winning lay in offering such a resolute and unyielding opposition that Newcastle would be prevented from developing their skilful attacks. Newcastle probably had about ninety per cent of the play, but the ten per cent for which Wolves were responsible, plus their dash and their more direct methods, proved sufficient to undo the Tynesiders.

A brace of goals in the last five minutes of the first half – Hunt's long shot and Hedley's swift shot after eluding two tackles – suddenly put Wolves into a winning position, and, though Howie scored for Newcastle shortly after the interval, Harrison, the Wolves right-winger who played a brilliant match, later put the result beyond doubt. There were only four 'Hs' on the field, and yet, curiously, all of them scored.

Wolverhampton Wanderers: Lunn; Jones, Collins; K. R. G. Hunt, Wooldridge, Bishop; Harrison, Shelton, Hedley, Radford, Pedley
Newcastle United: Lawrence; McCracken, Pudan; Gardner, Veitch, McWilliam; Rutherford, Howie, Appleyard, Speedie, Wilson
Referee: T. P. Campbell (Blackburn)

1908–9

First Round
MAN UTD v Brighton & H Alb 1–0; Everton v Barnsley 3–1; Notts Co v Blackburn R 0–1; Hull C v Chelsea 1–1, 0–1; Man C v Spurs 3–4; Carlisle Utd v Fulham 1–4; Wolves v Crystal Palace 2–2, 2–4; Bristol R v Burnley 1–4; Newcastle Utd v Clapton Orient 5–0; Blackpool v Hastings 2–0; Oldham Ath v Leeds C 1–1, 0–2; QPR v W Ham 0–0, 0–1; Sheff Utd v Sunderland 2–3; PNE v Middlesbro 1–0; Workington v Bradford C 0–0, 0–2; WBA v Bolton Wand 3–1; BRISTOL C v Southampton 1–1, 2–0; Bury v Kettering 8–0; Norwich C v Reading 0–0, 1–1, 3–2; Liverpool v Lincoln C 5–1; Grimsby T v Stockport Co 2–2, 0–2; Chesterfield v Glossop 0–2; Birmingham v Portsmouth 2–5; Sheff Wed v Stoke 5–0; Northampton v Derby Co 1–1, 2–4; Watford v Leicester Fosse 1–1, 1–3; Plymouth Arg v Swindon 1–0; Wrexham v Exeter C 1–1, 1–2; Nott'm Forest v Aston Villa 2–0; Brentford v Gainsboro Tr 2–0; Luton v Millwall Ath 1–2; Croydon Com v Woolwich Arsenal 1–1, 0–2

Second Round
MAN UTD v Everton 1–0; Blackburn R v Chelsea 2–1; Spurs v Fulham 1–0; Crystal Palace v Burnley 0–0, 0–9; Newcastle Utd v Blackpool 2–1; Leeds C v W Ham 1–1. 1–2; PNE v Sunderland 1–2; WBA v Bradford C 1–2; BRISTOL C v Bury 2–2, 1–0; Liverpool v Norwich C 2–3; Stockport Co v Glossop 1–1, 0–1; Portsmouth v Sheff Wed 2–2, 0–3; Leicester Fosse v Derby Co 0–2; Plymouth Arg v Exeter C 2–0; Nott'm Forest v Brentford 1–0; Woolwich Arsenal v Millwall Ath 1–1, 0–1

Third Round
MAN UTD v Blackburn R 6–1; Spurs v Burnley 0–0, 1–3; W Ham v Newcastle Utd 0–0, 1–2; Bradford C v Sunderland 0–1; BRISTOL C v Norwich C 2–0; Sheff Wed v Glossop 0–1; Derby Co v Plymouth Arg 1–0; Nott'm Forest v Millwall Ath 3–1

Fourth Round
Burnley v MAN UTD 2–3; Newcastle Utd v Sunderland 2–2, 3–0; Glossop v BRISTOL C 0–0, 0–1; Derby Co v Nott'm Forest 3–0

Semi-Final
MAN UTD v Newcastle Utd 1–0; BRISTOL C v Derby Co 1–1, 2–1

MANCHESTER UNITED **1**
BRISTOL CITY **0**

The year 1909 brought two newcomers to the Final, and, for once, the favourites won. Manchester United, League winners the previous season, had the greater experience and the boost of a victory over Newcastle in the semi-final.

United won a disappointing, rough game – the ninth Final to be decided by a solitary goal – with Turnbull's twenty-second minute effort. Only two players stood out for their skill: Wedlock, the great little Bristol City centre-half who won nineteen caps for England, and the legendary Billy Meredith, who added another winners' medal to the one he had gained with the other Manchester club in 1904.

In the opening stages of the game Bristol set the pace, but United soon wore down their attack and began to assert themselves. A movement by the United right-wing pair left the inside-right Halse poised for a shot. The ball was struck firmly against the angle of crossbar and post, and 'Sandy' Turnbull hit an unstoppable drive into the net from the rebound.

The nearest Bristol came to emulating this was when Hardy, left unmarked in front of a goal after a fine bout of passing, had his hard shot turned aside in masterly fashion by a dive from Moger.

Manchester United: Moger; Stacey, Hayes; Duckworth, Roberts, Bell; Meredith, Halse, Turnbull (J.), Turnbull (A.), Wall
Bristol City: Clay; Annan, Cottle; Hanlin, Wedlock, Spear; Staniforth, Hardy, Gilligan, Burton, Hilton
Referee: J. Mason (Burslem)

1909–10

First Round
Stoke v NEWCASTLE UTD 1–1, 1–2; Chesterfield v Fulham 0–0, 1–2; Accrington S v Blackburn R 1–7; Notts Co v Bradford C 2–4; Birmingham v Leicester Fosse 1–4; Bury v Glossop 2–1; Leyton v New Brompton 0–0, 2–2, 1–0; Stockport Co v Bolton Wand 4–1; Crystal Palace v Swindon 1–3; Burnley v Man Utd 2–0; Plymouth Arg v Spurs 1–1, 1–7; Chelsea v Hull C 2–1; Workington v Man C 1–2; Brighton & H Alb v Southampton 0–1; Oldham Ath v Aston Villa 1–2; Derby Co v Millwall Ath 5–0; Blackpool v BARNSLEY 1–1, 0–6; Grimsby T v Bristol R 0–2; WBA v Clapton Orient 2–0; Bristol C v Liverpool 2–0; Norwich C v QPR 0–0, 0–3; Gainsboro Tr v Southend 1–1, 0–1; W Ham v Carlisle Utd 1–1, 5–0; Reading v Wolves 0–5; Everton v Middlesbro 1–1, 5–3; Woolwich Arsenal v Watford 3–1; Sunderland v Leeds C 1–0; Bradford PA v Bishop Auckland 8–0; PNE v Coventry 1–2; Portsmouth v Shrewsbury T 3–0; Nott'm Forest v Sheff Utd 3–2; Northampton v Sheff Wed 0–0, 1–0

Second Round
NEWCASTLE UTD v Fulham 4–0; Bradford C v Blackburn R 1–2; Leicester Fosse v Bury 3–2; Stockport v Leyton 0–2; Swindon v Burnley 2–0; Chelsea v Spurs 0–1; Southampton v Man C 0–5; Aston Villa v Derby Co 6–1; Bristol R v BARNSLEY 0–4; Bristol C v WBA 1–1, 2–4; Southend v QPR 0–0, 2–3; Wolves v W Ham 1–5; Everton v Woolwich Arsenal 5–0; Sunderland v Bradford PA 3–1; Portsmouth v Coventry 0–1; Northampton v Nott'm Forest 0–0, 0–1

Third Round
NEWCASTLE UTD v Blackburn R 3–1; Leicester Fosse v Leyton 1–0; Swindon v Spurs 3–2; Aston Villa v Man C 1–2; BARNSLEY v WBA 1–0; QPR v W Ham 1–1, 1–0; Everton v Sunderland 2–0; Coventry v Nott'm Forest 3–1

Fourth Round
NEWCASTLE UTD v Leicester Fosse 3–0; Swindon v Man C 2–0; BARNSLEY v QPR 1–0; Coventry v Everton 0–2

Semi-Final
NEWCASTLE UTD v Swindon 2–0; BARNSLEY v Everton 0–0, 3–0

NEWCASTLE UNITED **2**
BARNSLEY **0** (after a 1–1 draw)

Newcastle, in their fourth Final in six years, faced Barnsley, a Second Division club with all the dour, fighting qualities of Yorkshire. Yet again they failed to win at Crystal Palace. However, after a replay at Everton, the Cup *was* finally taken back to Tyneside.

Barnsley's rush and bustle had overpowered the artistry of the Newcastle stars for long periods in the first encounter. Barnsley had scored in the first half through inside-left Tuffnell, and it was late in the second period when Rutherford forced home the equalizer.

Newcastle won a hard-fought replay at Goodison Park on merit. They played well from the start, the forwards working better together than they had ever done at Crystal Palace. It was the sort of form they had often shown in the League championship but seldom managed to reproduce in the Cup Final. In truth, they seemed more at home in the North.

Barnsley themselves played a dashing game, full of enterprise and hard kicking. Their defence performed admirably, the full-backs in particular giving the opposing wing men little room in which to manoeuvre. Newcastle mixed their short game with long, sweeping passes, and with the right-wing pair of Rutherford and Howie in splendid form, they won deservedly with two goals by centre-forward Shepherd.

Newcastle United: Lawrence; McCracken, Carr; Veitch, Low, McWilliam; Rutherford, Howie, Shepherd, Higgins, Wilson. (Whitson was injured in first match and Carr took his place in the replay)
Barnsley: Mearns; Downs, Ness; Glendinning, Boyle, Utley; Bartrop, Gadsby, Lilycrop, Tuffnell, Forman
Referee: J. T. Ibbotson (Derby)

1910–1

First Round
New Brompton v Bradford PA 0–1; Norwich C v Sunderland 3–1; Grimsby T v Croydon C 3–0;
Bristol C v Crewe Alex 0–3; Burnley v Exeter C 2–1; Watford v Barnsley 0–2; Sheff Wed v
Coventry C 1–2; Leeds C v Brighton & H Alb 1–3; Southend Utd v Blackburn R 1–5; Spurs v
Millwall Ath 2–1; Middlesbro v Glossop 1–0; Leicester Fosse v Southampton 3–1; W Ham v
Nott'm Forest 2–1; Brentford v PNE 0–1; Blackpool v Man Utd 1–2; Portsmouth v Aston Villa 1–4;
NEWCASTLE UTD v Bury 6–1; Northampton T v Luton 5–1; Bristol R v Hull C 0–0, 0–1;
Birmingham v Oldham Ath 1–1, 0–2; Derby Co v Plymouth Arg 2–1; WBA v Fulham 4–1;
Crystal Palace v Everton 0–4; Liverpool v Gainsboro Tr 3–2; Chelsea v Leyton 0–0, 2–0;
Bolton Wand v Chesterfield 0–2; Wolves v Accrington S 2–0; Stoke v Man C 1–2; Swindon v
Notts Co 3–1; Clapton Orient v Woolwich Arsenal 1–2; Sheff Utd v Darlington 0–1;
BRADFORD C v QPR 5–3

Second Round
BRADFORD C v Norwich C 2–1; Crewe Alex v Grimsby T 1–5; Burnley v Barnsley 2–0; Brighton v
Coventry C 0–0, 0–2; Blackburn R v Spurs 0–0, 2–0; Middlesbro v Leicester Fosse 0–0, 2–1;
W Ham v PNE 3–0; Man Utd v Aston Villa 2–1; NEWCASTLE UTD v Northampton 1–1, 1–0; Hull C
v Oldham Ath 1–0; Derby Co v WBA 2–0; Everton v Liverpool 2–1; Chesterfield v Chelsea 1–4;
Wolves v Man C 1–0; Swindon v Woolwich Arsenal 1–0; Darlington v Bradford PA 2–1

Third Round
BRADFORD C v Grimsby T 1–0; Burnley v Coventry C 5–0; Middlesbro v Blackburn R 0–3; W Ham
v Man Utd 2–1; NEWCASTLE UTD v Hull C 3–2; Derby Co v Everton 5–0; Wolves v Chelsea 0–2;
Darlington v Swindon 0–3

Fourth Round
BRADFORD C v Burnley 1–0; W Ham v Blackburn R 2–3; NEWCASTLE UTD v Derby Co 4–0;
Chelsea v Swindon 3–1

Semi-Final
BRADFORD C v Blackburn R 3–0; NEWCASTLE UTD v Chelsea 3–0

BRADFORD CITY **1**
NEWCASTLE UNITED **0** (after a 0–0 draw)

In July 1910 the Football Association Challenge Cup, having been dupli-cated without the consent of the Association, was withdrawn from the competition and a new Cup offered. This third trophy was the work of Messrs Fattorini & Sons of Bradford – how appropriate, therefore, that its first winners should be Bradford City.

In the 1911 Final, Newcastle once more failed to do themselves justice at Crystal Palace. An uneventful, goalless match led to a replay for the second successive year. This time it was held in Manchester, where a bad mistake by Lawrence, the Newcastle goalkeeper, gave Bradford's centre-forward O'Rourke the chance to score the only goal of the game with about fifteen minutes gone and thousands still clamouring to get into the Old Trafford ground.

The attendance of 66,646 was the highest for a midweek match in England; those who failed to gain entry missed little beyond an exhibition of hard, forthright tackling by both sides. The Bradford defence again performed heroically, and centre-half Torrance, who had missed the match at Crystal Palace, was outstanding.

Bradford, with a team containing eight Scotsmen, had therefore achieved in their first and only Final what Newcastle had been struggling to do for so long.

Bradford City: Mellors; Campbell, Taylor; Robinson, Torrance, McDonald; Logan, Spiers, O'Rourke, Devine, Thompson. (Gildea played centre-half in the first match.)
Newcastle United: Lawrence; McCracken, Whitson; Veitch, Low, Willis; Rutherford, Jobey, Stewart, Higgins, Wilson
Referee: J. H. Pearson (Crewe)

Bradford seemed poised to score in the replay

1911–2

First Round
Manchester Utd v Huddersfield T 3–1; Southampton v Coventry C 0–2; Aston Villa v Walsall 6–0;
Southport v Reading 0–2; Blackburn R v Norwich C 4–1; Derby Co v Newcastle Utd 3–0; Watford v
Wolves 0–0, 0–10; Lincoln C v Stockport Co 2–0; WBA v Spurs 3–0; Leeds C v Glossop 1–0;
Sunderland v Plymouth Arg 3–1; Brentford v Crystal Palace 0–0, 0–4; Fulham v Burnley 2–1;
Liverpool v Leyton 1–0; Northampton T v Bristol C 1–0; Darlington v Brighton & H Alb 2–1;
Swindon T v Sutton Junction 5–0; Luton v Notts Co 2–4; W Ham v Gainsboro Tr 2–1; Middlesbro v
Sheff Wed 0–0, 2–1; Clapton Orient v Everton 1–2; Bury v Millwall Ath 2–1; Oldham Ath v Hull C
1–1, 1–0; PNE v Man C 0–1; QPR v Bradford C 0–0, 0–4; Chelsea v Sheff Utd 1–0; Nott'm Forest v
Bradford PA 0–1; Bristol R v Portsmouth 1–2; Birmingham v BARNSLEY 0–0, 1–3;
Croydon Common v Leicester Fosse 2–2, 1–6; Bolton Wand v Woolwich Arsenal 1–0;
Crewe Alex v Blackpool 1–1, 1–2

Second Round
Coventry C v Man Utd 1–5; Aston Villa v Reading 1–1, 0–1; Derby Co v Blackburn R 1–2; Wolves v
Lincoln C 2–1; Leeds C v WBA 0–1; Crystal Palace v Sunderland 0–0, 0–1; Fulham v Liverpool
3–0; Darlington v Northampton T 1–1, 0–2; Swindon T v Notts Co 2–0; Middlesbro v W Ham
1–1, 1–2; Everton v Bury 1–1, 6–0; Manchester C v Oldham Ath 0–1; Bradford C v Chelsea 2–0;
Bradford PA v Portsmouth 2–0; BARNSLEY v Leicester Fosse 1–0; Bolton Wand v Blackpool 1–0

Third Round
Reading v Man Utd 1–1, 0–3; Blackburn R v Wolves 3–2; Sunderland v WBA 1–2; Fulham v
Northampton T 2–1; W Ham v Swindon T 1–1, 0–4; Oldham Ath v Everton 0–2; Bradford PA v
Bradford C 0–1; Bolton Wand v BARNSLEY 1–2

Fourth Round
Man Utd v Blackburn R 1–1, 2–4; WBA v Fulham 3–0; Swindon T v Everton 2–1; BARNSLEY v
Bradford C 0–0, 0–0, 0–0, 3–2

Semi-Final
Blackburn R v WBA 0–0, 0–1; Swindon T v BARNSLEY 0–0, 0–1

BARNSLEY **1**
WEST BROMWICH ALBION **0** (after a 0–0 draw)

The Cup stayed in Yorkshire for another season as Second Division Barnsley, losing finalists in 1910, beat West Bromwich Albion after a draw. It was the third year running that the Final had been drawn, strange when one realizes that it was to be fifty-eight years before it was drawn again.

In the second game in Sheffield, the score sheet was still blank at the end of normal time. Two minutes from the end of extra time, Glendinning, the Barnsley right-half, beat two opponents and pushed a pass forward to Tuffnell, his inside-right. Away he went on a long dribble through the Albion ranks, finally evading defenders Pennington and Cook to put a fast ground shot past Pearson.

By their victory Barnsley became the third team from the Second Division to lift the Cup. They won it because of their stamina throughout the competition – their fourth round tie with Bradford City, for example, had been a four-game marathon lasting seven hours – and a superb defence conceding just four goals in twelve matches.

What Albion goalkeeper Hubert Pearson failed to achieve that day, his son Harold gained some twenty years later as Albion's goalkeeper when they beat Birmingham at Wembley in 1931.

Barnsley: Cooper; Downs, Taylor; Glendinning, Bratley, Utley; Bartrop, Tuffnell, Lillycrop, Travers, Moore
West Bromwich Albion: Pearson; Cook, Pennington; Baddeley, Buck, McNeal; Jephcott, Wright, Pailor, Bowser, Shearman
Referee: J. R. Schumacher (London)

1912-3

First Round
Derby Co v ASTON VILLA 1–3; WBA v W. Ham 1–1, 2–2, 0–3; Crystal Palace v Glossop 2–0; Southampton v Bury 1–1, 1–2; Bradford PA v Barrow 1–1, 1–0; Wolves v London Caledonian 3–1; Sheff Wed v Grimsby T 5–1; Chelsea v Southend Utd 5–2; Oldham Ath v Bolton Wand 2–0; Chesterfield v Nott'm Forest 1–4; Man Utd v Coventry C 1–1, 2–1; Plymouth Arg v PNE 2–0; Everton v Stockport Co 5–1; Portsmouth v Brighton & H Alb 1–2; Bristol R v Notts Co 2–0; Leicester Fosse v Norwich C 1–4; SUNDERLAND v Clapton Orient 6–0; Man C v Birmingham 4–0; Rochdale v Swindon T 0–2; Huddersfield T v Sheff Utd 3–1; Newcastle Utd v Bradford C 1–0; Fulham v Hull C 0–2; Liverpool v Bristol C 3–0; Croydon Common v Woolwich Arsenal 0–0, 1–2; Leeds C v Burnley 2–3; South Shields v Gainsboro Tr 0–1; Millwall Ath v Middlesbro 0–0, 1–4; Halifax T v QPR 2–4; Blackburn R v Northampton T 7–2; Gillingham v Barnsley 0–0, 1–3; Stoke C v Reading 2–2, 0–3; Spurs v Blackpool 1–1, 6–1

Second Round
ASTON VILLA v W. Ham 5–0; Crystal Palace v Bury 2–0; Bradford PA v Wolves 3–0; Chelsea v Sheff Wed 1–1, 0–6; Oldham Ath v Nott'm Forest 5–1; Plymouth Arg v Man Utd 0–2; Brighton & H Alb v Everton 0–0, 0–1; Bristol R v Norwich C 1–1, 2–2, 1–0; SUNDERLAND v Man C 2–0; Huddersfield T v Swindon T 1–2; Hull C v Newcastle Utd 0–0, 0–3; Woolwich Arsenal v Liverpool 1–4; Burnley v Gainsboro Tr 4–1; Middlesbro v QPR 3–2; Barnsley v Blackburn R 2–3; Reading v Spurs 1–0

Third Round
ASTON VILLA v Crystal Palace 5–0; Bradford PA v Sheff Wed 2–1; Oldham Ath v Man Utd 0–0, 2–1; Bristol R v Everton 0–4; SUNDERLAND v Swindon T 4–2; Liverpool v Newcastle Utd 1–1, 0–1; Burnley v Middlesbro 3–1; Reading v Blackburn R 1–2

Fourth Round
Bradford PA v ASTON VILLA 0–5; Everton v Oldham Ath 0–1; SUNDERLAND v Newcastle Utd 0–0, 2–2, 3–0; Blackburn R v Burnley 0–1

Semi-Final
ASTON VILLA v Oldham Ath 1–0; SUNDERLAND v Burnley 0–0, 3–2

ASTON VILLA **1**
SUNDERLAND **0**

For the first time the current top two clubs in the League contested the Cup Final. Sunderland, with a great tradition of fine performances in the League, had reached their first Final. Villa, the most popular side in the country, were back in the Final after an interval of eight years.

This veritable 'battle of the giants' attracted a record crowd for a Final (120,081), so large that many hardly caught a glimpse of the ball during the whole match.

Villa won, but only after a tremendous fight. First Wallace failed with a penalty-kick that would have given them an early advantage, then Sam Hardy, their great international goalkeeper, had to leave the field for ten minutes in the second half with a leg injury. Harrop took over in goal in his absence.

Richardson and Buchan both missed 'gifts' for Sunderland, and the great chance had gone. Barber, Villa's right-half, headed home a perfect Wallace corner-kick in the closing minutes, and Villa were victors for the fifth time, equalling the record of the Wanderers and Blackburn Rovers.

The play in the first ten minutes was such a delight to watch, that the massive crowd had cheered almost non-stop. Then the football lost its crispness, and there were frequent free-kicks for fouls and offside.

Aston Villa: Hardy; Lyons, Weston; Barber, Harrop, Leach; Wallace, Halse, Hampton, Stephenson (C.), Bache
Sunderland: Butler; Gladwin, Ness; Cuggy, Thompson, Low; Mordue, Buchan, Richardson, Holley, Martin
Referee: A. Adams (Nottingham)

1913–4

First Round
Newcastle Utd v Sheff Utd 0–5; Bradford PA v Reading 5–1; Millwall Ath v Chelsea 0–0, 1–0; Bradford C v Woolwich Arsenal 2–0; Man C v Fulham 2–0; Leicester Fosse v Spurs 5–5, 0–2; Blackburn R v Middlesbro 3–0; Hull C v Bury 0–0, 1–2; BURNLEY v South Shields 3–1; Derby Co v Northampton T 1–0; Bolton Wand v Port Vale 3–0; Swindon T v Man Utd 1–0; Sunderland v Chatham 9–0; Plymouth Arg v Lincoln C 4–1; PNE v Bristol R 5–2; Glossop v Everton 2–1; Aston Villa v Stoke C 4–0; Portsmouth v Exeter C 0–4; WBA v Grimsby T 2–0; Gainsboro Tr v Leeds C 2–4; Sheff Wed v Notts Co 3–2; Wolves v Southampton 3–0; Oldham Ath v Brighton & H Alb 1–1, 0–1; Clapton Orient v Nott'm Forest 2–2, 1–0; LIVERPOOL v Barnsley 1–1, 1–0; Gillingham v Blackpool 1–0; W. Ham v Chesterfield 8–1; Crystal Palace v Norwich C 2–1; QPR v Bristol R 2–2, 2–0; Swansea T v Merthyr Tydfil 2–0; Birmingham v Southend Utd 2–1; Huddersfield T v London Caledonian 3–0

Second Round
Sheff Utd v Bradford PA 3–1; Millwall Ath v Bradford C 1–0; Man C v Spurs 2–1; Blackburn R v Bury 2–0; BURNLEY v Derby Co 3–2; Bolton Wand v Swindon T 4–2; Sunderland v Plymouth Arg 2–1; Glossop v PNE 0–1; Exeter C v Aston Villa 1–2; Leeds C v WBA 0–2; Wolves v Sheff Wed 1–1, 0–1; Brighton & H Alb v Clapton Orient 3–1; LIVERPOOL v Gillingham 2–0; W. Ham v Crystal Palace 2–0; Swansea T v QPR 1–2; Birmingham v Huddersfield T 1–0

Third Round
Millwall Ath v Sheff Utd 0–4; Blackburn R v Man C 1–2; BURNLEY v Bolton Wand 3–0; Sunderland v PNE 2–0; Aston Villa v WBA 2–1; Sheff Wed v Brighton & H Alb 3–0; W. Ham v LIVERPOOL 1–1, 1–5; Birmingham v QPR 1–2

Fourth Round
Man C v Sheff Utd 0–0, 0–0, 0–1; Sunderland v BURNLEY 0–0, 1–2; Sheff Wed v Aston Villa 0–1; LIVERPOOL v QPR 2–1

Semi-Final
Sheff Utd v BURNLEY 0–0, 0–1; Aston Villa v LIVERPOOL 0–2

BURNLEY **1**
LIVERPOOL **0**

By 1914 the Qualifying Competition had been enlarged from ten to twenty-four divisions, and, that season, from a record entry of 476 clubs, Burnley and Liverpool emerged as the two protagonists in a second all-Lancashire Final. For the first time the Final was honoured by the presence of a ruling monarch, King George V – regal recognition of the place football had assumed in the life of the nation.

A fierce shot just after half-time by centre-forward Freeman gave Burnley a narrow victory in an otherwise undistinguished match in which two teams with low positions in the League slogged it out in midfield, neither set of forwards being capable of mounting a sustained attack.

After Freeman had shot past Campbell and put Burnley in the lead, the standard of play improved considerably. The last half-hour certainly had the crowd on its toes as Liverpool battled hard for an equaliser.

The Burnley defence remained resolute to the end, and their captain and centre-half Boyle, became the first man ever to receive the Cup from royal hands. It was the last Final to be played at the old Crystal Palace.

Burnley: Sewell; Bamford, Taylor; Halley, Boyle, Watson; Nesbit, Lindley, Freeman, Hodgson, Mosscrop
Liverpool: Campbell; Longworth, Pursell; Fairfoul, Ferguson, McKinlay; Sheldon, Metcalf, Miller, Lacey, Nicholl
Referee: H. S. Bamlett (Gateshead)

Freeman scores the only goal of the game

1914-5

First Round
Blackpool v SHEFF UTD 1–2; Liverpool v Stockport Co 3–0; Bradford PA v Portsmouth 1–0; Bury v Plymouth Arg 1–1, 2–1; Croydon Common v Oldham Ath 0–3; Rochdale v Gillingham 2–0; Birmingham v Crystal Palace 2–2, 3–0; Brighton & H Alb v Lincoln C 2–1; Bolton Wand v Notts Co 2–1; Millwall Ath v Clapton Orient 2–1; Burnley v Huddersfield T 3–1; Bristol R v Southend Utd 0–0, 0–3; Hull C v WBA 1–0; Grimsby T v Northampton T 0–3; Southampton v Luton T 3–0; South Shields v Fulham 1–2; CHELSEA v Swindon T 1–1, 5–2; Arsenal v Merthyr Tydfil 3–0; PNE v Man C 0–0, 0–3; Aston Villa v Exeter C 2–0; W. Ham v Newcastle Utd 2–2, 2–3; Swansea T v Blackburn R 1–0; Sheff Wed v Man Utd 1–0; Reading v Wolves 0–1; Everton v Barnsley 3–0; Bristol C v Cardiff C 2–0; QPR v Glossop 2–1; Derby Co v Leeds C 1–2; Darlington v Bradford C 0–1; Middlesbro v Goole T 9–3; Nott'm Forest v Norwich C 1–4; Spurs v Sunderland 2–1

Second Round
SHEFF UTD v Liverpool 1–0; Bury v Bradford PA 0–1; Oldham Ath v Rochdale 3–0; Brighton & H Alb v Birmingham 0–0, 0–3; Bolton Wand v Millwall Ath 0–0, 2–2, 4–1; Burnley v Southend Utd 6–0; Hull C v Northampton 2–1; Fulham v Southampton 2–3; CHELSEA v Arsenal 1–0; Man C v Aston Villa 1–0; Newcastle Utd v Swansea T 1–1, 2–0; Sheff Wed v Wolves 2–0; Everton v Bristol C 4–0; QPR v Leeds C 1–0; Bradford C v Middlesbro 1–0; Norwich C v Spurs 3–2

Third Round
SHEFF UTD v Bradford PA 1–0; Birmingham v Oldham Ath 2–3; Bolton Wand v Burnley 2–1; Southampton v Hull C 2–2, 0–4; Man C v CHELSEA 0–1; Sheff Wed v Newcastle Utd 1–2; QPR v Everton 1–2; Bradford C v Norwich C 1–1, 0–0, 2–0

Fourth Round
Oldham Ath v SHEFF UTD 0–0, 0–3; Bolton Wand v Hull C 4–2; CHELSEA v Newcastle Utd 1–1, 1–0; Bradford C v Everton 0–2

Semi-Final
SHEFF UTD v Bolton Wand 2–1; CHELSEA v Everton 2–0

SHEFFIELD UNITED **3**
CHELSEA **0**

Sheffield United won the 'Khaki' Final amid controversy as to whether organized football should be continued in time of war. The Football Association had decided that it was better to carry on somehow, to provide relief for the workers and the warriors.

In the League, Chelsea struggled for most of the season and finished only one from the bottom. In the Cup, however, they stayed right through to the last hurdle for the first time. It was fifty-five years before they were to reach the Final again.

Nobody had expected Chelsea to do well in the Cup. The players were considered too small – Ford, at 5 ft 7 in, was the tallest of five forwards – to have much chance in the hurly-burly of cup-tie football.

On the grounds that it would otherwise interfere with war work, the Final venue was switched from London to Old Trafford, Manchester. In a one-sided game Chelsea played a long way below their best Cup form.

Molyneux should have prevented Simmons's opener for Sheffield ten minutes before half-time. Yet Chelsea's defence did keep them in with a chance until six minutes from the end. Then Fazackerley and Kitchen added further goals to give Sheffield their third Cup victory.

Sheffield United: Gough; Cook, English; Sturgess, Brelsford, Utley; Simmons, Fazackerley, Kitchen, Masterman, Evans
Chelsea: Molyneux; Bettridge, Harrow; Taylor, Logan, Walker; Ford, Halse, Thompson, Croal, McNeil
Referee: H. H. Taylor (Altrincham)

1919–20

First Round
ASTON VILLA v QPR 2–1; Port Vale v Man Utd 1–2; Sunderland v Hull C 6–2; Thorneycroft's (W) v Burnley 0–0, 0–5; Bristol R v Spurs 1–4; West Stanley v Gillingham 3–1; Southampton v W. Ham 0–0, 1–3; Bury v Stoke C 2–0; Bolton Wand v Chelsea 0–1; Fulham v Swindon T 1–2; Newport Co v Leicester C 0–0, 0–2; Man C v Clapton Orient 4–1; Bradford PA v Nott'm Forest 3–0; Castleford T v Hednesford T 2–0; Notts Co v Millwall Ath 2–0; Middlesbro v Lincoln C 4–1; Grimsby T v Bristol C 1–2; Arsenal v Rochdale 4–2; Cardiff C v Oldham Ath 2–0; Blackburn R v Wolves 2–2, 0–1; Bradford C v Portsmouth 2–2, 2–0; Sheff Utd v Southend Utd 3–0; PNE v Stockport Co 3–1; Blackpool v Derby Co 0–0, 4–1; HUDDERSFIELD T v Brentford 5–1; Newcastle Utd v Crystal Palace 2–0; Plymouth Arg v Reading 2–0; WBA v Barnsley 0–1; South Shields v Liverpool 1–1, 0–2; Luton T v Coventry C 2–2, 1–0; Birmingham v Everton 2–0; Darlington v Sheff Wed 0–0, 2–0

Second Round
Man Utd v ASTON VILLA 1–2; Burnley v Sunderland 1–1, 0–2; Spurs v West Stanley 4–0; W. Ham v Bury 6–0; Chelsea v Swindon T 4–0; Leicester C v Man C 3–0; Bradford PA v Castleford T 3–2; Notts Co v Middlesbro 1–0; Bristol C v Arsenal 1–0; Wolves v Cardiff C 1–2; Bradford C v Sheff Utd 2–1; PNE v Blackpool 2–1; Newcastle Utd v HUDDERSFIELD T 0–1; Plymouth Arg v Barnsley 4–1; Luton T v Liverpool 0–2; Birmingham v Darlington 4–0

Third Round
ASTON VILLA v Sunderland 1–0; Spurs v W. Ham 3–0; Chelsea v Leicester C 3–0; Notts Co v Bradford PA 3–4; Bristol C v Cardiff C 2–1; PNE v Bradford C 0–3; HUDDERSFIELD T v Plymouth Arg 3–1; Liverpool v Birmingham 2–0

Fourth Round
Spurs v ASTON VILLA 0–1; Chelsea v Bradford PA 4–1; Bristol C v Bradford C 2–0; HUDDERSFIELD T v Liverpool 2–1

Semi-Final
ASTON VILLA v Chelsea 3–1; Bristol C v HUDDERSFIELD T 1–2

Andy Ducat,
the winning captain in 1920

Huddersfield clear the ball away following a corner

ASTON VILLA **1**
HUDDERSFIELD TOWN **0**

The substitution of Stamford Bridge for the Crystal Palace, then a War Service Depôt and no longer available, signalled the end of the picnic-like atmosphere that had existed at the Final since 1895. Now the match was more important than any 'side-show'.

Huddersfield Town's achievement in reaching the 1920 Final was a remarkable one as the club had only recently been threatened with dissolution through lack of funds. The townspeople of Huddersfield had rallied to the club's aid, and their reward was promotion from the Second Division and a first-ever appearance in the Cup Final in the same season.

In the early autumn of the 1919–20 season, Villa's League position had been desperate – bottom of the First Division, with eight defeats in ten matches. But Villa won this first post-war Final with a fluke goal scored in the seventh minute of extra time.

Villa's quick interpassing had Huddersfield at full stretch early on, and only three magnificent saves from Mutch, defying Kirton, Stephenson and Walker, and Wilson's sterling play at centre-half, gave the nervous Huddersfield team time to settle. Soon their strong spoiling style jolted Villa out of their rhythm, and there was no score at the end of normal time. Villa had been the better, more positive side throughout, but too often they were forced to shoot under pressure or from long range, and the close covering of the Huddersfield defence cut openings down to a minimum. Villa were a shade too casual in everything they did, and it was just as well that Ducat and Moss were so much on top in midfield.

Villa won the Cup for the sixth time, with a goal scored almost involuntarily. When Dorrell's corner hung tantalizingly in front of goal, Wilson went up for the ball with Kirton, Villa's best forward. It seemed to go into the net off Wilson's head, but was actually diverted off Wilson's face from Kirton's head – or so the players concerned said afterwards.

In the few minutes that remained, Huddersfield threw everything into an all-out attack on the Villa goal. Mann beat Hardy, but Weston stuck out a leg to block his goal-bound shot. Huddersfield didn't come as close to a goal again.

Andy Ducat, one of the select few to have represented England at both football and cricket, came up to collect the Cup from Prince Henry. There were four members of the winning side of 1913 behind him – Weston, Wallace, Stephenson and the 'Keeper of Keepers', Sam Hardy.

Aston Villa: Hardy; Smart, Weston; Ducat, Barson, Moss; Wallace, Kirton, Walker, Stephenson (C.), Dorrell
Huddersfield Town: Mutch; Wood, Bullock; Slade, Wilson, Watson; Richardson, Mann, Taylor, Swan, Islip
Referee: J. T. Howcroft (Bolton)

1920–1

First Round
Southend Utd v Eccles 5–1; Darlington v Blackpool 2–2, 1–2; SPURS v Bristol R 6–2; Bradford C v Barnsley 3–1; Notts Co v WBA 3–0; Aston Villa v Bristol C 2–0; Bradford PA v Clapton Orient 1–0; Brentford v Huddersfield T 1–2; Crystal Palace v Man C 2–0; Hull C v Bath C 3–0; Leicester C v Burnley 3–7; QPR v Arsenal 2–0; South Shields v Portsmouth 3–0; Luton T v Birmingham 2–1; PNE v Bolton Wand 2–0; Watford v Exeter C 3–0; Everton v Stockport Co 1–0; Sheff Wed v W. Ham 1–0; Newcastle Utd v Nott'm Forest 1–1, 2–0; Liverpool v Man Utd 1–1, 2–1; Millwall Ath v Lincoln C 0–3; Blackburn R v Fulham 1–1, 0–1; Derby Co v Middlesbro 2–0; WOLVES v Stoke C 3–2; Grimsby T v Norwich C 1–0; Northampton T v Southampton 0–0, 1–4; Brighton & H Alb v Oldham Ath 4–1; Sunderland v Cardiff C 0–1; Swansea T v Bury 3–0; Plymouth Arg v Rochdale 2–0; Swindon T v Sheff Utd 1–0; Reading v Chelsea 0–0, 2–2, 1–3

Second Round
Southend Utd v Blackpool 1–0; SPURS v Bradford C 4–0; Notts Co v Aston Villa 0–0, 0–1; Bradford PA v Huddersfield T 0–1; Crystal Palace v Hull C 0–2; Burnley v QPR 4–2; South Shields v Luton T 0–4; PNE v Watford 4–1; Everton v Sheff Wed 1–1, 1–0; Newcastle Utd v Liverpool 1–0; Lincoln C v Fulham 0–0, 0–1; Derby Co v WOLVES 1–1, 0–1; Grimsby T v Southampton 1–3; Brighton & H Alb v Cardiff C 0–0, 0–1; Swansea T v Plymouth Arg 1–2; Swindon T v Chelsea 0–2

Third Round
Southend Utd v SPURS 1–4; Aston Villa v Huddersfield T 2–0; Hull C v Burnley 3–0; Luton T v PNE 2–3; Everton v Newcastle Utd 3–0; Fulham v WOLVES 0–1; Southampton v Cardiff C 0–1; Plymouth Arg v Chelsea 0–0, 0–0, 1–2

Fourth Round
SPURS v Aston Villa 1–0; Hull C v PNE 0–0, 0–1; Everton v WOLVES 0–1; Cardiff C v Chelsea 1–0

Semi-Final
SPURS v PNE 2–1; WOLVES v Cardiff C 0–0, 3–1

TOTTENHAM HOTSPUR **1**
WOLVERHAMPTON WANDERERS **0**

Tottenham reached the Final at Stamford Bridge after difficult ties in earlier rounds against Aston Villa, avenging their fourth round defeat the previous year, and Preston in the semi-final at Hillsborough. Now they were up against the Wolves, still a Second Division side and in their first Final for twenty years.

In spite of an increase in the admission price to keep down the numbers, the crowd was still large enough to spill on to the cinder track around the pitch.

Tottenham, with such great players as Seed, Grimsdell the captain, and the left-wing pair Bliss and Dimmock, were the artists, but the match produced only three memorable incidents: a cloudburst that reduced the pitch to a quagmire; Dimmock's winning goal; and Brooks, just before the finish, having his close-range shot brilliantly blocked by Tottenham centre-half Walters.

Dimmock had tried unsuccessfully for most of the match to dribble his way through the clinging mud and the Wolves defence. Ten minutes after half-time he finally broke through to score. Taking a long crossfield pass from Seed, he appeared to have lost the ball to Woodward, but then quickly regained possession before sending a shot flying into the far corner of the net.

Tottenham Hotspur: Hunter; Clay, M'Donald; Smith, Walters, Grimsdell; Banks, Seed, Cantrell, Bliss, Dimmock
Wolverhampton Wanderers: George; Woodward, Marshall; Gregory, Hodnett, Riley; Lea, Burrill, Edmonds, Potts, Brooks
Referee: J. Davies (Rainhill)

1921–2

First Round

Everton v Crystal Palace 0–6; Millwall Ath v Ashington 4–2; Worksop T v Southend Utd 1–2; Swansea T v W. Ham 0–0, 1–1, 1–0; Blackburn R v Southport 1–1, 2–0; Swindon T v Leeds Utd 2–1; Brighton & H Alb v Sheff Utd 1–0; Burnley v HUDDERSFIELD T 2–2, 2–3; Aston Villa v Derby Co 6–1; Portsmouth v Luton T 1–1, 1–2; Port Vale v Stoke C 2–4; Northampton T v Reading 3–0; Chelsea v WBA 2–4; Sunderland v Liverpool 1–1, 0–5; Walsall v Bradford C 3–3, 0–4; Grimsby T v Notts Co 1–1, 0–3; Bradford PA v Sheff Wed 1–0; Arsenal v QPR 0–0, 2–1; Plymouth Arg v Fulham 1–1, 0–1; Leicester C v Clapton Orient 2–0; Barnsley v Norwich C 1–1, 2–1; Gillingham v Oldham Ath 1–3; Newcastle Utd v Newport Co 6–0; PNE v Wolves 3–0; Man Utd v Cardiff C 1–4; Southampton v South Shields 3–1; Hull C v Middlesbro 5–0; Bristol C v Nott'm Forest 0–0, 1–3; Man C v Darlington 3–1; Bolton Wand v Bury 1–0; Blackpool v Watford 1–2; Brentford v Spurs 0–2

Second Round

Crystal Palace v Millwall Ath 0–0, 0–2; Southend Utd v Swansea T 0–1; Swindon T v Blackburn R 0–1; Brighton & H Alb v HUDDERSFIELD T 0–0, 0–2; Aston Villa v Luton T 1–0; Northampton T v Stoke C 2–2, 0–3; Liverpool v WBA 0–1; Bradford C v Notts Co 1–1, 1–1, 0–1; Bradford PA v Arsenal 2–3; Leicester C v Fulham 2–0; Barnsley v Oldham Ath 3–1; PNE v Newcastle Utd 3–1; Southampton v Cardiff C 1–1, 0–2; Nott'm Forest v Hull C 3–0; Bolton Wand v Man C 1–3; Spurs v Watford 1–0

Third Round

Millwall Ath v Swansea T 4–0; Blackburn R v HUDDERSFIELD T 1–1, 0–5; Stoke C v Aston Villa 0–0, 0–4; WBA v Notts C 1–1, 0–2; Arsenal v Leicester C 3–0; Barnsley v PNE 1–1, 0–3; Cardiff C v Nott'm Forest 4–1; Spurs v Man C 2–1;

Fourth Round

HUDDERSFIELD T v Millwall Ath 3–0; Notts Co v Aston Villa 2–2, 4–3; Arsenal v PNE 1–1, 1–2; Cardiff C v Spurs 1–1, 1–2

Semi-Final

HUDDERSFIELD T v Notts Co 3–1; PNE v Spurs 2–1

HUDDERSFIELD TOWN **1**
PRESTON NORTH END **0**

The year 1922 saw Preston take their place in the Final – the last at Stamford Bridge – for the first time since 1889. Their opponents, Huddersfield, were now heading for their great triumphs. They had some splendid players in Wadsworth and Smith, both England Internationals, and inside-left Clem Stephenson, who had already won Cup medals with Villa in 1913 and 1920.

The match itself was rough and undistinguished. In some way it was fitting that it should have been the first Final to be decided by a penalty-kick. Both sides were determined to stop each other at all costs, and the referee, for his part, was far too lenient with offenders.

Mr Fowler's penalty award was controversial. Huddersfield's outside-left, Billy Smith, had set off on a long dribble and was racing into the penalty-area when Hamilton, Preston's right-back, brought him down from behind. Despite the bespectacled Mitchell's efforts to distract the taker by jumping up and down on his line, Smith blasted the spot-kick into the net.

Was it a penalty? Smith had certainly fallen inside the area, but marks on the pitch suggested that the foul may have been committed outside.

Huddersfield Town: Mutch; Wood, Wadsworth; Slade, Wilson, Watson; Richardson, Mann, Islip, Stephenson, Smith (W. H.)
Preston North End: J. F. Mitchell; Hamilton, Doolan; Duxbury, McCall, Williamson; Rawlings, Jefferis, Roberts, Woodhouse, Quinn
Referee: J. W. D. Fowler (Sunderland)

1922-3

First Round
Norwich C v BOLTON WAND 0–2; Portsmouth v Leeds Utd 0–0, 1–3; Clapton Orient v Millwall Ath 0–2; Huddersfield T v Birmingham 2–1; Man C v Charlton Ath 1–2; Aberdare v PNE 1–3; WBA v Stalybridge Celtic 0–0, 2–0; Sunderland v Burnley 3–1; Oldham Ath v Middlesbro 0–1; Nott'm Forest v Sheff Utd 0–0, 0–0, 1–1, 0–1; Liverpool v Arsenal 0–0, 4–1; Merthyr Tydfil v Wolves 0–1; QPR v Crystal Palace 1–0; Wigan Borough v Bath C 4–1; South Shields v Halifax T 3–1; Aston Villa v Blackburn R 0–1; Bury v Luton T 2–1; Blyth Spartans v Stoke C 0–3; Chelsea v Rotherham C 1–0; Newcastle Utd v Southampton 0–0, 1–3; Brighton & H Alb v Corinthians 1–1, 1–1, 1–0; Hull C v W. HAM 2–3; Plymouth Arg v Notts Co 0–0, 1–0; Everton v Bradford PA 1–1, 0–1; Derby Co v Blackpool 2–0; Bristol C v Wrexham 5–1; Sheff Wed v New Brighton 3–0; Swindon T v Barnsley 0–0, 0–2; Spurs v Worksop T 0–0, 9–0; Bradford C v Man Utd 1–1, 0–2; Cardiff C v Watford 1–1, 2–2, 2–1; Leicester C v Fulham 4–0

Second Round
BOLTON WAND v Leeds Utd 3–1; Millwall Ath v Huddersfield T 0–0, 0–3; Charlton Ath v PNE 2–0; WBA v Sunderland 2–0; Middlesbro v Sheff Utd 1–1, 0–3; Wolves v Liverpool 0–2; Wigan Borough v QPR 2–4; South Shields v Blackburn R 0–0, 1–0; Bury v Stoke City 3–1; Chelsea v Southampton 0–0, 0–1; Brighton & H Alb v W. HAM 1–1, 0–1; Plymouth Arg v Bradford PA 4–1; Bristol C v Derby Co 0–3; Sheff Wed v Barnsley 2–1; Spurs v Man Utd 4–0; Leicester C v Cardiff C 0–1

Third Round
Huddersfield T v BOLTON WAND 1–1, 0–1; Charlton Ath v WBA 1–0; Liverpool v Sheff Utd 1–2; QPR v South Shields 3–0; Bury v Southampton 0–0, 0–1; W. HAM v Plymouth Arg 2–0; Derby Co v Sheff Wed 1–0; Cardiff C v Spurs 2–3

Fourth Round
Charlton Ath v BOLTON WAND 0–1; QPR v Sheff Utd 0–1; Southampton v W. HAM 1–1, 1–1, 0–1; Spurs v Derby Co 0–1

Semi-Final
BOLTON WAND v Sheff Utd 1–0; W. HAM v Derby Co 5–2

Jack is on target after only two minutes

BOLTON WANDERERS **2**
WEST HAM UNITED **0**

The first Final at the new stadium at Wembley, played on 28 April 1923, was marked by disorderly scenes unparalleled in the history of the game. Before the match a crowd of 100,000 outside the stadium rushed the gates, burst the barriers, and swarmed on to the field of play. In all about 200,000 people – a record football crowd – squeezed into a space supposed to accommodate 127,000.

The stadium had been completed in 300 working days at a cost of £750,000. The workmen had made use of 25,000 tons of concrete, 1,500 tons of steel and half a million rivets. A few days before the Final a battalion of infantry marked time on the terraces for fifteen minutes to test their strength.

But for the anger of the mob of 200,000 people, and the presence of King George V in the Royal Box, the match would probably have been called off. Although it took three-quarters of an hour after the time fixed for the start of the match for mounted police to clear the pitch, it was virtually impossible to observe the rules of the game. When a player took a corner kick, for example, the crowd were so close up to the touch-line that he could not take his run until policemen had forced people away from the corner of the field.

Bolton won the match 2–0 and took the Cup for the first time, after two previous appearances in the Final. The first Wembley goal came only two minutes after the delayed start, and David Jack, Bolton's inside-right, was the scorer.

Jack later played in three more finals, one for Bolton and two for Arsenal. He was also the first player for whom a transfer fee of £10,000 was paid. It is said that, while he was shooting into the West Ham net in the 1923 Final, one of the West Ham defenders, Tresadern, was struggling to get back on to the pitch after finding himself the wrong side of part of the crowd on the touch-line.

When half-time came neither side left the field, and eight minutes after the interval Bolton scored a second. J. R. Smith, Bolton's centre-forward and the only Scotsman in the match, took a beautiful pass from Vizard on his left and shot home past Hufton. The ball rebounded into play so swiftly that few realized he had scored.

Bolton Wanderers: Pym; Haworth, Finney; Nuttall, Seddon, Jennings; Butler, Jack, Smith (J.R.), Smith (J.), Vizard
West Ham United: Hufton; Henderson, Young; Bishop, Kay, Tresadern; Richards, Brown, Watson (V.), Moore, Ruffell
Referee: D. H. Asson (West Bromwich)

1923–4

First Round

Derby C v Bury 2–1; Portsmouth v NEWCASTLE UTD 2–4; Exeter C v Grimsby T 1–0; Middlesbro v Watford 0–1; Chelsea v Southampton 1–1, 0–2; Blackpool v Sheff Utd 1–0; Liverpool v Bradford C 2–1; Hull C v Bolton Wand 2–2, 0–4; Man C v Nott'm Forest 2–0; Northampton T v Halifax T 1–1, 1–1, 2–4; Barnsley v Brighton & H Alb 0–0, 0–1; Everton v PNE 3–1; Cardiff C v Gillingham 0–0, 2–0; Arsenal v Luton T 4–1; Sheff Wed v Leicester C 4–1; Norwich C v Bristol C 0–1; Ashington v ASTON VILLA 1–5; Swansea T v Clapton Orient 1–1, 1–1, 2–1; W. Ham v Aberdare 5–0; Leeds Utd v Stoke C 1–0; Millwall Ath v WBA 0–1; Corinthians v Blackburn R 1–0; Accrington S v Charlton Ath 0–0, 0–1; Wolves v Darlington 3–1; Swindon T v Bradford PA 4–0; Oldham Ath v Sunderland 2–1; Crystal Palace v Spurs 2–0; QPR v Notts Co 1–2; Burnley v South Shields 3–2; Fulham v Llanelly 2–0; Huddersfield T v Birmingham 1–0; Man Utd v Plymouth Arg 1–0

Second Round

Derby Co v NEWCASTLE UTD 2–2, 2–2, 2–2, 3–5; Exeter C v Watford 0–0, 0–1; Southampton v Blackpool 3–1; Bolton Wand v Liverpool 1–4; Man C v Halifax T 2–2, 0–0, 3–0; Brighton & H Alb v Everton 5–2; Cardiff C v Arsenal 1–0; Sheff Wed v Bristol C 1–1, 0–2; Swansea T v ASTON VILLA 0–2; W. Ham v Leeds Utd 1–1, 0–1; WBA v Corinthians 5–0; Charlton Ath v Wolves 0–0, 0–1; Swindon T v Oldham Ath 2–0; Crystal Palace v Notts Co 0–0, 0–0, 0–0, 2–1; Burnley v Fulham 0–0, 1–0; Man Utd v Huddersfield T 0–3

Third Round

Watford v NEWCASTLE UTD 0–1; Southampton v Liverpool 0–0, 0–2; Brighton & H Alb v Man C 1–5; Cardiff C v Bristol C 3–0; ASTON VILLA v Leeds Utd 3–0; WBA v Wolves 1–1, 2–0; Crystal Palace v Swindon T 1–2; Burnley v Huddersfield T 1–0

Fourth Round

NEWCASTLE UTD v Liverpool 1–0; Man C v Cardiff C 0–0, 1–0; WBA v ASTON VILLA 0–2; Swindon T v Burnley 1–1, 1–3

Semi-Final

NEWCASTLE UTD v Man C 2–0; ASTON VILLA v Burnley 3–0

NEWCASTLE UNITED **2**
ASTON VILLA **0**

In 1924 Villa still had five players in their side from the victorious team of 1920, and Newcastle sprang a surprise by calling up their reserve goalkeeper, Bradley, on the morning of the match.

On a rain-soaked pitch the play was scintillating from start to finish, and, for the first half at least, Villa appeared to be heading for their seventh Cup Final victory.

Villa captain Walker collided with a post as he just missed connecting with a cross, and, though Villa continued to hold a slight advantage in some exciting exchanges, the prospect of extra time loomed large.

With eight minutes left, centre-half Spencer advanced upfield for Newcastle and put Harris through to score with a tremendous shot. Before Villa could recover from the shock, Newcastle had made it 2–0. Seymour, on the left wing, gathered a long pass without breaking stride and slammed another unstoppable shot into the Villa net. It was an exciting finish to an exciting match, and Newcastle had neatly reversed the 1905 result.

A few days prior to the Final, Villa had defeated Newcastle 6–1 in a League match at Villa Park. However, Bradley, Newcastle's inexperienced goalkeeper, had played a hero's game in the Final, keeping Villa's illustrious forward-line at bay.

Newcastle United: Bradley; Hampson, Hudspeth; Mooney, Spencer, Gibson; Low, Cowan, Harris, M'Donald, Seymour
Aston Villa: Jackson; Smart, Mort; Moss, Dr V. E. Milne, Blackburn; York, Kirton, Capewell, Walker, Dorrell
Referee: W. E. Russell (Swindon)

Harris gives Newcastle the lead eight minutes from time

1924–5

First Round
CARDIFF C v Darlington 0–0, 0–0, 2–0; Swindon T v Fulham 1–2; Doncaster R v Norwich C
1–2; Coventry C v Notts Co 0–2; Hull C v Wolves 1–1, 1–0; Crystal Palace v South Shields
2–1; Newcastle Utd v Hartlepools Utd 4–1; Leicester C v Stoke C 3–0; Blackpool v Barrow
0–0, 2–0; Bradford PA v Middlesbro 1–0; Nott'm Forest v Clapton Orient 1–0; W. Ham v
Arsenal 0–0, 2–2, 1–0; Spurs v Northampton 3–0; Bolton Wand v Huddersfield T 3–0;
Accrington S v Portsmouth 2–5; Blackburn R v Oldham Ath 1–0; Southampton v Exeter C 3–1;
Watford v Brighton & H Alb 1–1, 3–4; Millwall Ath v Barnsley 1–1, 1–2; Derby Co v Bradford C 0–1;
Birmingham v Chelsea 2–0; QPR v Stockport Co 1–3; Bristol R v Bristol C 0–1; Liverpool v
Leeds Utd 3–0; WBA v Luton T 4–0; PNE v Man C 4–1; Swansea T v Plymouth Arg 3–0; Aston Villa
v Port Vale 7–2; Everton v Burnley 2–1; Bury v Sunderland 0–3; Sheff Wed v Man Utd 2–0;
SHEFF UTD v Corinthians 5–0

Second Round
CARDIFF C v Fulham 1–0; Notts Co v Norwich C 4–0; Hull C v Crystal Palace 3–2; Newcastle Utd v
Leicester C 2–2, 0–1; Bradford PA v Blackpool 1–1, 1–2; Nott'm Forest v W. Ham 0–2; Spurs v
Bolton Wand 1–1, 1–0; Blackburn R v Portsmouth 0–0, 0–0, 1–0; Southampton v Brighton & H Alb
1–0; Barnsley v Bradford C 0–3; Birmingham v Stockport Co 1–0; Bristol C v Liverpool 0–1;
WBA v PNE 2–0; Swansea T v Aston Villa 1–3; Sunderland v Everton 0–0, 1–2; SHEFF UTD v
Sheff Wed 3–2

Third Round
Notts Co v CARDIFF C 0–2; Hull C v Leicester C 1–1, 1–3; W. Ham v Blackpool 1–1, 0–3;
Spurs v Blackburn R 2–2, 1–3; Southampton v Bradford C 2–0; Liverpool v Birmingham 2–1;
WBA v Aston Villa 1–1, 2–1; SHEFF UTD v Everton 1–0

Fourth Round
CARDIFF C v Leicester C 2–1; Blackburn R v Blackpool 1–0; Southampton v Liverpool 1–0;
SHEFF UTD v WBA 2–0

Semi-Final
CARDIFF C v Blackburn R 3–1; SHEFF UTD v Southampton 2–0

SHEFFIELD UNITED 1
CARDIFF CITY 0

Cardiff had won promotion to the First Division shortly after the war, they had only been beaten for the Championship by Huddersfield on goal average in 1924, and now they were playing in their first Final. Their clash with Sheffield United at Wembley in 1925 – a meeting of old masters and new hopefuls – almost amounted to an international match.

Not for the first time in a Wembley Final a mistake cost one team the match. A quarter of an hour before half-time, Pantling, Sheffield's right-half, hit a long, swinging pass out to the left. Tunstall, the new England outside-left, moved towards the ball as it dropped, trapped it and went on to pick his spot in the Cardiff net. Cardiff right-half Wake could probably have cut out the pass to Tunstall, but, fatally, he hesitated and Tunstall was through to score.

It was a terrific blow to the Welsh team, and, though Blair, Hardy and Keenor continued to play above themselves, Cardiff were unable to repro-duce any of the brilliant football that had recently brought them into the limelight. Sheffield, led by the supreme strategy of Gillespie at inside-left, deservedly won the Cup for the fourth time in their history. Cardiff's chance was to come two years later.

Sheffield United: Sutcliffe; Cook, Milton; Pantling, King, Green; Mercer, Boyle, Johnson, Gillespie, Tunstall
Cardiff City: Farquharson; Nelson, Blair; Wake, Keenor, Hardy; Davies (W.), Gill, Nicholson, Beadles, Evans (J.)
Referee: G. N. Watson (Nottingham)

1925–6

First Round
Aberdare v Bristol R 4–1; Accrington S v Wrexham 4–0; Blyth Spartans v Hartlepools Utd 2–2, 1–1, 1–1, 2–1; Bournemouth & Bos Ath v Merthyr T 3–0; Boston T v Mansfield T 5–2; Bradford PA v Lincoln C 2–2, 1–1, 2–1; Brentford v Barnet 3–1; Brighton & H Alb v Watford 1–1, 0–2; Carlisle Utd v Chilton Colliery 0–2; Clapton v Norwich C 3–1; Charlton Ath v Windsor and Eton 4–2; Chatham v Sittingbourne 0–3; Doncaster R v Wellington T 2–0; Exeter C v Swansea T 1–3; Farnham United Breweries v Swindon T 1–10; Gillingham v Southall 6–0; Halifax T v Rotherham Utd 0–3; Horden Ath v Darlington 2–3; Leyton v St Albans C 1–0; London Caledonians v Ilford Utd 1–2; Luton T v Folkestone 3–0; New Brighton v Barrow 2–0; Northampton T v Barnsley 3–1; Northfleet v QPR 2–2, 0–2; Oldham Ath v Lytham 10–1; Rochdale v West Stanley 4–0; Southend Utd v Dulwich Hamlet 5–1; Southport v Mold 1–0; Torquay Utd v Reading 1–1, 1–1, 1–2; Tranmere R v Crewe Alex 0–0, 1–2; Walsall v Grimsby T 0–1; Wath Athletic v Chesterfield 0–5; Weymouth v Newport Co 0–1; Worksop T v Coventry C 1–0; Durham C v Ashington 4–1; Wigan Borough v Nelson 3–0; South Bank v Stockton 1–4; Worcester C v Kettering T 0–0, 0–0, 0–2

Second Round
Aberdare v Luton T 1–0; Accrington S v Blyth Spartans 5–0; Brentford v Bournemouth & Bos Ath 1–2; Crewe Alex v Wigan Borough 2–2, 1–2; Stockton v Oldham Ath 4–6; Boston T v Bradford PA 1–0; Swindon T v Sittingbourne 7–0; Reading v Leyton 6–0; Swansea T v Watford 3–2; Southend Utd v Gillingham 1–0; Clapton v Ilford Utd 1–0; QPR v Charlton Ath 1–1, 0–1; Chilton Colliery v Rochdale 1–1, 2–1; Kettering T v Grimsby T 1–1, 1–3; New Brighton v Darlington 2–0; Doncaster R v Rotherham Utd 0–2; Worksop T v Chesterfield 1–2; Durham C v Southport 0–3; Northampton T v Newport Co 3–1

Third Round
Accrington S v BOLTON WAND 0–1; Bournemouth & Bos Ath v Reading 2–0; South Shields v Chilton Colliery 3–0; Birmingham v Grimsby T 2–0; Nott'm Forest v Bradford C 1–0; Clapton v Swindon T 2–3; Southend Utd v Southport 5–2; Derby Co v Portsmouth 0–0, 1–1, 2–0; Blackpool v Swansea T 0–2; Wigan Borough v Stoke C 2–5; Millwall v Oldham Ath 1–1, 1–0; Rotherham Utd v Bury 2–3; Wolves v Arsenal 1–1, 0–1; Blackburn R v PNE 1–1, 4–1; Hull C v Aston Villa 0–3; WBA v Bristol C 4–1; Corinthians v MAN C 3–3, 0–4; Charlton Ath v Huddersfield T 0–1; Northampton T v Crystal Palace 3–3, 1–2; Plymouth Arg v Chelsea 1–2; Chesterfield v Clapton Orient 0–1; Middlesborough v Leeds Utd 5–1; Newcastle Utd v Aberdare 4–1; Cardiff C v Burnley 2–2, 2–0; Port Vale v Man Utd 2–3; Spurs v W. Ham 5–0; Sunderland v Boston T 8–1; Sheff Utd v Stockport Co 2–0; Everton v Fulham 1–1, 0–1; Southampton v Liverpool 0–0, 0–1; Notts Co v Leicester C 2–0; New Brighton v Sheff Wed 2–1

Fourth Round
Bournemouth & Bos Ath v BOLTON WAND 2–2, 2–6; South Shields v Birmingham 2–1; Nott'm Forest v Swindon T 2–0; Southend Utd v Derby Co 4–1; Swansea T v Stoke C 6–3; Bury v Millwall 3–3, 0–2; Arsenal v Blackburn R 3–1; WBA v Aston Villa 1–2; MAN C v Huddersfield T 4–0; Crystal Palace v Chelsea 2–1; Clapton Orient v Middlesbro 4–2; Cardiff C v Newcastle Utd 0–2; Spurs v Man Utd 2–2, 0–2; Sheff Utd v Sunderland 1–2; Fulham v Liverpool 3–1; Notts Co v New Brighton 2–0

Fifth Round
BOLTON WAND v South Shields 3–0; Southend Utd v Nott'm Forest 0–1; Millwall v Swansea T 0–1; Aston Villa v Arsenal 1–1, 0–2; MAN C v Crystal Palace 11–4; Clapton Orient v Newcastle Utd 2–0; Sunderland v Man Utd 3–3, 1–2; Notts Co v Fulham 0–1

Sixth Round
Nott'm Forest v BOLTON WAND 2–2, 0–0, 0–1; Swansea T v Arsenal 2–1; Clapton Orient v MAN C 1–6; Fulham v Man Utd 1–2

Semi-Final
BOLTON WAND v Swansea T 3–0; MAN C v Man Utd 3–0

BOLTON WANDERERS 1
MANCHESTER CITY 0

Bolton reversed the 1904 result, in the first Final to be played under the new offside law, and it was the great David Jack who did the trick again. With less than fifteen minutes left, Vizard's low centre from the left gave Jack the chance to send a shot hurtling into the roof of the net.

Pym, the Devon fisherman in Bolton's goal, performed miracles at the other end as Manchester fought desperately to save their necks. But Bolton were quicker on the ball in the first quarter of an hour, and looked the better side as they got within shooting range several times, mainly through the effectiveness of the left-wing pair Smith and Vizard. Then City rallied to test Pym, playing at the top of his form.

Immediately after half-time, Vizard tricked his way through the City ranks, slipped the ball through to Smith (J. R.), and the latter powered in a shot against the keeper's body.

Bolton's half-back line now began to dominate the game, and only inaccurate finishing prevented them from scoring on a number of occasions.

At Burnden Park, meanwhile, 10,000 spectators at a Central League fixture against Huddersfield went wild when they heard the Marconiphone announcement that Jack had scored at Wembley.

Bolton Wanderers: Pym; Haworth, Greenhalgh; Nuttall, Seddon, Jennings; Butler, Jack, Smith (J.R.), Smith (J.), Vizard
Manchester City: Goodchild; Cookson, McCloy; Pringle, Cowan, McMullan; Austin, Browell, Roberts, Johnson, Hicks
Referee: I. Baker (Crewe)

1926–7

First Round

Accrington S v Rochdale 4–3; Annfield Plain v Chilton Colliery 2–4; Barking T v Gillingham 0–0, 0–2; Bishop Auckland v Bedlington Utd 1–0; Boston T v Northampton T 1–1, 1–2; Bournemouth & Bos Ath v Swindon T 1–1, 4–3; Brighton & H Alb v Barnet 3–0; Carlisle Utd v Hartlepools Utd 6–2; Chatham v St Albans C 3–1; Chesterfield v Mexborough 0–0, 2–1; Clapton v Brentford 1–1, 3–7; Crewe Alex v Northern Nomads 0–0, 4–1; Crystal Palace v Norwich C 0–0, 0–1; Desborough v Doncaster R 0–3; Dulwich Hamlet v Southend Utd 1–4; Exeter C v Aberdare Ath 3–0; Grimsby T v Halifax T 3–2; Kettering T v Coventry C 2–3; Lincoln C v Rotherham Utd 2–0; Luton T v London Caledonians 4–2; Merthyr T v Bristol C 0–2; Nelson v Stockport Co 4–1; Nunhead v Kingstonian 9–0; Poole v Newport Co 1–0; Reading v Weymouth 4–4, 5–0; Rhyl Ath v Stoke C 1–1, 1–1, 2–1; Sittingbourne v Northfleet Utd 1–3; Southport v Tranmere R 1–1, 2–1; Stockton v Ashington 1–2; Torquay Utd v Bristol R 1–1, 0–1; Watford v Lowestoft 10–1; Walsall v Bradford PA 1–0; Wellington T v Mansfield T 1–2; Wigan Borough v Barrow 0–0, 2–2, 1–0; Woking v Charlton Ath 1–3; Workington v Crook T 1–2; Wrexham v New Brighton 1–1, 2–2, 3–1; York C v Worksop T 1–1, 4–1

Second Round

Ashington v Nelson 2–1; Bristol C v Bournemouth & Bos Ath 1–1, 0–2; Bristol R v Charlton Ath 4–1; Carlisle Utd v Bedlington Utd 4–0; Crewe Alex v Wigan Borough 4–1; Coventry C v Lincoln C 1–1, 1–2; Doncaster R v Chesterfield 0–1; Chilton Colliery v Accrington S 0–3; Exeter C v Northampton T 1–0; Gillingham v Brentford 1–1, 0–1; Grimsby T v York C 2–1; Luton T v Northfleet Utd 6–2; Norwich C v Chatham 5–0; Nunhead v Poole 1–2; Reading v Southend Utd 3–2; Rhyl Ath v Wrexham 3–1; Southport v Crook T 2–0; Walsall v Mansfield T 2–0; Watford v Brighton & H Alb 0–1

Third Round

Chelsea v Luton T 4–0; Exeter C v Accrington S 0–2; Fulham v Chesterfield 4–3; Burnley v Grimsby T 3–1; Leeds Utd v Sunderland 3–2; Blackpool v Bolton Wand 1–3; Darlington v Rhyl Ath 2–1; CARDIFF C v Aston Villa 2–1; Sheff Wed v Brighton & H Alb 2–0; South Shields v Plymouth Arg 3–1; Barnsley v Crewe Alex 6–1; Swansea T v Bury 4–1; Reading v Man Utd 1–1, 2–2, 2–1; Bristol R v Portsmouth 3–3, 0–4; W. Ham v Spurs 3–2; Oldham v Brentford 2–2, 2–4; Clapton Orient v Port Vale 1–1, 1–5; Sheff Utd v ARSENAL 2–3; Bournemouth & Bos Ath v Liverpool 1–1, 1–4; Southport v Blackburn R 2–0; Carlisle Utd v Wolves 0–2; Ashington v Nott'm Forest 0–2; Hull C v WBA 2–1; Everton v Poole 3–1; Bradford C v Derby C 2–6; Millwall v Huddersfield T 3–1; Lincoln C v PNE 2–4; Middlesbro v Leicester C 5–3; Southampton v Norwich C 3–0; Birmingham v Man C 4–1; Walsall v Corinthians 0–4; Newcastle Utd v Notts Co 8–1

Fourth Round

Chelsea v Accrington S 7–2; Fulham v Burnley 0–4; Leeds Utd v Bolton Wand 0–0, 0–3; Darlington v CARDIFF C 0–2; Sheff Wed v South Shields 1–1, 0–1; Barnsley v Swansea T 1–3; Reading v Portsmouth 3–1; W. Ham v Brentford 1–1, 0–2; Port Vale v ARSENAL 2–2, 0–1; Liverpool v Southport 3–1; Wolves v Nott'm Forest 2–0; Hull C v Everton 1–1, 2–2, 3–2; Derby Co v Millwall 0–3; PNE v Middlesbro 0–2; Southampton v Birmingham 4–3; Corinthians v Newcastle Utd 1–3

Fifth Round

Chelsea v Burnley 2–1; Bolton Wand v CARDIFF C 0–2; South Shields v Swansea T 2–2, 1–2; Reading v Brentford 1–0; ARSENAL v Liverpool 2–0; Wolves v Hull C 1–0; Millwall v Middlesbro 3–2; Southampton v Newcastle Utd 2–1

Sixth Round

Chelsea v CARDIFF C 0–0, 2–3; Swansea T v Reading 1–3; ARSENAL v Wolves 2–1; Millwall v Southampton 0–0, 0–2

Semi-Final

CARDIFF C v Reading 3–0; ARSENAL v Southampton 2–1

CARDIFF CITY **1**
ARSENAL **0**

Arsenal, now under the magic touch of Herbert Chapman, were captained by the famous Charles Buchan, and had other star players in Hulme, Parker and John. Cardiff, with practically the same defence as in 1925 but now with a new forward-line, were at the peak of their fame.

For Arsenal, however, only Buchan lived up to his reputation, setting up at least three clear chances for his colleagues. The Welsh supporters massed on the Wembley banks had little to sing about, with both defences well in command and play for the most part incoherent. Then, out of the blue, the decisive goal came in the seventy-third minute.

Following a Cardiff throw-in, Ferguson tried a hurried shot at goal before he could be tackled. His drive was a hard one, low and diagonal, but Lewis, Arsenal's Welsh International goalkeeper, appeared to have it covered. However, with Davies and Irving challenging, the ball somehow twisted on his chest and trickled slowly over the line.

It was a classic example of the kind of luck that can win or lose a Final. Fred Keenor and his men went on to take the Cup, and the trophy went out of England for the first time.

Cardiff City: Farquharson; Nelson, Watson; Keenor, Sloan, Hardy; Curtis, Irving, Ferguson, Davies (L.), M'Lachlan
Arsenal: Lewis; Parker, Kennedy; Baker, Butler, John; Hulme, Buchan, Brain, Blyth, Hoar
Referee: W. F. Bunnell (Preston)

Ferguson (near penalty-spot with arms raised) watches Lewis fumble

1927–8

First Round
Aldershot v QPR 2–1; Bath C v Southall 2–0; Nelson v Bradford PA 0–3; Bradford C v Workington 6–0; Watford v Brighton & H Alb 1–2; Bristol R v Walsall 4–2; Carlisle Utd v Doncaster R 2–1; Coventry C v Bournemouth & Bos Ath 2–2, 0–2; Crewe Alex v Ashington 2–2, 2–0; Dartford v Crystal Palace 1–3; Darlington v Chesterfield 4–1; Durham C v Wrexham 1–1, 0–4; Exeter C v Aberdare 9–1; Gainsboro Tr v Stockton 6–0; Gillingham v Plymouth Arg 2–1; Halifax T v Hartlepools Utd 3–0; Ilford v Dulwich Hamlet 4–0; Kettering T v Chatham 2–0; Accrington S v Lincoln C 2–5; Northfleet Utd v London Caledonians 0–1; Luton T v Clapton Orient 9–0; Merthyr T v Charlton Ath 0–0, 0–2; Shildon v New Brighton 1–3; Northampton T v Leyton 8–0; Poole v Norwich C 1–1, 0–5; Botwell Mission v Peterborough & Fletton Utd 3–4; Rhyl Ath v Wigan Borough 4–3; Rochdale v Crook T 8–2; Southend Utd v Wellington T 1–0; Denaby Utd v Southport 2–3; Spennymoor Utd v Rotherham Utd 1–1, 2–4; Stockport Co v Oswestry T 5–2; Newport Co v Swindon T 0–1; Shirebrook v Tranmere R 1–3

Second Round
Bournemouth & Bos Ath v Bristol R 6–1; Charlton Ath v Kettering T 1–1, 2–1; Crewe Alex v Stockport Co 2–0; Darlington v Rochdale 2–1; Exeter C v Ilford 5–3; Gillingham v Southend Utd 2–0; Gainsboro Tr v Lincoln C 0–2; London Caledonians v Bath C 1–0; Luton T v Norwich C 6–0; New Brighton v Rhyl Ath 7–2; Northampton T v Brighton & H Alb 1–0; Peterborough & Fletton Utd v Aldershot 2–1; Bradford C v Rotherham Utd 2–3; Bradford PA v Southport 0–2; Swindon T v Crystal Palace 0–0, 2–1; Tranmere R v Halifax T 3–1; Wrexham v Carlisle Utd 1–0

Third Round
BLACKBURN R v Newcastle Utd 4–1; Rotherham Utd v Exeter C 3–3, 1–3; Port Vale v Barnsley 3–0; New Brighton v Corinthians 2–1; Man Utd v Brentford 7–1; Charlton Ath v Bury 1–1, 3–4; Wrexham v Swansea T 2–1; Birmingham v Peterborough & Fletton Utd 4–3; Arsenal v WBA 2–0; PNE v Everton 0–3; Burnley v Aston Villa 0–2; London Caledonians v Crewe Alex 2–3; Sunderland v Northampton T 3–3, 3–0; Man C v Leeds Utd 1–0; Stoke C v Gillingham 6–1; Bolton Wand v Luton T 2–1; HUDDERSFIELD T v Lincoln C 4–2; Portsmouth v W. Ham 0–2; Southport v Fulham 3–0; Middlesbro v South Shields 3–0; Reading v Grimsby T 4–0; Hull C v Leicester C 0–1; Bristol C v Spurs 1–2; Blackpool v Oldham Ath 1–4; Notts Co v Sheff Utd 2–3; Wolves v Chelsea 2–1; Swindon T v Clapton Orient 2–1; Sheff Wed v Bournemouth & Bos Ath 3–0; Nott'm Forest v Tranmere R 1–0; Millwall v Derby Co 1–2; Cardiff C v Southampton 2–1; Liverpool v Darlington 1–0

Fourth Round
Exeter C v BLACKBURN R 2–2, 1–3; Port Vale v New Brighton 3–0; Bury v Man Utd 1–1, 0–1; Wrexham v Birmingham 1–3; Arsenal v Everton 4–3; Aston Villa v Crewe Alex 3–0; Sunderland v Man C 1–2; Stoke C v Bolton Wand 4–2; HUDDERSFIELD T v W. Ham 2–1; Southport v Middlesbro 0–3; Reading v Leicester C 0–1; Spurs v Oldham Ath 3–0; Sheff Utd v Wolves 3–1; Swindon T v Sheff Wed 1–2; Nott'm Forest v Derby Co 0–0, 2–0; Cardiff C v Liverpool 2–1

Fifth Round
BLACKBURN R v Port Vale 2–1; Man Utd v Birmingham 1–0; Arsenal v Aston Villa 4–1; Man C v Stoke C 0–1; HUDDERSFIELD T v Middlesbro 4–0; Leicester C v Spurs 0–3; Sheff Wed v Sheff Utd 1–1, 1–4; Nott'm Forest v Cardiff C 2–1

Sixth Round
BLACKBURN R v Man Utd 2–0; Arsenal v Stoke C 4–1; HUDDERSFIELD T v Spurs 6–1; Sheff Utd v Nott'm Forest 3–0

Semi-Final
BLACKBURN R v Arsenal 1–0; HUDDERSFIELD T v Sheff Utd 2–2, 0–0, 1–0

BLACKBURN ROVERS **3**
HUDDERSFIELD TOWN **1**

Blackburn were hardly expected to beat Huddersfield, lying second in the League to Newcastle and demolishing all opposition in the earlier ties with one six- and two four-goal victories. A side that eventually avoided relegation by only three points could surely not stop Huddersfield's tremendous forward-line of five internationals.

But Blackburn, too, could boast their internationals: the full-back pair, Hutton and Jones; wing-halves, Healless and Campbell; Puddefoot and Rigby in attack. And they had knocked out both Newcastle and Arsenal en route to the Final.

Huddersfield never recovered from Roscamp's goal for Blackburn within the first thirty seconds – the fastest goal in a Wembley Final, and before half-time M'Lean had sent a skimming shot into the goal to add to Blackburn's lead. Blackburn's play was showing a relentless determination that wore down Huddersfield's famous forward-line.

Alex Jackson, switched from the wing into the centre after the interval, gave Huddersfield a fighting chance by closing the gap with a fast shot that hit the underside of the bar on its way into the net. The goal was also significant for another reason: it was the first time both sides had scored in a Final since 1910.

Even Jackson, a player with a genius for snatching goals from unexpected positions, failed to save the Yorkshire side. Roscamp made matters safe with his second goal of the game, and Rovers won the Cup for the sixth time.

Blackburn Rovers: Crawford; Hutton, Jones; Healless, Rankin, Campbell; Thornewell, Puddefoot, Roscamp, M'Lean, Rigby
Huddersfield Town: Mercer; Goodall, Barkas; Redfern, Wilson, Steele; Jackson (A.), Kelly, Brown, Stephenson, Smith (W. H.)
Referee: T. G. Bryan (Willenhall)

Roscamp's very early goal for Blackburn

1928–9

First Round

Accrington S v South Shields 2–1; York C v Barrow 0–1; Poole v Bournemouth & Bos Ath 1–4; Bradford C v Doncaster R 4–1; Brentford v Brighton & H Alb 4–1; Bristol R v Wellingborough T 2–1; Carlisle Utd v Wrexham 1–0; Peterborough & Fletton Utd v Charlton Ath 0–2; Chesterfield v Rochdale 3–2; Crystal Palace v Kettering T 2–0; Darlington v New Brighton 3–0; Exeter C v Barking T 6–0; Coventry C v Fulham 1–4; Gainsboro Tr v Crewe Alex 3–1; Grantham v Rhyl Ath 1–0; Guildford C v QPR 4–2; Lancaster T v Lincoln C 1–3; Luton T v Southend Utd 5–1; Shirebrook v Mansfield T 2–4; Merthyr T v Dulwich Hamlet 4–2; Newport Co v Woking 7–0; Northfleet Utd v Ilford 5–2; Norwich C v Chatham 6–1; Yeovil & Petters Utd v Plymouth Arg 1–4; Horwich RMI v Scarborough T 1–2; Sittingbourne v Southall 2–1; Annfield Plain v Southport 1–4; Spennymoor Utd v Hartlepools Utd 5–2; Stockport Co v Halifax T 1–0; Gillingham v Torquay Utd 0–0, 0–1; Tranmere R v Rotherham Utd 2–1; Walsall v Worcester C 3–1; Leyton v Watford 0–2; Wigan Borough v Ashington 2–0

Second Round

Accrington S v Spennymoor Utd 7–0; Bradford C v Tranmere R 1–0; Guildford C v Bournemouth & Bos Ath 1–5; Northfleet Utd v Charlton Ath 1–5; Gainsboro T v Chesterfield 2–3; Crystal Palace v Bristol R 3–1; Scarborough T v Darlington 2–2, 1–2; Torquay Utd v Exeter C 0–1; Carlisle Utd v Lincoln C 0–1; Fulham v Luton T 0–0, 1–4; Barrow v Mansfield T 1–2; Norwich C v Newport Co 6–0; Brentford v Plymouth Arg 0–1; Stockport Co v Southport 3–0; Walsall v Sittingbourne 2–1; Watford v Merthyr T 2–0; Wigan Borough v Grantham 2–1

Third Round

Blackburn R v Barnsley 1–0; Derby Co v Notts Co 4–3; Port Vale v Man Utd 0–3; Darlington v Bury 2–6; Lincoln C v Leicester C 0–1; Nott'm Forest v Swansea T 1–2; Bristol C v Liverpool 0–2; BOLTON WAND v Oldham Ath 2–0; Grimsby T v WBA 1–1, 0–2; Walsall v Middlesbro 1–1, 1–5; Plymouth Arg v Blackpool 3–0; Hull C v Bradford PA 1–1, 1–3; Chesterfield v Huddersfield T 1–7; Exeter C v Leeds Utd 2–2, 1–5; Millwall v Northampton T 1–1, 2–2, 2–0; Luton T v Crystal Palace 0–0, 0–7; Chelsea v Everton 2–0; Birmingham v Man C 3–1; PORTSMOUTH v Charlton Ath 2–1; Bradford C v Stockport Co 2–0; Accrington S v Bournemouth & Bos Ath 1–1, 0–2; Watford v PNE 1–0; W. Ham v Sunderland 1–0; Norwich C v Corinthians 0–5; Reading v Spurs 2–0; Wigan Borough v Sheff Wed 1–3; Aston Villa v Cardiff C 6–1; Southampton v Clapton Orient 0–0, 1–2; Burnley v Sheff Utd 2–1; Swindon T v Newcastle Utd 2–0; Arsenal v Stoke C 2–1; Wolves v Mansfield T 0–1

Fourth Round

Blackburn R v Derby Co 1–1, 3–0; Man Utd v Bury 0–1; Leicester C v Swansea T 1–0; Liverpool v BOLTON WAND 0–0, 2–5; WBA v Middlesbro 1–0; Plymouth Arg v Bradford PA 0–1; Huddersfield T v Leeds Utd 3–0; Millwall v Crystal Palace 0–0, 3–5; Chelsea v Birmingham 1–0; PORTSMOUTH v Bradford C 2–0; Bournemouth & Bos Ath v Watford 6–4; W. Ham v Corinthians 3–0; Reading v Sheff Wed 1–0; Aston Villa v Clapton Orient 0–0, 8–0; Burnley v Swindon T 3–3, 2–3; Arsenal v Mansfield T 2–0

Fifth Round

Blackburn R v Bury 1–0; Leicester C v BOLTON WAND 1–2; WBA v Bradford PA 6–0; Huddersfield T v Crystal Palace 5–2; Chelsea v PORTSMOUTH 1–1, 0–1; Bournemouth & Bos Ath v W. Ham 1–1, 1–3; Reading v Aston Villa 1–3; Swindon T v Arsenal 0–0, 0–1

Sixth Round

Blackburn R v BOLTON WAND 1–1, 1–2; WBA v Huddersfield T 1–1, 1–2; PORTSMOUTH v W. Ham 3–2; Aston Villa v Arsenal 1–0

Semi-Final

BOLTON WAND v Huddersfield T 3–1; PORTSMOUTH v Aston Villa 1–0

BOLTON WANDERERS **2**
PORTSMOUTH **0**

Bolton achieved a remarkable sequence of Wembley triumphs, winning the Finals of 1923, 1926 and 1929, and, even more remarkable, achieved it with largely the same set of players.

As in their last Final, Bolton allowed the initiative to come from the opposition for most of the first half. But Portsmouth's Weddle, with his reputation as a forward with a scorching shot, was well policed by Finney, and half time arrived with no score. Bolton resumed with more urgency, and launched a series of fierce attacks. Gilfillan was peppered with shots from Gibson, M'Clelland and Blackmore.

During this period of second-half pressure from Bolton, Portsmouth left-back Bell was injured, and, after attention, switched to outside-left. The cohesion of the Portsmouth team was broken as a result, and Butler, a fiery and determined winger, cut inside to shoot Bolton into the lead with ten minutes to go. Mackie hacked the ball clear a fraction too late – it had already crossed the line.

In the last seconds Bolton made sure of victory with a second goal. Butler broke away to cross to Blackmore who promptly and characteristically cracked it left-footed into the net before Gilfillan could move.

Bolton Wanderers: Pym; Haworth, Finney; Kean, Seddon, Nuttall; Butler, M'Clelland, Blackmore, Gibson, Cook (W.)
Portsmouth: Gilfillan; Mackie, Bell; Nichol, McIlwaine, Thackeray; Forward, Smith (J.), Weddle, Watson, Cook (F.)
Referee: A. Josephs (South Shields)

1929–30

First Round

Accrington S v Rochdale 3–1; Barrow v Newark 1–0; Barry T v Dagenham 0–0, 1–0; Tunbridge Wells v Bath C 1–3; Bournemouth & Bos Ath v Torquay 2–0; Brighton & H Alb v Peterborough & Fletton Utd 4–0; Nunhead v Bristol R 0–2; Caernarvon v Darlington 4–2; Carlisle Utd v Halifax T 2–0; Southport v Chesterfield 0–0, 2–3; Clapton Orient v Folkestone 0–0, 2–2, 4–1; Norwich C v Coventry C 3–3, 0–2; Nelson v Crewe Alex 0–3; Doncaster R v Shildon 0–0, 1–1, 3–0; Fulham v Thames 4–0; Leyton v Merthyr T 4–1; Lincoln C v Wigan Borough 3–1; Mansfield T v Manchester Central 0–2; Gillingham v Margate 0–2; New Brighton v Lancaster T 4–1; Newport Co v Kettering T 3–2; Aldershot v Northampton T 0–1; Wimbledon v Northfleet Utd 1–4; Dulwich Hamlet v Plymouth Arg 0–3; Gainsboro Tr v Port Vale 0–0, 0–5; Rotherham Utd v Ashington 3–0; Luton T v QPR 2–3; Scunthorpe Utd v Hartlepools Utd 1–0; Southend Utd v Brentford 1–0; Wellington T v Stockport Co 1–4; Walsall v Exeter C 1–0; Ilford v Watford 0–3; South Shields v Wrexham 2–4; York C v Tranmere R 2–2, 1–0

Second Round

Caernarvon v Bournemouth & Bos Ath 1–1, 2–5; Brighton & H Alb v Barry T 4–1; Bristol R v Accrington S 4–1; Carlisle Utd v Crewe Alex 4–2; Clapton Orient v Northfleet Utd 2–0; Coventry C v Bath C 7–1; Doncaster R v New Brighton 1–0; Leyton v Fulham 1–4; Northampton T v Margate 6–0; QPR v Lincoln C 2–1; Watford v Plymouth Arg 1–1, 0–3; Scunthorpe Utd v Rotherham Utd 3–3, 4–5; Stockport Co v Barrow 4–0; Newport Co v Walsall 2–3; Manchester Central v Wrexham 0–1; Southend Utd v York C 1–4

Third Round

W. Ham v Notts Co 4–0; Leeds Utd v Crystal Palace 8–1; Corinthians v Millwall 2–2, 1–1, 1–5; Doncaster R v Stoke C 1–0; ARSENAL v Chelsea 2–0; Birmingham v Bolton Wand 1–0; Chesterfield v Middlesbro 1–1, 3–4; Charlton Ath v QPR 1–1, 3–0; Plymouth Arg v Hull C 3–4; Blackpool v Stockport Co 2–1; Spurs v Man C 2–2, 1–4; Man Utd v Swindon T 0–2; Newcastle Utd v York C 1–1, 2–1; Clapton Orient v Bristol R 1–0; Brighton & H Alb v Grimsby T 1–1, 1–0; Portsmouth v PNE 2–0; Aston Villa v Reading 5–1; Walsall v Swansea T 2–0; Blackburn R v Northampton T 4–1; Carlisle Utd v Everton 2–4; Bury v HUDDERSFIELD T 0–0, 1–3; Sheff Utd v Leicester C 2–1; Bradford C v Southampton 4–1; Wrexham v WBA 1–0; Rotherham Utd v Nott'm Forest 0–5; Fulham v Bournemouth & Bos Ath 1–1, 2–0; Coventry C v Sunderland 1–2; Liverpool v Cardiff C 1–2; Sheff Wed v Burnley 1–0; Oldham Ath v Wolves 1–0; Barnsley v Bradford PA 0–1; Derby Co v Bristol C 5–1

Fourth Round

W. Ham v Leeds Utd 4–1; Millwall v Doncaster R 4–0; ARSENAL v Birmingham 2–2, 1–0; Middlesbro v Charlton Ath 1–1, 1–1, 1–0; Hull C v Blackpool 3–1; Swindon T v Man C 1–1, 1–10; Newcastle Utd v Clapton Orient 3–1; Portsmouth v Brighton & H & Alb 0–1; Aston Villa v Walsall 3–1; Blackburn R v Everton 4–1; HUDDERSFIELD T v Sheff Utd 2–1; Wrexham v Bradford C 0–0, 1–2; Nott'm Forest v Fulham 2–1; Sunderland v Cardiff C 2–1; Oldham Ath v Sheff Wed 3–4; Derby Co v Bradford PA 1–1, 1–2

Fifth Round

W. Ham v Millwall 4–1; Middlesbro v ARSENAL 0–2; Man C v Hull C 1–2; Newcastle Utd v Brighton & H Alb 3–0; Aston Villa v Blackburn R 4–1; HUDDERSFIELD T v Bradford C 2–1; Sunderland v Nott'm Forest 2–2, 1–3; Sheff Wed v Bradford PA 5–1

Sixth Round

W. Ham v ARSENAL 0–3; Newcastle Utd v Hull C 1–1, 0–1; Aston Villa v HUDDERSFIELD T 1–2; Nott'm Forest v Sheff Wed 2–2, 1–3

Semi-Final

ARSENAL v Hull C 2–2, 1–0; HUDDERSFIELD T v Sheff Wed 2–1

ARSENAL **2**
HUDDERSFIELD TOWN **0**

Arsenal and Huddersfield, both fashioned on the Chapman tactical concept – defence based on careful planning and a 'W' formation attack with wing-halves and inside-forwards as the vital links – clashed head-on in the 1930 Final.

Arsenal's forward-line in this Final was perhaps their greatest ever. The young outside-left Bastin, with his uncanny sense of position and deadly shot, formed the spearhead of Arsenal's famous pincer movement with Hulme on the opposite wing. Alex James, a footballing genius in long baggy shorts, used his quick wits and his understanding with Bastin outside him to beat Huddersfield that sunny afternoon at Wembley.

James was fouled, quickly took the free-kick himself, received an inch-perfect return pass from Bastin and scored one of his rare goals before the Huddersfield defence realized the danger.

Huddersfield made strenuous efforts during the second half to wipe out Arsenal's lead, and they had their defence at full-stretch for long periods. Then a long pass by James opened the way for Lambert down the middle, and Arsenal made certain of the Cup for the first time.

Huddersfield's relentless endeavour had made for such an absorbing struggle that few in the crowd allowed themselves to be distracted when the sinister shape of the German airship 'Graf Zeppelin' floated overhead.

Arsenal: Preedy; Parker, Hapgood; Baker, Seddon, John; Hulme, Jack, Lambert, James, Bastin
Huddersfield Town: Turner; Goodall, Spence; Naylor, Wilson, Campbell; Jackson (A.), Kelly, Davies, Raw, Smith (W. H.)
Referee: T. Crew (Leicester)

James (out of picture) makes it 1–0 to Arsenal

1930-1

First Round

Accrington S v Lancaster T 3–1; Aldershot T v Peterborough & Fletton Utd 4–1; Ilford v Brentford 1–6; Bristol R v Merthyr Tydfil 4–1; Carlisle Utd v New Brighton 3–1; Northampton T v Coventry C 1–2; Crewe Alex v Jarrow 1–0; Crystal Palace v Taunton T 6–0; Rochdale v Doncaster R 1–2; Exeter C v Northfleet Utd 3–0; Folkestone v Sittingbourne 5–3; Fulham v Wimbledon 1–1, 6–0; Gainsboro Tr v Scunthorpe Utd 1–0; Tranmere R v Gateshead 4–4, 2–3; Gillingham v Guildford C 7–2; Halifax T v Mansfield T 2–2, 2–1; Lincoln C v Barrow 8–3; Luton T v Clapton Orient 2–2, 4–2; Nelson v Workington 4–0; Newport Co v Dulwich Hamlet 2–2, 4–1; Newark v Rotherham Utd 2–1; Norwich C v Swindon T 2–0; Chesterfield v Notts Co 1–2; QPR v Thames 5–0; Scarborough T v Rhyl Ath 6–0; Southport v Darlington 4–2; Hartlepools Utd v Stockport Co 2–3; Torquay Utd v Southend Utd 1–0; Tunbridge Wells R v Kingstonians 3–0; Watford v Walthamstow Ave 5–1; Walsall v Bournemouth & Bos Ath 1–0; Wellington T v Wombwell 0–0, 3–0; Wrexham v Wigan Borough 2–0; York C v Gresley R 3–1

Second Round

Gillingham v Aldershot T 1–3; Brentford v Norwich C 1–0; Bristol R v Stockport Co 4–2; Carlisle Utd v Tunbridge Wells R 4–2; Crystal Palace v Newark 6–0; Exeter C v Coventry C 1–1, 2–1; Fulham v Halifax T 4–0; Gateshead v Folkestone 3–2; Notts Co v Doncaster R 1–0; Crewe Alex v QPR 2–4; Scarborough T v Lincoln C 6–4; Gainsboro Tr v Southport 0–4; Accrington S v Torquay Utd 0–1; Walsall v Newport Co 4–0; Watford v Luton T 3–1; Wellington T v Wrexham 2–4; Nelson v York C 1–1, 0–3

Third Round

Liverpool v BIRMINGHAM 0–2; Corinthians v Port Vale 1–3; Oldham Ath v Watford 1–3; Leicester C v Brighton & H Alb 1–2; W. Ham v Chelsea 1–3; Arsenal v Aston Villa 2–2, 3–1; Blackburn R v Walsall 1–1, 3–0; Bristol R v QPR 3–1; Bolton Wand v Carlisle Utd 1–0; Sunderland v Southampton 2–0; Sheff Utd v York C 1–1, 2–0; Notts Co v Swansea T 3–1; Bury v Torquay Utd 1–1, 2–1; Exeter C v Derby Co 3–2; Leeds Utd v Huddersfield T 2–0; Newcastle Utd v Nott'm Forest 4–0; Crystal Palace v Reading 1–1, 1–1, 2–0; Plymouth Arg v Everton 0–2; Scarborough T v Grimsby T 1–2; Stoke C v Man Utd 3–3, 0–0, 2–4; Southport v Millwall 3–1; Hull C v Blackpool 1–2; Aldershot T v Bradford PA 0–1; Burnley v Man C 3–0; Brentford v Cardiff C 2–2, 2–1; Fulham v Portsmouth 0–2; WBA v Charlton Ath 2–2, 1–1, 3–1; Spurs v PNE 3–1; Barnsley v Bristol C 4–1; Gateshead v Sheff Wed 2–6; Middlesbro v Bradford C 1–1, 1–2; Wolves v Wrexham 9–1

Fourth Round

BIRMINGHAM v Port Vale 2–0; Watford v Brighton & H Alb 2–0; Chelsea v Arsenal 2–1; Blackburn R v Bristol R 5–1; Bolton Wand v Sunderland 1–1, 1–3; Sheff Utd v Notts Co 4–1; Bury v Exeter C 1–2; Leeds Utd v Newcastle Utd 4–2; Crystal Palace v Everton 0–6; Grimsby T v Man Utd 1–0; Southport v Blackpool 2–1; Bradford PA v Burnley 2–0; Brentford v Portsmouth 0–1; WBA v Spurs 1–0; Barnsley v Sheff Wed 2–1; Bradford PA v Wolves 0–0, 2–4

Fifth Round

BIRMINGHAM C v Watford 3–0; Chelsea v Blackburn R 3–0; Sunderland v Sheff Utd 2–1; Exeter C v Leeds Utd 3–1; Everton v Grimsby T 5–3; Southport v Bradford PA 1–0; Portsmouth v WBA 0–1; Barnsley v Wolves 1–3

Sixth Round

BIRMINGHAM v Chelsea 2–2, 3–0; Sunderland v Exeter C 1–1, 4–2; Everton v Southport 9–1; WBA v Wolves 1–1, 2–1

Semi-Final

BIRMINGHAM v Sunderland 2–0; Everton v WBA 0–1

WEST BROMWICH ALBION **2**
BIRMINGHAM **1**

At the Oval and Crystal Palace, West Bromwich had been famed for their battles with Aston Villa, and at Wembley they were now taking part in another battle with a purely local flavour. This time they beat Birmingham for the trophy, and, as a nice bonus, gained promotion from the Second Division in the same season. It was the first time that such a double feat had been achieved.

Albion were not a brilliant side, but they had tremendous team spirit. Inside-right Carter was the master general, and Richardson (W. G.) at centre-forward the man who translated most of those plans into reality.

In persistent rain, Richardson gave Albion the lead after a three-man move with Carter and Glidden, and Albion looked set for victory.

But Birmingham were by no means out of the hunt yet, and they proved the point when Bradford took a pass from Curtis and beat Pearson with a perfectly aimed shot. Then came one of those Wembley twists. Straight from the kick-off Richardson went through the middle to make it 2–1.

Hibbs' inspired goalkeeping saved Birmingham from a much heavier defeat. The impression given that forwards spent all their time shooting straight at him bore testimony to his great positional sense.

West Bromwich Albion: Pearson; Shaw, Trentham; Magee, Richardson (W.), Edwards; Glidden, Carter, Richardson (W. G.), Sandford, Wood
Birmingham: Hibbs; Liddell, Barkas; Cringan, Morrall, Leslie; Briggs, Crosbie, Bradford, Gregg, Curtis
Referee: A. H. Kingscott (Long Eaton)

1931–2

First Round
Aldershot v Chelmsford 7–0; Barnet v QPR 3–7; Bath C v Nunhead 9–0; Bournemouth & Bos Ath v Northfleet Utd 1–1, 1–0; Bristol R v Gillingham 5–1; Cardiff C v Enfield 8–0; Chester v Hartlepools Utd 4–1; Coventry C v Clapton Orient 2–2, 0–2; Crewe Alex v Gainsboro Tr 2–2, 0–1; Crook T v Stockport Co 3–1; Darlington v Walsall 1–0; Darwen v Peterborough and Fletton Utd 4–1; Folkestone v Brighton & H Alb 2–5; Fulham v Guildford C 2–0; Gateshead v Wrexham 3–2; Lancaster T v Blyth Spartans 0–3; Hull C v Mansfield T 4–1; Manchester Central v Lincoln C 0–3; Newark T v Halifax T 1–1, 1–2; New Brighton v York C 3–1; Northampton T v Metropolitan Police 9–0; Reading v Crystal Palace 0–1; Rotherham Utd v Accrington S 0–0, 0–5; Scunthorpe Utd v Rochdale 2–1; Swindon T v Luton T 0–5; Thames v Watford 2–2, 2–3; Tunbridge Wells Rangers v Brentford 1–1, 1–2; Torquay Utd v Southend Utd 1–3; Tranmere R v West Stanley 3–0; Wimbledon v Norwich C 1–3; Yeovil and Petters Utd v Hayes 3–1; Yorks Amateurs v Carlisle Utd 1–3; Barrow v Doncaster R 3–3, 1–1, 1–1, 0–1; Burton T v Wigan Borough wo

Second Round
Gainsboro Tr v Watford 2–5; Brighton & H Alb v Doncaster R 5–0; Brentford v Norwich C 4–1; Burton T v Gateshead 4–1; Scunthorpe Utd v QPR 1–4; Cardiff C v Clapton Orient 4–0; New Brighton v Hull C 0–4; Lincoln C v Luton T 2–2, 1–4; Halifax T v Accrington S 3–0; Northampton T v Southampton 3–0; Bath C v Crystal Palace 2–1; Darwen v Chester 2–1; Carlisle Utd v Darlington 0–2; Tranmere R v Bristol R 2–0; Aldershot v Crook T 1–1, 0–1; Bournemouth & Bos Ath v Blyth Spartans 1–0; Fulham v Yeovil and Petters Utd 0–0, 5–2

Third Round
Oldham Ath v Huddersfield T 1–1, 0–6; QPR v Leeds Utd 3–1; PNE v Bolton Wand 0–0, 5–2; Luton T v Wolves 1–2; Middlesbro v Portsmouth 1–1, 0–3; WBA v Aston Villa 1–2; ARSENAL v Darwen 11–1; Plymouth Arg v Man Utd 4–1; Bury v Swansea T 2–1; Sheff Utd v Corinthians 2–1; Sunderland v Southampton 0–0, 4–2; Stoke C v Hull C 3–0; Millwall v Man C 2–3; Brentford v Bath C 2–0; Burnley v Derby Co 0–4; Burton T v Blackburn R 0–4; Chesterfield v Nott'm Forest 5–2; Everton v Liverpool 1–2; Grimsby T v Exeter C 4–1; Birmingham v Bradford C 1–0; Spurs v Sheff Wed 2–2, 1–3; Halifax v Bournemouth & Bos Ath 1–3; Tranmere R v Chelsea 2–2, 3–5; Charlton Ath v W. Ham 1–2; Blackpool v NEWCASTLE UTD 1–1, 0–1; Barnsley v Southport 0–0, 1–4; Brighton & H Alb v Port Vale 1–2; Leicester C v Crook T 7–0; Watford v Fulham 1–1, 3–0; Notts Co v Bristol C 2–2, 2–3; Bradford PA v Cardiff C 2–0; Darlington v Northampton T 1–1, 0–2

Fourth Round
Huddersfield T v QPR 5–0; PNE v Wolves 2–0; Portsmouth v Aston Villa 1–1, 1–0; ARSENAL v Plymouth Arg 4–2; Bury v Sheff Utd 3–1; Sunderland v Stoke C 1–1, 1–1, 1–2; Man C v Brentford 6–1; Derby Co v Blackburn R 3–2; Chesterfield v Liverpool 2–4; Grimsby T v Birmingham 2–1; Sheff Wed v Bournemouth & Bos Ath 7–0; Chelsea v W. Ham 3–1; NEWCASTLE UTD v Southport 1–1, 1–1, 9–0; Port Vale v Leicester C 1–2; Watford v Bristol C 2–1; Bradford PA v Northampton T 4–2

Fifth Round
Huddersfield T v PNE 4–0; Portsmouth v ARSENAL 0–2; Bury v Stoke C 3–0; Man C v Derby Co 3–0; Liverpool v Grimsby T 1–0; Sheff Wed v Chelsea 1–1, 0–2; NEWCASTLE UTD v Leicester C 3–1; Watford v Bradford PA 1–0

Sixth Round
Huddersfield T v ARSENAL 0–1; Bury v Man C 3–4; Liverpool v Chelsea 0–2; NEWCASTLE UTD v Watford 5–0

Semi-Final
ARSENAL v Man C 1–0; Chelsea v NEWCASTLE UTD 1–2

NEWCASTLE UNITED **2**
ARSENAL **1**

Arsenal, second-placed in the League, were forced to take the field at Wembley without James, who was unfit, and that necessitated a change in the left flank of the attack. Newcastle, judged by their League performances, were nothing out of the ordinary. Few thought they stood a chance against the great Highbury side.

The match was merely following its expected course when Arsenal went ahead after fifteen minutes. 'Police Constable' Roberts, the Arsenal centre-half, sent a long pass out to Hulme who beat Fairhurst and centred. McInroy and Nelson both failed to cut it out, leaving John with a chance he couldn't miss.

Newcastle equalized seven minutes before the interval, when Allen at last 'lost' Roberts and scored with a header. This was Newcastle's famous 'over the line' goal – perhaps the most disputed goal in the history of football. Photographs later indicated that the ball had run over the dead-ball line before Richardson hooked it over from the right. Certainly the Arsenal defence relaxed, thinking that it had, and Allen was left unguarded in the middle.

From that moment the Cup slowly slipped from Arsenal's grasp, though the tension was sustained almost to breaking point. Allen snatched Newcastle's seventy-second minute winner, and for the first time the team scoring first at Wembley had lost.

Newcastle United: McInroy; Nelson, Fairhurst; McKenzie, Davidson, Weaver; Boyd, Richardson, Allen, McMenemy, Lang
Arsenal: Moss; Parker, Hapgood; Jones (C.), Roberts, Male; Hulme, Jack, Lambert, Bastin, John
Referee: W. P. Harper (Stourbridge)

1932–3

First Round

Accrington S v Hereford Utd 2–1; Barrow v Gateshead 0–1; Carlisle Utd v Denaby Utd 1–0; Chester v Rotherham Utd 4–0; Crewe Alex v Crook T 4–0; Darlington v Boston T 1–0; Doncaster R v Gainsboro Tr 4–1; Halifax T v Darwen 2–0; Marine, Liverpool v Hartlepools Utd 2–5; Rochdale v Stockport Co 0–2; Southport v Nelson 3–3; 4–0; Stalybridge Celtic v Hull C 2–8; Tranmere R v New Brighton 3–0; Walsall v Mansfield T 4–1; Workington v Scunthorpe Utd 5–1; Wrexham v Spennymoor Utd 3–0; York C v Scarborough 1–3; Bristol C v Romford 4–0; Cardiff C v Bristol R 1–1, 1–4; Clapton Orient v Aldershot 0–1; Crystal Palace v Brighton & H Alb 1–2; Dartford v Yeovil and Petters Utd 0–0, 2–4; Folkestone v Norwich C 1–0; Gillingham v Wycombe Wand 1–1, 4–2; Guildford C v Coventry C 1–2; Luton T v Kingstonians 2–2, 3–2; Margate v Ryde Sports 5–0; Merthyr T v QPR 1–1, 1–5; Newport Co v Ilford 4–2; Northampton T v Lloyds 8–1; Reading v Brentford 3–2; Southend Utd v Exeter C 1–1, 1–0; Swindon T v Dulwich Hamlet 4–1; Torquay Utd v Bournemouth & Bos Ath 0–0, 2–2, 3–2

Second Round

Gateshead v Margate 5–2; Southend Utd v Scarborough 4–1; Stockport Co v Luton T 2–3; Reading v Coventry C 2–2, 3–3, 1–0; Bristol C v Tranmere R 2–2, 2–3; Accrington S v Aldershot 1–2; Southport v Swindon T 1–2; Walsall v Hartlepools Utd 2–1; Chester v Yeovil and Petters Utd 2–1; Halifax T v Workington 2–1; Folkestone v Newport Co 2–1; Crewe Alex v Darlington 0–2; Carlisle Utd v Hull C 1–1, 1–2; Bristol R v Gillingham 1–1, 3–1; Torquay Utd v QPR 1–1, 1–3; Northampton T v Doncaster R 0–1; Brighton & H Alb v Wrexham 0–0, 3–2

Third Round

Swindon T v Burnley 1–2; Swansea T v Sheffield Utd 2–3; Darlington v QPR 2–0; Sheff Wed v Chesterfield 2–2, 2–4; Charlton Ath v Bolton Wand 1–5; Grimsby T v Portsmouth 3–2; Gateshead v MAN C 1–1, 0–9; Walsall v Arsenal 2–0; Watford v Southend Utd 1–1, 0–2; Wolves v Derby Co 3–6; Aldershot v Bristol R 1–0; Millwall v Reading 2–2, 1–1, 2–0; Bradford C v Aston Villa 2–2, 1–2; Hull C v Sunderland 0–2; Blackpool v Port Vale 2–1; Huddersfield T v Folkestone 2–0; Leicester C v EVERTON 2–3; Bury v Nott'm Forest 2–2, 2–1; Tranmere R v Notts Co 2–1; Newcastle Utd v Leeds Utd 0–3; Chester v Fulham 5–0; Doncaster R v Halifax T 0–3; Barnsley v Luton T 0–0, 0–2; Oldham Ath v Spurs 0–6; Brighton & H Alb v Chelsea 2–1; Bradford PA v Plymouth Arg 5–1; Corinthians v W. Ham 0–2; WBA v Liverpool 2–0; Man Utd v Middlesbro 1–4; Stoke C v Southampton 1–0; Birmingham v PNE 2–1; Lincoln C v Blackburn R 1–5

Fourth Round

Burnley v Sheff Utd 3–1; Darlington v Chesterfield 0–2; Bolton Wand v Grimsby T 2–0; MAN C v Walsall 3–2; Southend Utd v Derby Co 2–0; Aldershot v Millwall 1–3; Aston Villa v Sunderland 0–3; Blackpool v Huddersfield T 2–1; EVERTON v Bury 3–1; Tranmere R v Leeds Utd 0–0, 0–4; Chester v Halifax T 0–0, 2–3; Luton T v Spurs 2–0; Brighton & H Alb v Bradford PA 2–1; W. Ham v WBA 2–0; Middlesbro v Stoke C 4–1; Birmingham v Blackburn R 3–0

Fifth Round

Burnley v Chesterfield 1–0; Bolton v MAN C 2–4; Derby C v Aldershot 2–0; Sunderland v Blackpool 1–0; EVERTON v Leeds Utd 2–0; Halifax T v Luton T 0–2; Brighton & H Alb v W. Ham 2–2, 0–1; Middlesbro v Birmingham 0–0, 0–3;

Sixth Round

Burnley v MAN C 0–1; Derby Co v Sunderland 4–4, 1–0; EVERTON v Luton T 6–0; W. Ham v Birmingham 4–0

Semi-Final

MAN C v Derby Co 3–2; EVERTON v W. Ham 2–1

EVERTON **3**
MANCHESTER CITY **0**

At the time of their Final against Manchester City, Everton were at their very best. Promoted to the First Division in 1931 and League champions in the following year, they were now Cup-winners for the second time.

Everton's Cresswell had won his first England cap as far back as 1921, and yet still managed to stroll through the hardest match. Dean was a great centre-forward – his haul of sixty goals in the First Division in the 1927–8 season still stands as a League record.

Everton took control after City's opening series of attacks, and goals by Stein, Dean and Dunn gave them a victory that was emphatic and undisputed in a Final notably uneventful, judged by normal Wembley standards. Two of Everton's goals were the result of misjudgement on the part of City's goalkeeper Langford, who had kept too close to his line and failed to cut out most of the crosses to the immortal 'Dixie', but there were no sensations this year, no sudden twist or hectic finish.

For the first time the players' shirts were numbered – from 1 to 22 – and City were the high-numbered also-rans.

Everton: Sagar; Cook, Cresswell; Britton, White, Thomson; Geldard, Dunn, Dean, Johnson, Stein
Manchester City: Langford; Cann, Dale; Busby, Cowan, Bray; Toseland, Marshall, Herd, McMullan, Brook
Referee: E. Wood (Sheffield)

'Dixie' Dean falls after scoring Everton's second

1933-4

First Round
Barrow v Doncaster R 4–2; Bath C v Charlton Ath 0–0, 1–3; Bournemouth & Bos Ath v Hayes 3–0; Cardiff C v Aldershot 0–0, 1–3; Carlisle Utd v Wrexham 2–1; Cheltenham T v Barnet 5–1; Chester v Darlington 6–1; Clapton Orient v Epsom T 4–2; Coventry C v Crewe Alex 3–0; Crystal Palace v Norwich C 3–0; Dulwich Hamlet v Newport Co 2–2, 2–6; Folkestone v Bristol R 0–0, 1–3; Gainsboro Tr v Altrincham 1–0; Gateshead v Darwen 5–2; Halifax T v Barnsley 3–2; Ilford v Swindon T 2–4; Kingstonian v Bristol C 1–7; Lancaster T v Stockport Co 0–1; London PM v Southend Utd 0–1; New Brighton v Mansfield T 0–0, 4–3; Northampton T v Exeter C 2–0; Northfleet Utd v Dartford 0–2; North Shields v Scarborough 3–0; Oxford C v Gillingham 1–5; QPR v Kettering T 6–0; Rotherham Utd v South Bank St Peters 3–2; Scunthorpe Utd v Accrington S 1–1, 0–3; Sutton T v Rochdale 2–1; Torquay Utd v Margate 1–1, 2–0; Tranmere R v Newark T 7–0; Walsall v Spennymoor Utd 4–0; Watford v Reading 0–3; Workington v Southport 1–0; York C v Hartlepools Utd 2–3

Second Round
Bournemouth & Bos Ath v Tranmere R 2–4; Workington v Newport Co 3–1; Northampton T v Torquay Utd 3–0; Bristol C v Barrow 2–1; Rotherham Utd v Coventry C 2–1; Southend Utd v Chester 2–1; Stockport Co v Crystal Palace 1–2; Carlisle Utd v Cheltenham T 1–2; Sutton T v Reading 1–2; Gainsboro Tr v Aldershot 0–2; Halifax T v Hartlepools Utd 1–1, 2–1; QPR v New Brighton 1–1, 4–0; Charlton Ath v Gillingham 1–0; Accrington S v Bristol R 1–0; Gateshead v North Shields 1–0; Swindon T v Dartford 1–0; Walsall v Clapton Orient 0–0, 0–2

Third Round
Man Utd v PORTSMOUTH 1–1, 1–4; Grimsby T v Clapton Orient 1–0; Burnley v Bury 0–0, 2–3; Swansea T v Notts Co 1–0; Liverpool v Fulham 1–1, 3–2; Tranmere R v Southend Utd 3–0; Brighton & H Alb v Swindon T 3–1; Bolton Wand v Halifax T 3–1; Leeds Utd v PNE 0–1; Workington v Gateshead 4–1; Southampton v Northampton T 1–1, 0–1; Plymouth Arg v Huddersfield T 1–1, 2–6; Birmingham v Sheff Utd 2–1; Charlton Ath v Port Vale 2–0; Millwall v Accrington S 3–0; Leicester C v Lincoln C 3–0; Chesterfield v Aston Villa 2–2, 0–2; Sunderland v Middlesbro 1–1, 2–1; W. Ham v Bradford C 3–2; Spurs v Everton 3–0; Bristol C v Derby Co 1–1, 0–1; Wolves v Newcastle Utd 1–0; Crystal Palace v Aldershot 1–0; Luton T v Arsenal 0–1; Stoke C v Bradford PA 3–0; Cheltenham T v Blackpool 1–3; Nott'm Forest v QPR 4–0; Chelsea v WBA 1–1, 1–0; Rotherham Utd v Sheff Wed 0–3; Reading v Oldham Ath 1–2; Hull C v Brentford 1–0; MAN C v Blackburn R 3–1

Fourth Round
PORTSMOUTH v Grimsby T 2–0; Bury v Swansea T 1–1, 0–3; Liverpool v Tranmere R 3–1; Brighton & H Alb v Bolton Wand 1–1, 1–6; Workington v PNE 1–2; Huddersfield T v Northampton T 0–2; Birmingham v Charlton Ath 1–0; Millwall v Leicester C 3–6; Aston Villa v Sunderland 7–2; Spurs v W. Ham 4–1; Derby Co v Wolves 3–0; Arsenal v Crystal Palace 7–0; Stoke C v Blackpool 3–0; Chelsea v Nott'm Forest 1–1, 3–0; Oldham Ath v Sheff Wed 1–1, 1–6; Hull C v MAN C 2–2, 1–4

Fifth Round
Swansea T v PORTSMOUTH 0–1; Liverpool v Bolton Wand 0–3; PNE v Northampton T 4–0; Birmingham v Leicester C 1–2; Spurs v Aston Villa 0–1; Arsenal v Derby Co 1–0; Stoke C v Chelsea 3–1; Sheff Wed v MAN C 2–2, 0–2

Sixth Round
Bolton Wand v PORTSMOUTH 0–3; PNE v Leicester C 0–1; Arsenal v Aston Villa 1–2; MAN C v Stoke C 1–0

Semi Final
PORTSMOUTH v Leicester C 4–1; MAN C v Aston Villa 6–1

MANCHESTER CITY **2**
PORTSMOUTH **1**

City's central plan of attack, designed to outwit the 'stopper' centre-half, was based on the rapid switching and interchanging of positions by their forward-line. It had worked like a dream against Villa in the semi-final, and City had put six goals past their bemused defence, yet, when it came to the Final against Portsmouth, for a long time the plan simply wouldn't work.

The weather was nothing if not dramatic, with thunder and lightning playing around the stadium, and, fittingly, there were moments of drama on the field as well, as Portsmouth took a lead in the first half which they were to lose only very late in the second. Rutherford's cross-shot from the wing looked innocuous enough, but suddenly it spun away from Frank Swift in goal and veered into the net.

During the interval Tilson, City's centre-forward, promised the downcast Swift, then only nineteen and feeling that he ought to have saved the goal, that he would knock in a couple of goals in the second half and win the match for City. He was as good as his word.

Portsmouth led until the seventy-third minute. Then suddenly Allen, Portsmouth's tall centre-half , went down injured after an aerial collision with Cowan, and had to be carried to the touch-line. City, and left-winger Brook in particular, immediately realized that here was their chance.

It was Brook, a player with the gift of turning up at the right time in the most unlikely places, either to make goals or score them, who laid on City's equalizer. Stealing across the field from the left to the right wing, Brook received the ball from Busby's throw-in near the half-way line and set off on a controlled dribble. City's attacking plan was very much in evidence as the forwards ran towards the goal en bloc, switching positions at top speed. Brook's flick found Tilson in the inside-left channel, and he had time to pick his spot and shoot left-footed past Gilfillan into the far corner.

Three minutes from time Tilson fulfilled his dressing-room promise to score a second and winning goal with another unerring shot from his left foot. This time Herd's accurate cross-pass had created the chance.

The nervous tension of the last few minutes had been too much for the young Swift. At the final whistle he stooped into the net for his cap and gloves, and seconds later was lying flat-out on the ground. He had fainted.

Manchester City: Swift; Barnett, Dale; Busby, Cowan, Bray; Toseland, Marshall, Tilson, Herd, Brook
Portsmouth: Gilfillan; Mackie, Smith (W.); Nichol, Allen, Thackeray; Worrall, Smith (J.), Weddle, Easson, Rutherford
Referee: S. F. Rous (Herts)

1934–5

First Round
Southend Utd v Golders Green 10–1; Coventry C v Scunthorpe Utd 7–0; Mansfield T v Accrington S 6–1; Carlisle Utd v Wigan Ath 1–6; Ashford v Clapton Orient 1–4; Gateshead v Darlington 1–4; Wrexham v Rochdale 4–1; Bedford T v Dartford 2–3; Burton T v York C 2–3; Swindon T v Newport Co 4–0; Aldershot v Bournemouth & Bos Ath 4–0; Brighton & H Alb v Folkestone 3–1; Chester v Dinnington Ath 3–1; Tranmere R v Stalybridge Celtic 3–1; Charlton Ath v Exeter C 2–2, 2–5; Shildon Colliery v Lincoln C 2–2, 0–4; Yeovil & Petters United v Crystal Palace 3–0; Bristol R v Harwich and Parkeston 3–0; Crewe Alex v Walsall 1–2; Darwen v Boston Utd 1–2; Dulwich Hamlet v Torquay Utd 1–2; Guildford v Bath C 1–2; Cardiff C v Reading 1–2; QPR v Walthamstow Ave 2–0; Rotherham Utd v Spennymoor Utd 2–0; Watford v Corinthians 2–0; Workington v Birmingham Corporation Trams 2–0; Bristol C v Gillingham 2–0; Doncaster R v Barrow 0–2; Halifax T v Hartlepools Utd 1–1, 0–2; Southport v New Brighton 1–1, 1–1, 1–2; Wimbledon v Leyton 1–1, 1–0; Blyth Spartans v Stockport Co 1–1, 1–4; Barry v Northampton T 0–1

Second Round
Swindon T v Lincoln C 4–3; Wimbledon v Southend Utd 1–5; Mansfield T v Tranmere R 4–2; Yeovil & Petters United v Exeter C 4–1; Wigan Ath v Torquay Utd 3–2; Stockport Co v Darlington 3–2; Hartlepools Utd v Coventry C 0–4; Clapton Orient v Chester 1–3; Reading v Wrexham 3–0; Bath C v Boston Utd 2–1; QPR v Brighton & H Alb 1–2; Rotherham Utd v Bristol C 1–2; Barrow v Aldershot 0–2; Watford v Walsall 1–1, 1–0; York C v New Brighton 1–0; Dartford v Bristol R 0–1; Northampton T v Workington 0–0, 1–0

Third Round
SHEFF WED v Oldham Ath 3–1; Wolves v Notts Co 4–0; Norwich C v Bath C 2–0; Leeds Utd v Bradford PA 4–1; Aldershot v Reading 0–0, 1–3; Wigan Ath v Millwall 1–4; Leicester C v Blackpool 2–1; Brighton & H Alb v Arsenal 0–2; Birmingham v Coventry C 5–1; Walsall v Southampton 1–2; Yeovil & Petters Utd v Liverpool 2–6; Middlesbro v Blackburn R 1–1, 0–1; Chester v Nott'm Forest 0–4; Bristol R v Man Utd 1–3; Chelsea v Luton T 1–1, 0–2; Burnley v Mansfield T 4–2; Northampton T v Bolton Wand 0–2; Brentford v Plymouth Arg 0–1; Hull C v Newcastle Utd 1–5; Spurs v Man C 1–0; York C v Derby Co 0–1; Swansea T v Stoke C 4–1; Sunderland v Fulham 3–2; Everton v Grimsby T 6–3; PNE v Barnsley 0–0, 1–0; Swindon T v Chesterfield 2–1; Portsmouth v Huddersfield T 1–1, 3–2; Bristol C v Bury 1–1, 2–2, 2–1; W. Ham v Stockport Co 1–1, 0–1; Aston Villa v Bradford C 1–3; Southend Utd v Sheff Utd 0–4; WBA v Port Vale 2–1

Fourth Round
Wolves v SHEFF WED 1–2; Norwich C v Leeds Utd 3–3, 2–1; Reading v Millwall 1–0; Leicester C v Arsenal 0–1; Southampton v Birmingham 0–3; Nott'm Forest v Liverpool 1–0; Man Utd 0–0, 3–0; Burnley v Luton T 3–1; Plymouth Arg v Bolton Wand 1–4; Spurs v Newcastle Utd 2–0; Derby Co v Swansea T 3–0; Sunderland v Everton 1–1, 4–6; Swindon T v PNE 0–2; Portsmouth v Bristol C 0–0, 0–2; Bradford C v Stockport Co 0–0, 2–3; WBA v Sheff Utd 7–1

Fifth Round
Norwich C v SHEFF WED 0–1; Reading v Arsenal 0–1; Blackburn R v Birmingham 1–2; Nott'm Forest v Burnley 0–0, 0–3; Spurs v Bolton Wand 1–1, 1–1, 0–2; Everton v Derby Co 3–1; Bristol C v PNE 0–0, 0–5; WBA v Stockport Co 5–0

Sixth Round
SHEFF WED v Arsenal 2–1; Burnley v Birmingham 3–2; Everton v Bolton Wand 1–2; WBA v PNE 1–0

Semi-Final
SHEFF WED v Burnley 3–0, Bolton Wand v WBA 1–1, 0–2

SHEFFIELD WEDNESDAY 4
WEST BROMWICH ALBION 2

For some seasons now Wednesday had done well in the League – they were champions in 1929 and 1930 – and in the year of their Final against the Albion they were lying in third position. Albion, for their part, were appearing in their eighth Final, and came to Wembley with nine of the players who had beaten Birmingham in 1931. The scene was set for a great fight.

Five minutes from time the score was 2–2. Up to that moment it had been attack and counter-attack all the way, at an astonishing pace, with Albion twice forcing equalizers.

The Wednesday forwards were soon in gear and playing brilliant football against a harassed Albion defence which seemed powerless when Starling, Surtees and Palethorpe worked the ball between them for Palethorpe to shoot Wednesday into a second-minute lead. But before half-time, with Albion beginning to find their Wembley feet, they drew level when Boyes, the outside-left, took a pass from the limping Carter and raced half the length of the field before slashing a rising shot into the Wednesday net. It was one of the finest goals seen at Wembley.

Sheffield were now beginning to have more of the play, and twenty minutes from time Hooper, moving in from the right wing, took an intelligent pass from Starling and netted with a snap shot which went in off a post. Cock-a-hoop Wednesday were 2–1 up.

With only a quarter of an hour left Sandford shot home from twenty yards and Albion were level once more. Five agonizing minutes left and then, surely, an extra half-hour. Soon after Richardson's glaring miss for Albion, Rimmer, the Wednesday outside-left, chased a long bouncing pass down the centre into the Albion penalty-area. Pearson came smartly out of his goal, but Rimmer's head beat him to the ball by a whisker, and Wednesday were ahead for the third time in the match. Rimmer had set a record by scoring in every round.

Almost at once Rimmer scored again, and, with that, Albion's fighting spirit vanished. Except, that is, for centre-forward Billy Richardson, who retrieved the ball which the frustrated Pearson had just kicked into the net again and then dashed back to the centre-spot and kicked-off. But only thirty seconds remained, and Richardson's gesture had been heroic but futile.

Sheffield Wednesday: Brown; Nibloe, Catlin; Sharp, Millership, Burrows; Hooper, Surtees, Palethorpe, Starling, Rimmer
West Bromwich Albion: Pearson; Shaw, Trentham; Murphy, Richardson (W.), Edwards; Glidden, Carter, Richardson (W.G.), Sandford, Boyes
Referee: A. E. Fogg (Bolton)

1935–6

First Round
Barrow v Wrexham 4–1; Brighton & H Alb v Cheltenham 0–0, 6–0; Bristol C v Crystal Palace 0–1; Cardiff C v Dartford 0–3; Chester v Gateshead 1–0; Chesterfield v Southport 3–0; Clapton Orient v Aldershot 0–0, 1–0; Coventry C v Scunthorpe Utd 1–1, 2–4; Crewe Alex v Boston Utd 4–2; Darlington v Accrington S 4–2; Dulwich Hamlet v Torquay Utd 2–3; Exeter C v Gillingham 0–4; Gainsboro Tr v Blyth Spartans 3–1; Grantham v Notts Co 0–2; Halifax T v Rochdale 4–0; Kidderminster Harriers v Bishop Auckland 4–1; Mansfield T v Hartlepools Utd 2–3; Margate v QPR 3–1; New Brighton v Workington 1–3; Newport Co v Southend Utd 0–1; Northampton T v Bristol R 0–0, 1–3; Nunhead v Watford 2–4; Oldham Ath v Ferryhill Ath 6–1; Reading v Corinthians 8–3; Romford v Folkestone 3–3, 1–2; Scarborough v Darwen 2–0; Southall v Swindon T 3–1; Stalybridge Celtic v Kells Utd 4–0; Tranmere R v Carlisle Utd 3–0; Walsall v Lincoln C 2–0; Walthamstow Ave v Bournemouth & Bos Ath 1–1, 1–8; Wigan Ath v Rotherham Utd 1–2; Yeovil & Petters Utd v Newport (IoW) 0–1; York C v Burton T 1–5

Second Round
Southall v Newport (IoW) 8–0; Tranmere R v Scunthorpe Utd 6–2; Bournemouth & Bos Ath v Barrow 5–2; Workington v Kidderminster Harriers 5–1; Chester v Reading 3–3, 0–3; Southend Utd v Burton T 5–0; Dartford v Gainsboro Tr 4–0; Margate v Crystal Palace 3–1; Notts Co v Torquay Utd 3–0; Crewe Alex v Gillingham 2–1; Folkestone v Clapton Orient 1–2; Halifax T v Hartlepools Utd 1–1, 0–0, 4–1; Oldham Ath v Bristol R 1–1, 1–4; Rotherham Utd v Watford 1–1, 0–1; Scarborough v Brighton & H Alb 1–1, 0–3; Stalybridge Celtic v Darlington 0–1; Chesterfield v Walsall 0–0, 1–2

Third Round
Bristol R v ARSENAL 1–5; Liverpool v Swansea T 1–0; Crewe Alex v Sheff Wed 1–1, 1–3; Walsall v Newcastle Utd 0–2; Barnsley v Birmingham 3–3, 2–0; Notts Co v Tranmere R 0–0, 3–4; Millwall v Stoke C 0–0, 0–4; Reading v Man Utd 1–3; Hartlepools Utd v Grimsby T 0–0, 1–4; Sunderland v Port Vale 2–2, 0–2; Man C v Portsmouth 3–1; W. Ham v Luton T 2–2, 0–4; Middlesbro v Southampton 1–0; Clapton Orient v Charlton Ath 3–0; Leicester C v Brentford 1–0; Southall v Watford 1–4; Fulham v Brighton & H Alb 2–1; Blackpool v Margate 5–1; Norwich C v Chelsea 1–1, 1–3; Stockport Co v Plymouth Arg 2–3; Bradford C v Bournemouth & Bos Ath 1–0; Blackburn R v Bolton Wand 1–1, 1–0; Derby Co v Dartford 3–2; Doncaster R v Nott'm Forest 1–2; Everton v PNE 1–3; Burnley v SHEFF UTD 0–0, 1–2; Wolves v Leeds Utd 1–1, 1–3; Darlington v Bury 2–3; Spurs v Southend Utd 4–4, 2–1; Aston Villa v Huddersfield T 0–1; Bradford PA v Workington 3–2; WBA v Hull C 2–0

Fourth Round
Liverpool v ARSENAL 0–2; Sheff Wed v Newcastle Utd 1–1, 1–3; Tranmere R v Barnsley 2–4; Stoke C v Man Utd 0–0, 2–0; Port Vale v Grimsby T 0–4; Man C v Luton T 2–1; Middlesbro v Clapton Orient 3–0; Leicester C v Watford 6–3; Fulham v Blackpool 5–2; Chelsea v Plymouth Arg 4–1; Bradford C v Blackburn R 3–1; Derby C v Nott'm Forest 2–0; PNE v SHEFF UTD 0–0, 0–2; Leeds Utd v Bury 3–2; Spurs v Huddersfield T 1–0; Bradford PA v WBA 1–1, 1–1, 2–0

Fifth Round
Newcastle Utd v ARSENAL 3–3, 0–3; Barnsley v Stoke C 2–1; Grimsby T v Man C 3–2; Middlesbro v Leicester C 2–1; Chelsea v Fulham 0–0, 2–3; Bradford C v Derby Co 0–1; SHEFF UTD v Leeds Utd 3–1; Bradford PA v Spurs 0–0, 1–2

Sixth Round
ARSENAL v Barnsley 4–1; Grimsby T v Middlesbro 3–1; Fulham v Derby Co 3–0; SHEFF UTD v Spurs 3–1

Semi-Final
ARSENAL v Grimsby T 1–0; Fulham v SHEFF UTD 1–2

ARSENAL **1**
SHEFFIELD UNITED **0**

Arsenal, at this period, were regularly called upon to supply at least half the England side. Most of the old guard were still there, though David Jack had hung up his boots, and now they had the free-scoring Drake at centre-forward.

Arsenal's opponents in 1936 were Sheffield United from the Second Division. They made Arsenal fight all the way that afternoon.

Sheffield's strength was in attack, and in Barclay and Pickering they had two of the most constructive inside-forwards of the day. Dodds, a free transfer signing from Huddersfield, was the discovery of the season at centre-forward.

Arsenal were slow to settle down, but their attack came more into the picture after twenty minutes play. Bastin and Hulme, the latter appearing in his fourth Final and still as speedy as ever, began to put the Sheffield defence under pressure. It was only with a quarter of an hour left that Drake, playing with a heavily strapped knee, took a pass from Bastin and shot home a left-foot thunderbolt for the only goal of the match.

Sheffield twice came near to equalizing. Almost immediately after Drake's goal, Dodds hit the bar, and then Pickering ballooned his shot over from a good position.

Arsenal: Wilson; Male, Hapgood; Crayston, Roberts, Copping; Hulme, Bowden, Drake, James, Bastin
Sheffield United: Smith; Hooper, Wilkinson; Jackson, Johnson, McPherson; Barton, Barclay, Dodds, Pickering, Williams
Referee: H. Nattrass (New Seaham)

1936–7

First Round
Accrington S v Wellington T 3–1; Aldershot v Millwall 1–6; Barrow v Mansfield T 0–4; Bath C v Tunbridge Wells Rangers 1–2; Blyth Spartans v Wrexham 0–2; Boston Utd v Spennymoor Utd 1–1, 0–2; Bournemouth & Bos Ath v Harwich and Parkeston 5–1; Burton T v Wigan Ath 5–1; Cardiff C v Southall 3–1; Carlisle Utd v Stockport Co 2–1; Clapton Orient v Torquay Utd 2–1; Corinthians v Bristol R 0–2; Crewe Alex v Rochdale 5–1; Crystal Palace v Southend Utd 1–1, 0–2; Dartford v Peterborough Utd 3–0; Exeter C v Folkestone 3–0; Frickley Colliery v Southport 0–2; Gateshead v Notts Co 2–0; Halifax T v Darlington 1–2; Ilford v Reading 2–4; Ipswich T v Watford 2–1; Lincoln C v New Brighton 1–1, 3–2; Newport Co v Bristol C 3–0; Oldham Ath v Tranmere R 1–0; QPR v Brighton & H Alb 5–1; Rotherham Utd v Hartlepools Utd 4–4, 0–2; Ryde Sports v Gillingham 1–5; Shildon v Stalybridge Celtic 4–2; South Liverpool v Morecambe 1–0; Swindon T v Dulwich Hamlet 6–0; Walsall v Scunthorpe Utd 3–0; Walthamstow Ave v Northampton T 6–1; Yeovil & Petters Utd v Worthing 4–3; York C v Hull C 5–2

Second Round
Reading v Newport Co 7–2; Millwall v Gateshead 7–0; Southend Utd v York C 3–3, 2–1; Carlisle Utd v Clapton Orient 4–1; Lincoln C v Oldham Ath 2–3; Bristol R v Southport 2–1; Cardiff C v Swindon T 2–1; Burton T v Darlington 1–2; Ipswich T v Spennymoor Utd 1–2; Mansfield T v Bournemouth & Bos Ath 0–3; Shildon v Dartford 0–3; Wrexham v Gillingham 2–0; Crewe Alex v Hartlepools Utd 1–1, 2–1; Walsall v Yeovil & Petters Utd 1–1, 1–0; Walthamstow Ave v Exeter C 1–1, 2–3; Accrington S v Tunbridge Wells Rangers 1–0; South Liverpool v QPR 0–1

Third Round
Southampton v SUNDERLAND 2–3; Luton T v Blackpool 3–3, 2–1; Swansea T v Carlisle Utd 1–0; Bradford C v York C 2–2, 0–1; Cardiff C v Grimsby T 1–3; Walsall v Barnsley 3–1; Wolves v Middlesbro 6–1; Nott'm Forest v Sheff Utd 2–4; Millwall v Fulham 2–0; Chelsea v Leeds Utd 4–0; Bradford PA v Derby Co 0–4; Brentford v Huddersfield T 5–0; W. Ham v Bolton Wand 0–0, 0–1; Norwich C v Liverpool 3–0; Wrexham v Man C 1–3; Blackburn R v Accrington S 2–2, 1–3; Portsmouth v Spurs 0–5; Crewe Alex v Plymouth Arg 0–2; Everton v Bournemouth & Bos Ath 5–0; Sheff Wed v Port Vale 2–0; PNE v Newcastle Utd 2–0; Stoke C v Birmingham 4–1; Exeter C v Oldham Ath 3–0; Bristol R v Leicester C 2–5; Coventry C v Charlton Ath 2–0; Chester v Doncaster R 4–0; WBA v Spennymoor Utd 7–1; Dartford v Darlington 0–1; Aston Villa v Burnley 2–3; Bury v QPR 1–0; Chesterfield v Arsenal 1–5; Man Utd v Reading 1–0

Fourth Round
Luton T v SUNDERLAND 2–2, 1–3; Swansea T v York C 0–0, 3–1; Grimsby T v Walsall 5–1; Wolves v Sheff Utd 2–2, 2–1; Millwall v Chelsea 3–0; Derby Co v Brentford 3–0; Bolton Wand v Norwich C 1–1, 2–1; Man C v Accrington S 2–0; Spurs v Plymouth Arg 1–0; Everton v Sheff Wed 3–0; PNE v Stoke C 5–1; Exeter C v Leicester C 3–1; Coventry C v Chester 2–0; WBA v Darlington 3–2; Burnley v Bury 4–1; Arsenal v Man Utd 5–0

Fifth Round
SUNDERLAND v Swansea T 3–0; Grimsby T v Wolves 1–1, 2–6; Millwall v Derby Co 2–1; Bolton Wand v Man C 0–5; Everton v Spurs 1–1, 3–4; PNE v Exeter C 5–3; Coventry C v WBA 2–3; Burnley v Arsenal 1–7

Sixth Round
Wolves v SUNDERLAND 1–1, 2–2, 0–4; Millwall v Man C 2–0; Spurs v PNE 1–2; WBA v Arsenal 3–1

Semi-Final
SUNDERLAND v Millwall 2–1; PNE v WBA 4–1

SUNDERLAND **3**
PRESTON NORTH END **1**

For all their great traditions in the League, Sunderland had never yet lifted the Cup. With Preston well in command early on in the 1937 Final, it seemed that once again 'the pot' was going to elude them.

Just before half-time, F. O'Donnell, veering into the inside-right position, collected the pass from the left that he had cleverly anticipated, and drove home a magnificent shot giving Mapson in the Sunderland goal no chance. Preston were a goal ahead, and only two sides had ever lost at Wembley in a Final after being in front.

But Sunderland were transformed in the second half. The wing-halves, Thomson and McNab, began to push forward and lend their weight to the attack, and the forwards, under the astute generalship of their England inside-right Horatio Carter, at last found their confidence. Within six minutes Gurney had wiped out Preston's lead. Twenty minutes from time Carter put Sunderland ahead, and, near the end, Burbanks shot home brilliantly from a difficult angle to make it 3–1.

'Raich' Carter, a master technician and great inside-forward, had stamped his personality on the game. Sunderland-born, he led a Sunderland side, League champions the year before, to their moment of triumph.

Sunderland: Mapson; Gorman, Hall; Thomson, Johnson, McNab; Duns, Carter, Gurney, Gallacher, Burbanks
Preston North End: Burns; Gallimore, Beattie (A.); Shankly, Tremelling, Milne; Dougal, Beresford, O'Donnell (F.), Fagan, O'Donnell (H.)
Referee: R. G. Rudd (Kenton)

Carter (behind the goalkeeper) scores to make it 2–1 to Sunderland

1937-8

First Round
Accrington S v Lancaster T 1–1, 1–1, 4–0; Barrow v Crewe Alex 0–1; Bournemouth & Bos Ath v Dartford 0–0, 6–0; Brighton & H Alb v Tunbridge Wells Rangers 5–1; Bristol C v Enfield 3–0; Bristol R v QPR 1–8; Burton T v Rotherham Utd 1–1, 0–3; Corinthians v Southend Utd 0–2; Crystal Palace v Kettering T 2–2, 4–0; Darlington v Scarborough 0–2; Doncaster R v Blyth Spartans 7–0; Dulwich Hamlet v Aldershot 1–2; Exeter C v Folkestone 1–0; Gillingham v Swindon T 3–4; Guildford C v Reading 1–0; Hartlepools Utd v Southport 3–1; Hull C v Scunthorpe Utd 4–0; Kidderminster Harriers v Newport Co 2–2, 1–4; King's Lynn v Bromley 0–4; New Brighton v Workington 5–0; Northampton T v Cardiff C 1–2; Port Vale v Gainsborough Tr 1–1, 1–2; Rochdale v Lincoln C 1–1, 0–2; Torquay Utd v Clapton Orient 1–2; Tranmere Rovers v Carlisle Utd 2–1; Walker Celtic v Bradford C 1–1, 3–11; Walsall v Gateshead 4–0; Watford v Cheltenham T 3–0; Wellington T v Mansfield T 1–2; Westbury Utd v Walthamstow Ave 1–3; Wigan Ath v South Liverpool 1–4; Wrexham v Oldham Ath 2–1; Yeovil & Petters Utd v Ipswich T 2–1; York C v Halifax T 1–1, 1–0

Second Round
Accrington S v Crystal Palace 0–1; Cardiff C v Bristol C 1–1, 2–0; Clapton Orient v York C 2–2, 0–1; Crewe Alex v New Brighton 2–2, 1–4; Doncaster R v Guildford C 4–0; Exeter C v Hull C 1–2; Mansfield T v Lincoln C 2–1; Newport Co v Bournemouth & Bos Ath 2–1; Rotherham Utd v Aldershot 1–3; Scarborough v Bromley 4–1; South Liverpool v Brighton & H Alb 1–1, 0–6; Swindon T v QPR 2–1; Tranmere R v Hartlepools Utd 3–1; Walthamstow Ave v Southend Utd 0–1; Watford v Walsall 3–0; Wrexham v Bradford C 1–2; Yeovil & Petters Utd v Gainsboro Tr 2–1

Third Round
PNE v W. Ham 3–0; Mansfield T v Leicester C 1–2; Swansea T v Wolves 0–4; Arsenal v Bolton Wand 3–1; Man Utd v Yeovil & Petters Utd 3–0; Southend Utd v Barnsley 2–2, 1–2; Tranmere R v Portsmouth 1–2; Brentford v Fulham 3–1; Millwall v Man C 2–2, 1–3; Bury v Brighton & H Alb 2–0; Grimsby T v Swindon T 1–1, 1–2; Scarborough v Luton T 1–1, 1–5; Charlton Ath v Cardiff C 5–0; Leeds Utd v Chester 3–1; Birmingham v Blackpool 0–1; Norwich C v Aston Villa 2–3; Sunderland v Watford 1–0; Chelsea v Everton 0–1; Derby Co v Stoke C 1–2; Bradford PA v Newport Co 7–4; Bradford C v Chesterfield 1–1, 1–1, 0–2; Sheff Wed v Burnley 1–1, 1–3; New Brighton v Plymouth Arg 1–0; Spurs v Blackburn R 3–2; York C v Coventry C 3–2; WBA v Newcastle Utd 1–0; Nott'm Forest v Southampton 3–1; Middlesbro v Stockport Co 2–0; Crystal Palace v Liverpool 0–0, 1–3; Doncaster R v Sheff Utd 0–2; Aldershot v Notts Co 1–3; HUDDERSFIELD T v Hull C 3–1

Fourth Round
PNE v Leicester C 2–0; Wolves v Arsenal 1–2; Barnsley v Man Utd 2–2, 0–1; Brentford v Portsmouth 2–1; Man C v Bury 3–1; Luton T v Swindon T 2–1; Charlton Ath v Leeds Utd 2–1; Aston Villa v Blackpool 4–0; Everton v Sunderland 0–1; Bradford PA v Stoke C 1–1, 2–1; Chesterfield v Burnley 3–2; New Brighton v Spurs 0–0, 2–5; York C v WBA 3–2; Nott'm Forest v Middlesbro 1–3; Sheff Utd v Liverpool 1–1, 0–1; HUDDERSFIELD T v Notts Co 1–0

Fifth Round
Arsenal v PNE 0–1; Brentford v Man Utd 2–0; Luton T v Man C 1–3; Charlton Ath v Aston Villa 1–1, 2–2, 1–4; Sunderland v Bradford PA 1–0; Chesterfield v Spurs 2–2, 1–2; York C v Middlesbro 1–0; Liverpool v HUDDERSFIELD T 0–1

Sixth Round
Brentford v PNE 0–3; Aston Villa v Man C 3–2; Spurs v Sunderland 0–1; York C v HUDDERSFIELD T 0–0, 1–2

Semi-Final
PNE v Aston Villa 2–1; Sunderland v HUDDERSFIELD T 1–3

PRESTON NORTH END **1**
HUDDERSFIELD TOWN **0**

Preston were back at Wembley in 1938 to make amends. This time they faced Huddersfield, just as they had done at Stamford Bridge in 1922. Once again it was a match best forgotten – dull and without pattern.

In fact, the 1938 Final produced another coincidence. Huddersfield won the first time with a penalty; now Preston won with a penalty, scored by Mutch sixty seconds from the end of extra time.

Had the Huddersfield inside-forwards taken advantage of two or three clear openings made by Hulme, the former Arsenal player now appearing in his fifth Final, Preston would have met with a surprise defeat.

Mutch, the Preston inside-right, set off on a long dribble. Thousands were already on their way towards the exits, as a little more than a minute of extra time remained of a drab Final. On and on he went until Young, the Huddersfield centre-half and captain, moved in to the tackle. Mutch went down, and the referee pointed to the penalty-spot.

The aggrieved player took the spot kick himself, and, with the crowd hushed, struck the ball firmly against the underside of the bar and over the line. Preston had won and an old debt had been settled.

Preston North End: Holdcroft; Gallimore, Beattie (A.); Shankly, Smith, Batey; Watmough, Mutch, Maxwell, Beattie (R.), O'Donnell (H.)
Huddersfield Town: Hesford; Craig; Mountford; Willingham, Young, Boot; Hulme, Isaac, McFadyen, Barclay, Beasley
Referee: A. J. Jewell (London)

Mutch's dramatic last-minute penalty

1938-9

First Round

Aldershot v Guildford C 1—1, 4—3; Bournemouth & Bos Ath v Bristol C 2—1; Bristol R v Peterborough Utd 4—1; Bromley v Apsley 2—1; Chester v Bradford C 3—1; Chelmsford C v Kidderminster Harriers 4—0; Cheltenham T v Cardiff C 1—1, 0—1; Clapton Orient v Hayes 3—1; Crystal Palace v QPR 1—1, 0—3; Darlington v Stalybridge Celtic 4—0; Doncaster R v New Brighton 4—2; Folkestone v Colchester Utd 2—1; Gainsboro Tr v Gateshead 2—1; Halifax T v Rochdale 7—3; Hartlepools Utd v Accrington S 2—1; Horden Welfare v Chorley 1—1, 2—1; Hull C v Rotherham Utd 4—1; Ipswich T v Street 7—0; Lincoln C v Barrow 4—1; North Shields v Stockport Co 1—4; Oldham Ath v Crewe Alex 2—2, 0—1; Reading v Newport Co 3—3, 1—3; Runcorn v Wellington T 3—0; Scarborough v Southport 0—0, 3—5; Scunthorpe Utd v Lancaster C 4—2; Southend Utd v Corinthians 3—0; Swindon T v Lowestoft T 6—0; Torquay Utd v Exeter C 3—1; Walthamstow Ave v Tunbridge Wells Rangers 4—1; Walsall v Carlisle Utd 4—1; Watford v Northampton T 4—1; Workington v Mansfield T 1—1, 1—2; Wrexham v Port Vale 1—2; Yeovil and Petters United v Brighton & H Alb 2—1

Second Round

Bristol R v Bournemouth & Bos Ath 0—3; Cardiff C v Crewe Alex 1—0; Chelmsford C v Darlington 3—1; Chester v Hull C 2—2, 1—0; Folkestone v Yeovil & Petters Utd 1—1, 0—1; Gainsboro Tr v Doncaster R 0—1; Halifax T v Mansfield T 1—1, 3—3, 2—1; Hartlepools Utd v QPR 0—2; Horden Welfare v Newport Co 2—3; Ipswich T v Torquay Utd 4—1; Lincoln C v Bromley 8—1; Port Vale v Southend Utd 0—1; Runcorn v Aldershot 3—1; Scunthorpe Utd v Watford 1—2; Southport v Swindon T 2—0; Stockport Co v Walthamstow Ave 0—0, 3—1; Walsall v Clapton Orient 4—2

Third Round

PORTSMOUTH v Lincoln C 4—0; WBA v Man Utd 0—0, 5—0; QPR v W. Ham 1—2; Spurs v Watford 7—1; Runcorn v PNE 2—4; Aston Villa v Ipswich T 1—1, 2—1; Cardiff C v Charlton Ath 1—0; Brentford v Newcastle Utd 0—2; Leeds Utd v Bournemouth & Bos Ath 3—1; Huddersfield T v Nott'm Forest 0—0, 3—0; Notts Co v Burnley 3—1; Newport Co v Walsall 0—2; Middlesbro v Bolton Wand 0—0, 0—0, 1—0; Sunderland v Plymouth Arg 3—0; Blackburn R v Swansea T 2—0; Chesterfield v Southend Utd 1—1, 3—4; WOLVES v Bradford PA 3—1; Stoke C v Leicester C 1—1, 1—2; Liverpool v Luton T 3—0; Barnsley v Stockport Co 1—2; Derby Co v Everton 0—1; Southport v Doncaster R 1—1, 1—2; Birmingham v Halifax T 2—0; Chelmsford C v Southampton 4—1; Chelsea v Arsenal 2—1; Fulham v Bury 6—0; Sheff Wed v Yeovil & Petters Utd 1—1, 2—1; Chester v Coventry C 1—0; Blackpool v Sheff Utd 1—2; Norwich C v Man C 0—5; York C v Millwall 0—5; Grimsby T v Tranmere R 6—0

Fourth Round

PORTSMOUTH v WBA 2—0; W. Ham v Spurs 3—3, 1—1, 2—1; PNE v Aston Villa 2—0; Cardiff C v Newcastle Utd 0—0, 1—4; Leeds Utd v Huddersfield T 2—4; Notts Co v Walsall 0—0, 0—4; Middlesbro v Sunderland 0—2; Blackburn R v Southend Utd 4—2; WOLVES v Leicester C 5—1; Liverpool v Stockport Co 5—1; Everton v Doncaster R 8—0; Birmingham v Chelmsford C 6—0; Chelsea v Fulham 3—0; Sheff Wed v Chester 1—1, 1—1, 2—0; Sheff Utd v Man C 2—0; Millwall v Grimsby T 2—2, 2—3

Fifth Round

PORTSMOUTH v W. Ham 2—0; Newcastle Utd v PNE 1—2; Huddersfield T v Walsall 3—0; Sunderland v Blackburn R 1—1, 0—0, 0—1; WOLVES v Liverpool 4—1; Birmingham v Everton 2—2, 1—2; Chelsea v Sheff Wed 1—1, 0—0, 3—1; Sheff Utd v Grimsby T 0—0, 0—1

Sixth Round

PORTSMOUTH v PNE 1—0; Huddersfield T v Blackburn R 1—1, 2—1; WOLVES v Everton 2—0; Chelsea v Grimsby T 0—1

Semi-Final

PORTSMOUTH v Huddersfield T 2—1; WOLVES v Grimsby T 5—0

PORTSMOUTH **4**
WOLVERHAMPTON WANDERERS **1**

Wolves came to Wembley the hottest favourites for the Cup since Huddersfield faced Blackburn in 1928. Built round their great centre-half Stan Cullis, they were a brilliant and youthful side. Wolves were lying second in the League, whereas Portsmouth were struggling in the relegation danger zone.

Perhaps the label of favourites was too much of a burden for the young Wolves team, for they flopped badly in the Final. Barlow, who had actually begun the season as a Wolves player, scored Portsmouth's first goal and was their ace in the pack after that. Anderson added a second before half-time after McAlinden's chip from the right had left the advancing Scott in no-man's land.

Immediately after the interval Scott fumbled a shot on the goal-line and had to stretch out an arm and place a hand on the ball to keep it in play. Parker, dashing in from the left wing, audaciously kicked the ball from under Scott's hand and into the net.

Portsmouth were now home and dry with a three-goal lead. Dorsett got one back for Wolves, but Worrall, with a lucky sixpence in his boot, capped a great exhibition of wing-play by centring perfectly for Parker to run in and head home Portsmouth's fourth.

Portsmouth: Walker; Morgan, Rochford; Guthrie, Rowe, Wharton; Worrall, McAlinden, Anderson, Barlow, Parker
Wolverhampton Wanderers: Scott; Morris, Taylor; Galley, Cullis, Gardiner; Burton, McIntosh, Westcott, Dorsett, Maguire
Referee: T. Thompson (Lemington-on-Tyne)

1945–6

First Round
Barnet v QPR 2–6, 1–2 (3–8 agg); Barrow v Netherfield 1–0, 2–2 (3–2); Bath C v Cheltenham T 3–2, 2–0 (5–2); Brighton & H Alb v Romford 3–1, 1–1 (4–2); Bromley v Slough Utd 6–1, 0–1 (6–2); Carlisle Utd v South Shields 5–1, 3–2 (8–3); Chorley v Accrington S 2–1, 0–2 (2–3); Clapton Orient v Newport (IoW) 2–1, 0–2 (2–3); Crewe Alex v Wrexham 4–2, 0–3 (4–5); Darlington v Stockton 2–0, 4–1 (6–1); Doncaster R v Rotherham Utd 0–1, 1–2 (1–3); Halifax T v York C 1–0, 2–4 (3–4); Hartlepools Utd v Gateshead 1–2, 2–6 (3–8); Kettering T v Grantham 1–5, 2–2, (3–7); Lovell's Ath v Bournemouth & Bos Ath 4–1, 2–3 (6–4); Mansfield T v Gainsboro Tr 3–0, 2–4 (5–4); Marine (Crosby) v Stalybridge Celtic 4–0, 3–3 (7–3); Northampton T v Chelmsford 5–1, 5–0 (10–1); Notts Co v Bradford C 2–2, 2–1 (4–3); Port Vale v Wellington T 4–0, 2–0 (6–0); Reading v Aldershot 3–1, 3–7 (6–8); Shrewsbury T v Walsall 5–0, 1–4 (6–4); South Liverpool v Tranmere R 1–1, 1–6 (2–7); Southport v Oldham Ath 1–2, 1–3 (2–5); Stockport Co v Rochdale 1–2, 1–1 (2–3); Sutton Utd v Walthamstow Ave 1–4, 2–7 (3–11); Swindon T v Bristol R 1–0, 1–4 (2–4); Torquay Utd v Newport Co 0–1, 1–1 (1–2); Trowbridge v Exeter C 1–3, 2–7 (3–10); Watford v Southend Utd 1–1, 3–0 (4–1); Willington v Bishop Auckland 0–5, 2–0 (2–5); Wisbech v Ipswich T 0–3, 0–5 (0–8); Yeovil & Petters Utd v Bristol C 2–2, 0–3 (2–5); Yorkshire Amateurs v Lincoln C 1–0, 1–5 (2–5)

Second Round
Aldershot v Newport (IoW) 7–0, 5–0 (12–0); Barrow v Carlisle Utd 4–2, 4–3 (8–5); Bishop Auckland v York C 1–2, 0–3 (1–5); Bristol C v Bristol R 4–2, 2–0 (6–2); Bromley v Watford 1–3, 1–1 (2–4); Darlington v Gateshead 2–4, 2–1 (4–5); Grantham v Mansfield T 1–2, 1–2 (2–4); Lovell's Athletic v Bath C 2–1, 5–2 (7–3); Newport Co v Exeter C 5–1, 3–1 (8–2); Northampton T v Notts Co 3–1, 0–1 (3–2); Oldham Ath v Accrington S 2–1, 1–3 (3–4); Port Vale v Marine (Crosby) 3–1, 1–1 (4–2); QPR v Ipswich T 4–0, 2–0 (6–0); Rotherham Utd v Lincoln C 2–1, 1–1 (3–2); Shrewsbury T v Wrexham 0–1, 1–1 (1–2); Tranmere R v Rochdale 3–1, 0–3 (3–4); Walthamstow Ave v Brighton & H Alb 1–1, 2–4 (3–5)

Third Round
Accrington S v Man Utd 2–2, 1–5 (3–7); Aldershot v Plymouth Arg 2–0, 1–0 (3–0); Birmingham C v Portsmouth 1–0, 0–0 (1–0); Bolton Wand v Blackburn R 1–0, 3–1 (4–1); Bradford PA v Port Vale 2–1, 1–1 (3–2); Bristol C v Swansea T 5–1, 2–2 (7–3); Bury v Rochdale 3–3, 4–2 (7–5); Cardiff C v WBA 1–1, 0–4 (1–5); CHARLTON ATH v Fulham 3–1, 1–2 (4–3); Chelsea v Leicester C 1–1, 2–0 (3–1); Chester v Liverpool 0–2, 1–2 (1–4); Chesterfield v York C 1–1, 2–3 (3–4); Coventry C v Aston Villa 2–1, 0–2 (2–3); Grimsby T v Sunderland 1–3, 1–2 (2–5); Huddersfield T v Sheff Utd 1–1, 0–2 (1–3); Leeds Utd v Middlesbro 4–4, 2–7 (6–11); Lovell's Ath v Wolves 2–4, 1–8 (3–12); Luton T v DERBY CO 0–6, 0–3 (0–9); Man C v Barrow 6–2, 2–2 (8–4); Mansfield T v Sheff Wed 0–0, 0–5 (0–5); Newcastle Utd v Barnsley 4–2, 0–3 (4–5); Northampton T v Millwall 2–2, 0–3 (2–5); Norwich C v Brighton & H Alb 1–2, 1–4 (2–6); Nott'm Forest v Watford 1–1, 1–1, 0–1 (2–3); PNE v Everton 2–1, 2–2 (4–3); QPR v Crystal Palace 0–0, 0–0, 1–0 (1–0); Rotherham Utd v Gateshead 2–2, 2–0 (4–2); Southampton v Newport Co 4–3, 2–1 (6–4); Stoke C v Burnley 3–1, 1–2 (4–3); Spurs v Brentford 2–2, 0–2 (2–4); W. Ham v Arsenal 6–0, 1–0 (7–0); Wrexham v Blackpool 1–4, 1–4 (2–8)

Fourth Round
Barnsley v Rotherham Utd 3–0, 1–2 (4–2); Birmingham C v Watford 5–0, 1–1 (6–1); Blackpool v Middlesbro 3–2, 2–3, 0–1 (5–6); Bolton Wand v Liverpool 5–0, 0–2 (5–2); Bradford PA v Man C 1–3, 8–2 (9–5); Brighton & H Alb v Aldershot 3–0, 4–1 (7–1); Bristol C v Brentford 2–1, 0–5 (2–6); CHARLTON ATH v Wolves 5–2, 1–1, (6–3); Chelsea v W. Ham 2–0, 0–1 (2–1); DERBY CO v WBA 1–0, 3–1 (4–1); Man Utd v PNE 1–0, 1–3 (2–3); Millwall v Aston Villa 2–4, 1–9 (3–13); Sheff Wed v York C 5–1, 6–1 (11–2); Southampton v QPR 0–1, 3–4 (3–5); Stoke C v Sheff Utd 2–0, 2–3 (4–3); Sunderland v Bury 3–1, 4–5 (7–6)

Fifth Round
Barnsley v Bradford PA 0–1, 1–1 (1–2); Bolton Wand v Middlesbro 1–0, 1–1 (2–1); Brighton & H Alb v DERBY CO 1–4, 0–6 (1–10); Chelsea v Aston Villa 0–1, 0–1 (0–2); PNE v CHARLTON ATH 1–1, 0–6 (1–7); QPR v Brentford 1–3, 0–0 (1–3); Stoke C v Sheff Wed 2–0, 0–0 (2–0); Sunderland v Birmingham C 1–0, 1–3 (2–3)

DERBY COUNTY **4**
CHARLTON ATHLETIC **1**

In the first post-war Cup competition, extra time was to be played if teams were level after ninety minutes. For this one season only, ties were also to be played on a home and away basis, with aggregate scores deciding, from the first to the sixth round inclusive. This piece of legislation changed the whole character of the competition – there was to be no 'sudden death'.

Derby needed an extra half-hour before they could clinch victory in the Final. They would not have needed the extension had their own poor shooting and some gallant defence by Charlton not kept them without a goal in the first half.

With ten minutes to go the match burst into life with Turner's amazing double. First he diverted Duncan's shot into his own net, and then, sixty second later, he rammed a free-kick through Derby's defensive wall for the equalizer.

There were no further goals in normal time, but one odd thing happened – the ball burst. Stamps might have scored, had the ball retained its shape. Instead, it burst as he connected and Bartram caught the deflated object without great difficulty.

Derby ran riot in extra time. Doherty scored almost immediately from Stamps' cross, and ten minutes later Doherty returned the compliment, setting up a scoring chance for Stamps. Then Stamps made it 4–1 and, though Charlton still kept on, they couldn't even manage a consolation goal.

Derby County: Woodley; Nicholas, Howe; Bullions, Leuty, Musson; Harrison, Carter, Stamps, Doherty, Duncan
Charlton Athletic: Bartram; Phipps, Shreeve; Turner (H.), Oakes, Johnson; Fell, Brown, Turner (A.A.), Welsh, Duffy
Referee: E. D. Smith (Whitehaven)

Sixth Round
Aston Villa v DERBY CO 3–4, 1–1 (4–5); Bradford PA v Birmingham C 2–2, 0–6 (2–8); CHARLTON ATH v Brentford 6–3, 3–1 (9–4); Stoke C v Bolton Wand 0–2, 0–0 (0–2)

Semi-Final
Bolton Wand v CHARLTON ATH 0–2; DERBY CO v Birmingham C 1–1, 4–0

1946-7

First Round
Aldershot v Cheltenham T 4–2; Barnet v Sutton Utd 3–0; Barrow v Halifax T 0–0, 0–1;
Bournemouth & Bos Ath v Exeter C 4–2; Bristol C v Hayes 9–3; Brush Sports v Southend Utd 1–6;
Carlisle Utd v Runcorn 4–0; Doncaster R v Accrington S 2–2, 5–0; Gainsboro Tr v Darlington
1–2; Gateshead v Bradford C 3–1; Gillingham v Gravesend & Northfleet 4–1; Hartlepools Utd v
North Shields 6–0; Hull C v New Brighton 0–0, 2–1; Ipswich T v Torquay Utd 2–0; Lancaster C v
Spennymoor Utd 1–0; Leyton Orient v Notts Co 1–2; Leytonstone v Walsall 1–6; Merthyr Tydfil v
Bristol R 3–1; Northampton T v Mansfield T 2–0; Norwich C v Brighton & H Alb 7–2; Oldham Ath v
Tranmere R 1–0; Port Vale v Finchley 5–0; QPR v Poole T 2–2, 6–0; Reading v Colchester U 5–0;
Rochdale v Bishop Auckland 2–1; Rotherham Utd v Crewe Alex 2–0; South Liverpool v Workington
2–1; Stockport Co v Southport 2–0; Stockton v Lincoln C 2–4; Swindon T v Cambridge T 4–1;
Wellington T v Watford 1–1, 0–1; Wrexham v Marine (Crosby) 5–0; Yeovil T v Peterborough
2–2, 0–1; York C v Scunthorpe 0–1

Second Round
Barnet v Southend U 2–9; Bournemouth & Bos Ath v Aldershot 4–2; Bristol C v Gillingham 1–2;
Darlington v Hull C 1–2; Gateshead v Lancaster C 4–0; Halifax T v Stockport Co 1–1, 1–2; Lincoln C
v Wrexham 1–1, 3–3, 2–1; Merthyr Tydfil v Reading 1–3; Norwich C v QPR 4–4, 0–2; Notts Co v
Swindon T 2–1; Oldham Ath v Doncaster R 1–2; Peterborough v Northampton T 1–1, 1–1, 1–8;
Rochdale v Hartlepools Utd 6–1; Rotherham Utd v Scunthorpe Utd 4–1; South Liverpool v
Carlisle Utd 2–3; Walsall v Ipswich T 0–0, 1–0; Watford v Port Vale 1–1, 1–2

Third Round
CHARLTON ATH v Rochdale 3–1; WBA v Leeds Utd 2–1; Blackburn R v Hull C 1–1, 3–0; Millwall v
Port Vale 0–3; Northampton T v PNE 1–2; Huddersfield T v Barnsley 3–4; Sheff Wed v Blackpool
4–1; Everton v Southend U 4–2; Newcastle Utd v Crystal Palace 6–2; Southampton v Bury 5–1;
W Ham v Leicester C 1–2; Brentford v Cardiff C 1–0; Sheff Utd v Carlisle Utd 3–0; Wolves v
Rotherham Utd 3–0; Spurs v Stoke C 2–2, 1–0; Chester v Plymouth Arg 2–0; BURNLEY v
Aston Villa 5–1; Coventry C v Newport Co 5–2; Luton T v Notts Co 6–0; Swansea T v Gillingham
4–1; QPR v Middlesbro 1–1, 1–3; Chesterfield v Sunderland 2–1; Lincoln C v Nott'm Forest 0–1;
Bradford PA v Man Utd 0–3; Walsall v Liverpool 2–5; Reading v Grimsby T 2–2, 1–3;
Bournemouth & Bos Ath v Derby Co 0–2; Chelsea v Arsenal 1–1, 1–1, 2–0; Fulham v
Birmingham C 1–2; Doncaster R v Portsmouth 2–3; Man C v Gateshead 3–0; Bolton Wand v
Stockport Co 5–1

Fourth Round
WBA v CHARLTON ATH 1–2; Blackburn R v Port Vale 2–0; PNE v Barnsley 6–0; Sheff Wed v
Everton 2–1; Newcastle Utd v Southampton 3–1; Leicester v Brentford 0–0, 0–0, 4–1; Sheff Utd v
Wolves 0–0, 2–0; Stoke C v Chester 0–0, 3–2; BURNLEY v Coventry C 2–0; Luton T v Swansea T
2–0; Middlesbro v Chesterfield 2–1; Nott'm Forest v Man Utd 2–0; Liverpool v Grimsby T 2–0;
Derby Co v Chelsea 2–2, 1–0; Birmingham C v Portsmouth 1–0; Man C v Bolton Wand 3–3, 1–0

Fifth Round
CHARLTON ATH v Blackburn R 1–0; PNE v Sheff Wed 2–0; Newcastle Utd v Leicester C 1–1, 2–1;
Sheff Utd v Stoke C 1–0; BURNLEY v Luton T 0–0, 3–0; Middlesbro v Nott'm Forest 2–2, 6–2;
Liverpool v Derby Co 1–0; Birmingham C v Man C 5–0

Sixth Round
CHARLTON ATH v PNE 2–1; Sheff Utd v Newcastle Utd 0–2; Middlesbro v BURNLEY 1–1, 0–1;
Liverpool v Birmingham C 4–1

Semi-Final
CHARLTON ATH v Newcastle Utd 4–0; BURNLEY v Liverpool 0–0, 1–0

CHARLTON ATHLETIC **1**
BURNLEY **0**

Charlton, beaten finalists in 1946, returned the following year to defeat Second Division Burnley by the only goal of a match thought generally to have been one of the least memorable Wembley finals.

Their convincing display against high-scoring Newcastle in the semi-final, allied to the 'unknown' tag attached to their Lancashire opponents, made Charlton slight favourites.

The Final was played in tremendous heat, with the players of both teams apparently drained of energy long before the end of a mediocre match. As in 1946, extra time was needed, and until Duffy's spectacular winning goal the additional period had been played practically at walking pace.

The only two incidents worthy of note in normal time had been Potts' drive smacking against the Charlton crossbar and the bursting of the ball for the second successive year.

With the first Final replay since 1912 looking a distinct possibility as the stalemate continued, Charlton broke the deadlock six minutes from the end of extra time. Welsh flicked on Robinson's high cross and Duffy's volley from near the penalty-spot sailed past Strong's left shoulder and into the net.

In the short time that remained, Burnley launched a frantic series of attacks, and in one of these Morris send a header looping over Bartram . . . and over the bar.

Charlton Athletic: Bartram; Croker, Shreeve; Johnson, Phipps, Whittaker; Hurst, Dawson, Robinson (W.), Welsh, Duffy
Burnley: Strong; Woodruff, Mather; Attwell, Brown, Bray; Chew, Morris, Harrison, Potts, F. P. Kippax
Referee: J. M. Wiltshire (Sherbourne)

Duffy's extra-time winner

1947-8

First Round
Aldershot v Bromsgrove R 2–1; Barrow v Carlisle Utd 3–2; Bournemouth & Bos Ath v Guildford C 2–0; Bristol R v Leytonstone 3–2; Bromley v Reading 3–3, 0–3; Cheltenham T v Street 5–0; Chester v Bishop Auckland 3–1; Colchester Utd v Banbury Spencer 2–1; Crewe Alex v South Shields 4–1; Crystal Palace v Port Vale 2–1; Dartford v Bristol C 0–0, 2–9; Exeter C v Northampton T 1–1, 0–2; Gateshead v Bradford C 1–3; Gillingham v Leyton Orient 1–0; Gt Yarmouth v Shrewsbury T 1–4; Hartlepools Utd v Darlington 1–0; Hull C v Southport 1–1, 3–2; Lincoln C v Workington 0–2; New Brighton v Marine (Crosby) 4–0; Newport Co v Southend Utd 3–2; Norwich C v Merthyr Tydfil 3–0; Notts Co v Horsham 9–1; Oldham Ath v Lancaster C 6–0; Runcorn v Scunthorpe Utd 4–2; Stockport Co v Accrington S 3–1; Stockton v Grantham 2–1; Swindon T v Ipswich T 4–2; Tranmere R v Stalybridge Celtic 2–0; Trowbridge v Brighton & H Alb 1–1, 0–5; Vauxhall Motors (Luton) v Walsall 1–2; Watford v Torquay Utd 1–1, 0–3; Wimbledon v Mansfield T 0–1; Wrexham v Halifax T 5–0; York C v Rochdale 0–1

Second Round
Aldershot v Swindon T 0–0, 0–2; Bournemouth & Bos Ath v Bradford C 1–0; Bristol C v Crystal Palace 0–1; Bristol R v New Brighton 4–0; Colchester Utd v Wrexham 1–0; Hartlepools Utd v Brighton & H Alb 1–1, 1–2; Hull C v Cheltenham T 4–2; Northampton T v Torquay Utd 1–1, 0–2; Norwich C v Walsall 2–2, 2–3; Notts Co v Stockton 1–1, 4–1; Oldham Ath v Mansfield T 0–1; Reading v Newport Co 3–0; Rochdale v Gillingham 1–1, 0–3; Runcorn v Barrow 0–1; Stockport Co v Shrewsbury T 1–1, 2–2, 3–2; Tranmere R v Chester 0–1; Workington v Crewe Alex 1–2

Third Round
Gillingham v QPR 1–1, 1–3; Mansfield T v Stoke C 2–4; Plymouth Arg v Luton T 2–4; Coventry C v Walsall 2–1; Rotherham Utd v Brentford 0–3; Hull C v Middlesbro 1–3; Crewe A v Sheff Utd 3–1; Derby Co v Chesterfield 2–0; Aston Villa v MAN UTD 4–6; Liverpool v Nott'm Forest 4–1; Charlton Ath v Newcastle Utd 2–1; Stockport Co v Torquay Utd 3–0; Man C v Barnsley 2–1; Chelsea v Barrow 5–0; Portsmouth v Brighton & H Alb 4–1; Millwall v PNE 1–2; Fulham v Doncaster R 2–0; Bristol R v Swansea T 3–0; Bournemouth & Bos Ath v Wolves 1–2; Grimsby T v Everton 1–4; BLACKPOOL v Leeds Utd 4–0; Crystal Palace v Chester 0–1; Colchester Utd v Huddersfield T 1–0; Arsenal v Bradford PA 0–1; Southampton v Sunderland 1–0; Blackburn R v W. Ham 0–0, 4–2; Burnley v Swindon T 0–2; Birmingham v Notts Co 0–2; Bolton Wand v Spurs 0–2; WBA v Reading 2–0; Leicester C v Bury 1–0; Cardiff C v Sheff Wed 1–2

Fourth Round
QPR v Stoke C 3–0; Luton T v Coventry C 3–2; Brentford v Middlesbro 1–2; Crewe Alex v Derby Co 0–3; MAN UTD v Liverpool 3–0; Charlton Ath v Stockport Co 3–0; Man C v Chelsea 2–0; Portsmouth v PNE 1–3; Fulham v Bristol R 5–2; Wolves v Everton 1–1, 2–3; BLACKPOOL v Chester 4–0; Colchester Utd v Bradford PA 3–2; Southampton v Blackburn R 3–2; Swindon T v Notts Co 1–0; Spurs v WBA 3–1; Leicester C v Sheff Wed 2–1

Fifth Round
QPR v Luton T 3–1; Middlesbro v Derby Co 1–2; MAN UTD v Charlton Ath 2–0; Man C v PNE 0–1; Fulham v Everton 1–1, 1–0; BLACKPOOL v Colchester Utd 5–0; Southampton v Swindon T 3–0; Spurs v Leicester C 5–2

Sixth Round
QPR v Derby Co 1–1, 0–5; MAN UTD v PNE 4–1; Fulham v BLACKPOOL 0–2; Southampton v Spurs 0–1

Semi-Final
Derby Co v MAN UTD 1–3; BLACKPOOL v Spurs 3–1

Rowley heads United level at 2–2

MANCHESTER UNITED **4**
BLACKPOOL **2**

The all-Lancashire Cup Final of 1948 was one of the best exhibitions of football seen at Wembley. It isn't often that the football in the Final reaches the noblest heights; the excitement, the importance of the occasion and the huge crowd all too often combine to cause 'Wembley nerves'.

United had been among the Final probables from the start of the competition and rapidly became the favourites. In the first half at Wembley, which ended with Blackpool in the lead 2–1, United's brilliant play had not been rewarded as it should have been. After fifteen minutes Mortensen was tackled from behind inside the area, and Shimwell scored from the spot to put Blackpool in front. Five minutes after Rowley had equalized from Delaney's pass, Blackpool scored again with Mortensen's cross-shot.

Rowley darted between two defenders to head United level again from a quickly taken free-kick, and it was Crompton's save from England international Mortensen's fine shot in the eightieth minute that proved to be the turning point. Play immediately switched to the other end, and Pearson's hard shot from twenty yards flew into the Blackpool net via an upright. Three minutes later Anderson made the final score 4–2 to United.

United, with their extra stamina and power in attack, had just about deserved their exciting victory – their twelve corner-kicks to Blackpool's four had been a fair reflection of the play.

Manchester United: Crompton; Carey, Aston; Anderson, Chilton, Cockburn; Delaney, Morris, Rowley, Pearson, Mitten
Blackpool: Robinson; Shimwell, Crosland; Johnston, Hayward, Kelly; Matthews, Munro, Mortensen, Dick, Rickett
Referee: C. J. Barrick (Northampton)

1948–9

First Round
Barnet v Exeter C 2–6; Bradford C v Doncaster R 4–3; Colchester Utd v Reading 2–4; Crewe Alex v Billingham Synthonia 5–0; Crystal Palace v Bristol City 0–1; Dartford v Leyton Orient 2–3; Gainsboro Tr v Witton Alb 1–0; Gateshead v Netherfield 3–0; Halifax T v Scunthorpe Utd 0–0, 0–1; Hartlepools Utd v Chester 1–3; Hull C v Accrington S 3–1; Ipswich T v Aldershot 0–3; Kidderminster Harriers v Hereford Utd 0–3; Leytonstone v Watford 2–1; Mansfield T v Gloucester C 4–0; Millwall v Tooting and Mitcham 1–0; New Brighton v Carlisle Utd 1–0; Newport Co v Brighton & H Alb 3–1; Northampton T v Dulwich Hamlet 1–0; Norwich C v Wellington T 1–0; Notts Co v Port Vale 2–1; Peterborough Utd v Torquay Utd 0–1; Rochdale v Barrow 1–1, 0–2; Rhyl Ath v Scarborough 0–2; Southend Utd v Swansea T 1–2; Southport v Horden Colliery Welfare 2–1; Tranmere R v Darlington 1–3; Walsall v Bristol R 2–1; Walthamstow Ave v Cambridge T 3–2; Weymouth v Chelmsford C 2–1; Workington v Stockport Co 0–3; Wrexham v Oldham Ath 0–3; Yeovil T v Romford 4–0; York C v Runcorn 2–1

Second Round
Aldershot v Chester 1–0; Bradford C v New Brighton 0–0, 0–1; Bristol C v Swansea T 3–1; Crewe Alex v Millwall 3–2; Darlington v Leyton Orient 1–0; Exeter C v Hereford Utd 2–1; Gateshead v Scarborough 3–0; Hull C v Reading 0–0, 2–1; Leytonstone v Newport Co 3–4; Mansfield T v Northampton T 2–1; Notts Co v Barrow 3–2; Scunthorpe Utd v Stockport Co 0–1; Southport v York C 2–2, 2–0; Torquay Utd v Norwich C 3–1; Walsall v Gainsboro Tr 4–3; Walthamstow Ave v Oldham Ath 2–2, 1–3; Weymouth v Yeovil T 0–4

Third Round
Man Utd v Bournemouth & Bos Ath 6–0; Newcastle Utd v Bradford PA 0–2; Yeovil T v Bury 3–1; Crewe Alex v Sunderland 0–2; Blackburn R v Hull C 1–2; Grimsby T v Exeter C 2–1; Swindon T v Stoke C 1–3; Barnsley v Blackpool 0–1; WOLVES v Chesterfield 6–0; Sheff Utd v New Brighton 5–2; Nott'm Forest v Liverpool 2–2, 0–4; Plymouth Arg v Notts Co 0–1; Lincoln C v WBA 0–1; Gateshead v Aldershot 3–1; Bristol C v Chelsea 1–3; Everton v Man C 1–0; LEICESTER C v Birmingham 1–1, 1–1, 2–1; PNE v Mansfield T 2–1; Luton T v W. Ham 3–1; Fulham v Walsall 0–1; Brentford v Middlesbro 3–2; Torquay Utd v Coventry C 1–0; Burnley v Charlton Ath 2–1; Rotherham v Darlington 4–2; Portsmouth v Stockport Co 7–0; Sheff Wed v Southampton 2–1; Leeds Utd v Newport Co 1–3; QPR v Huddersfield 0–0, 0–5; Derby Co v Southport 4–1; Arsenal v Spurs 3–0; Oldham Ath v Cardiff C 2–3; Aston Villa v Bolton 1–1, 0–0, 2–1

Fourth Round
Man Utd v Bradford PA 1–1, 1–1, 5–0; Yeovil T v Sunderland 2–1; Grimsby T v Hull C 2–3; Stoke C v Blackpool 1–1, 1–0; Sheff Utd v WOLVES 0–3; Liverpool v Notts Co 1–0; Gateshead v WBA 1–3; Chelsea v Everton 2–0; LEICESTER C v PNE 2–0; Luton T v Walsall 4–0; Brentford v Torquay Utd 1–0; Rotherham v Burnley 0–1; Portsmouth v Sheff Wed 2–1; Newport Co v Huddersfield 3–3, 3–1; Derby Co v Arsenal 1–0; Aston Villa v Cardiff C 1–2

Fifth Round
Man Utd v Yeovil T 8–0; Stoke C v Hull C 0–2; WOLVES v Liverpool 3–1; WBA v Chelsea 3–0; Luton T v LEICESTER C 5–5, 3–5; Brentford v Burnley 4–2; Portsmouth v Newport Co 3–2; Derby Co v Cardiff C 2–1

Sixth Round
Hull C v Man Utd 0–1; WOLVES v WBA 1–0; Brentford v LEICESTER C 0–2; Portsmouth v Derby Co 2–1

Semi-Final
Man Utd v WOLVES 1–1, 0–1; LEICESTER C v Portsmouth 3–1

WOLVERHAMPTON WANDERERS **3**
LEICESTER CITY **1**

Wolverhampton, with their extra speed and ability to play together as a team, beat Midland rivals Leicester as expected and carried off the Cup for the third time in their history

Except for a twenty-minute spell just after half-time, when the under-dog team, Leicester, threatened to achieve the impossible, the match lacked the sustained excitement of some other Finals.

Wolves showed from the start that they meant business and took an early lead when Pye neatly headed in from Hancocks' perfectly-placed centre in the thirteenth minute. Three minutes before half-time Wolves forced two corners, and from the second of these Pye again scored. The Cup, it seemed, was as good as won.

There was a dramatic change after the break, as Leicester staged a wonderful rally. Within two minutes they had secured the goal they needed so badly. Chisholm's initial shot was blocked by Williams, but the ball ran on to Griffiths who, with split-second timing, hooked it into the net.

Now Leicester were inspired to launch a series of attacks on both flanks, but, seconds after Chisholm's apparent equalizer had been adjudged offside, Wolves' volatile Irishman Sammy Smyth beat three men and shot home with his left foot to make the final score 3–1 to Wolves.

The remainder of the game was something of an anti-climax, Leicester never looking as though they would reduce the two-goal deficit again.

Wolverhampton Wanderers: Williams; Pritchard, Springthorpe; Crook (W.), Shorthouse, Wright; Hancocks, Smyth, Pye, Dunn, Mullen
Leicester City: Bradley; Jelly, Scott; Harrison (W.), Plummer, King; Griffiths, Lee, Harrison (J.), Chisholm, Adam
Referee: R. A. Mortimer (Huddersfield)

Smyth smacks the ball past Lee for Wolves' third

1949–50

First Round

Accrington S v Hartlepools Utd 0–1; Bradford C v Fleetwood 9–0; Bromley v Watford 1–2; Carlisle Utd v Lincoln C 1–0; Chester v Goole T 4–1; Crystal Palace v Newport Co 0–3; Darlington v Crewe Alex 2–2, 0–1; Doncaster R v New Brighton 5–1; Gateshead v York C 3–1; Gloucester C v Norwich C 2–3; Gravesend & Northfleet Utd v Torquay Utd 1–3; Hastings Utd v Gillingham 1–3; Hereford Utd v Bromsgrove R 3–0; Ipswich T v Brighton & H Alb 2–1; Leyton Orient v Southend Utd 0–2; Leytonstone v Chelmsford C 1–2; Mansfield T v Walsall 4–1; Millwall v Exeter C 3–5; Netherfield v North Shields 4–3; Northampton T v Walthamstow Ave 4–1; Notts Co v Tilbury 4–0; Nott'm Forest v Bristol C 1–0; Nuneaton Boro v King's Lynn 2–1; Oldham Ath v Stockton 4–0; Port Vale v Wealdstone 1–0; Rhyl v Rochdale 0–3; Southport v Barrow 1–1, 1–0; Stockport Co v Billingham Synthonia Recreation 3–0; Swindon T v Bristol R 1–0; Tranmere R v Halifax T 2–1; Weymouth v Aldershot 2–2, 3–2; Witton Alb v Mossley 0–1; Wrexham v Grantham 4–1; Yeovil T v Romford 4–1

Second Round

Carlisle Utd v Swindon T 2–0; Chelmsford C v Ipswich T 1–1, 0–1; Crewe Alex v Oldham Ath 1–1, 0–0, 0–3; Doncaster R v Mansfield T 1–0; Exeter C v Chester 2–0; Hartlepools Utd v Norwich C 1–1, 1–5; Newport Co v Gateshead 1–1, 2–1; Northampton T v Torquay Utd 4–2; Nott'm Forest v Stockport Co 0–2; Nuneaton Boro v Mossley 0–0, 3–0; Port Vale v Tranmere R 1–0; Rochdale v Notts Co 1–2; Southport v Bradford C 2–1; Watford v Netherfield 6–0; Weymouth v Hereford Utd 2–1; Wrexham v Southend Utd 2–2, 0–2; Yeovil T v Gillingham 3–1

Third Round

ARSENAL v Sheff Wed 1–0; Swansea T v Birmingham C 3–0; Notts Co v Burnley 1–4; Newport Co v Port Vale 1–2; Carlisle Utd v Leeds Utd 2–5; Coventry C v Bolton Wand 1–2; Cardiff C v WBA 2–2, 1–0; Charlton Ath v Fulham 2–2, 2–1; Brentford v Chelsea 0–1; Oldham Ath v Newcastle Utd 2–7; Chesterfield v Yeovil 3–1; Aston Villa v Middlebro 2–2, 0–0, 2–3; Man Utd v Weymouth 4–0; Watford v PNE 2–2, 1–0; Portsmouth v Norwich C 1–1, 2–0; Luton T v Grimsby T 3–4; Blackburn R v LIVERPOOL 0–0, 1–2; Exeter C v Nuneaton Boro 3–0; Stockport Co v Barnsley 4–2; Southport v Hull 0–0, 0–5; Blackpool v Southend Utd 4–0; Reading v Doncaster R 2–3; Plymouth Arg v Wolves 1–1, 0–3; Sheff Utd v Leicester C 3–1; QPR v Everton 0–2; W. Ham v Ipswich T 5–1; Stoke C v Spurs 0–1; Sunderland v Huddersfield T 6–0; Man C v Derby Co 3–5; Bury v Rotherham 5–4; Northampton T v Southampton 1–1, 3–2; Bradford PA v Bournemouth & Bos Ath 0–1

Fourth Round

ARSENAL v Swansea T 2–1; Burnley v Port Vale 2–1; Leeds Utd v Bolton Wand 1–1, 3–2; Charlton Ath v Cardiff C 1–1, 0–2; Chelsea v Newcastle Utd 3–0; Chesterfield v Middlesbro 3–2; Watford v Man Utd 0–1; Portsmouth v Grimsby T 5–0; LIVERPOOL v Exeter C 3–1; Stockport Co v Hull C 0–0, 2–0; Blackpool v Doncaster R 2–1; Wolves v Sheff Utd 0–0, 4–3; W. Ham v Everton 1–2; Spurs v Sunderland 5–1; Bury v Derby Co 2–2, 2–5; Bournemouth & Bos Ath v Northampton T 1–1, 1–2

Fifth Round

ARSENAL v Burnley 2–0; Leeds Utd v Cardiff C 3–1; Chesterfield v Chelsea 1–1, 0–3; Man Utd v Portsmouth 3–3, 3–1; Stockport Co v LIVERPOOL 1–2; Wolves v Blackpool 0–0, 0–1; Everton v Spurs 1–0; Derby Co v Northampton T 4–2

Sixth Round

ARSENAL v Leeds Utd 1–0; Chelsea v Man Utd 2–0; LIVERPOOL v Blackpool 2–1; Derby Co v Everton 1–2

Semi-Final

ARSENAL v Chelsea 2–2, 1–0; LIVERPOOL v Everton 2–0

Stubbins (on ground) fails to connect, much to Barnes' relief

ARSENAL **2**
LIVERPOOL **0**

Arsenal registered their third Wembley win, equalling Bolton's record, in a defence-oriented Final against Liverpool.

The 2–0 scoreline was a fair reflection of the play, though Liverpool were certainly on top in the early stages. After eighteen minutes, however, Arsenal scored their opening goal. Goring lured Hughes away from the midfield, leaving the Liverpool defence open and allowing Lewis to slide unnoticed into the penalty-area, take Logie's measured pass into his stride and shoot unerringly into the net past Sidlow.

Liverpool struck back immediately, with Stubbins twice desperately close with headers, but Arsenal remained calm and unruffled in defence and by half-time the impression had emerged that, psychologically, they held the upper hand.

Swindin, for Arsenal, made a wonderful save from Payne early in the second half after Liddell's fine centre had left him all at sea, and then a series of Arsenal counter-attacks served as a prelude to a second goal after sixty-three minutes. Mercer began the movement which ended with Lewis running in to beat Sidlow with a low shot into the corner.

Liverpool refused to admit defeat and beat against the Arsenal defence until the end. Three times they nearly scored, with Liddell and Payne prominent, but their last-minute effort was in vain. Forbes at half-back had been outstanding for Arsenal, while Mercer's leadership had been as impressive as ever.

Arsenal: Swindin; Scott, Barnes; Forbes, Compton (L.), Mercer; Cox, Logie, Goring, Lewis, Compton (D.)
Liverpool: Sidlow; Lambert, Spicer; Taylor, Hughes, Jones; Payne, Baron, Stubbins, Fagan, Liddell
Referee: H. Pearce (Luton)

1950-1

First Round

Aldershot v Bromley 2–2, 1–0; Bishop Auckland v York C 2–2, 1–2; Bournemouth & Bos Ath v Colchester Utd 1–0; Bradford C v Oldham Ath 2–2, 1–2; Bristol C v Gloucester C 4–0; Bristol R v Llanelly 1–1, 1–1, 3–1; Bromsgrove R v Hereford Utd 1–3; Carlisle Utd v Barrow 2–1; Chelmsford C v Tonbridge 2–2, 1–0; Chester v Bradford PA 1–2; Cleator Moor Celtic v Tranmere R 0–5; Crewe Alex v North Shields 4–0; Crystal Palace v Millwall 1–4; Darlington v Rotherham Utd 2–7; Gainsboro Tr v Plymouth Arg 0–3; Glastonbury v Exeter C 1–2; Guildford C v Dartford 1–5; Halifax T v Ashington 2–3; Leyton Orient v Ipswich T 1–2; Linby Colliery v Gillingham 1–4; Lincoln C v Southport 1–1, 2–3; Mansfield T v Walthamstow Ave 1–0; Newport Co v Walsall 4–2; Norwich C v Watford 2–0; Nott'm Forest v Torquay Utd 6–1; Port Vale v New Brighton 3–2; Reading v Cheltenham T 3–1; Rochdale v Willington 3–1; Scarborough v Rhyl 1–2; Tooting and Mitcham v Brighton & H Alb 2–3; Witton Alb v Nelson 1–2; Southend Utd v Swindon T 0–3; Worcester C v Hartlepools Utd 1–4; Wrexham v Accrington S 1–0

Second Round

Aldershot v Bournemouth & Bos Ath 3–0; Ashington v Rochdale 1–2; Brighton & H Alb v Ipswich T 2–0; Bristol C v Wrexham 2–1; Bristol R v Gillingham 2–2, 1–1, 2–1; Chelmsford C v Mansfield T 1–4; Crewe Alex v Plymouth Arg 2–2, 0–3; Exeter C v Swindon T 3–0; Hartlepools Utd v Oldham Ath 1–2; Hereford Utd v Newport Co 0–3; Millwall Ath v Bradford PA 1–1, 1–0; Port Vale v Nelson 3–2; Reading v Dartford 4–0; Rhyl v Norwich C 0–1; Rotherham Utd v Nott'm Forest 3–1; Southport v Carlisle Utd 1–3; York C v Tranmere R 2–1

Third Round

NEWCASTLE UTD v Bury 4–1; Bolton Wand v York C 2–0; Stoke C v Port Vale 2–2, 1–0; W. Ham v Cardiff C 2–1; Luton T v Portsmouth 2–0; Bristol R v Aldershot 5–1; Hull C v Everton 2–0; Rotherham Utd v Doncaster R 2–1; Plymouth Arg v Wolves 1–2; Aston Villa v Burnley 2–0; Leicester C v PNE 0–3; Huddersfield T v Spurs 2–0; Sunderland v Coventry C 2–0; Notts Co v Southampton 3–4; Newport Co v Reading 3–2; Norwich C v Liverpool 3–1; Charlton Ath v BLACKPOOL 2–2, 0–3; Stockport Co v Brentford 2–1; Mansfield T v Swansea T 2–0; Sheff Utd v Gateshead 1–0; Grimsby T v Exeter C 3–3, 2–4; Rochdale v Chelsea 2–3; QPR v Millwall 3–4; Fulham v Sheff Wed 1–0; Derby Co v WBA 2–2, 1–0; Birmingham C v Man C 2–0; Bristol C v Blackburn R 2–1; Brighton & H Alb v Chesterfield 2–1; Man Utd v Oldham Ath 4–1; Leeds Utd v Middlesbro 1–0; Arsenal v Carlisle Utd 0–0, 4–1; Northampton T v Barnsley 3–1

Fourth Round

NEWCASTLE UTD v Bolton Wand 3–2; Stoke C v W. Ham 1–0; Luton T v Bristol R 1–2; Hull C v Rotherham Utd 2–0; Wolves v Aston V 3–1; PNE v Huddersfield T 0–2; Sunderland v Southampton 2–0; Newport Co v Norwich C 0–2; BLACKPOOL v Stockport Co 2–1; Sheff Utd v Mansfield T 0–0, 1–2; Exeter C v Chelsea 1–1, 0–2; Millwall v Fulham 0–1; Derby Co v Birmingham C 1–3; Bristol C v Brighton & H Alb 1–0; Man Utd v Leeds Utd 4–0; Arsenal v Northampton T 3–2

Fifth Round

Stoke C v NEWCASTLE UTD 2–4; Bristol R v Hull C 3–0; Wolves v Huddersfield T 2–0; Sunderland v Norwich C 3–1; BLACKPOOL v Mansfield T 2–0; Chelsea v Fulham 1–1, 0–3; Birmingham C v Bristol C 2–0; Man Utd v Arsenal 1–0

Sixth Round

NEWCASTLE UTD v Bristol R 0–0, 3–1; Sunderland v Wolves 1–1, 1–3; BLACKPOOL v Fulham 1–0; Birmingham C v Man Utd 1–0

Semi-Final

NEWCASTLE UTD v Wolves 0–0, 2–1; BLACKPOOL v Birmingham C 0–0, 2–1

Farm has no chance with this effort from Milburn

NEWCASTLE UNITED 2
BLACKPOOL 0

Newcastle won the Cup for the fourth time in a Final fought out by two very evenly matched teams. On the whole, Newcastle showed themselves the tougher, cleverer and speedier side, and at its best their forward-line was a dazzling and irresistible combination.

The game began with a display of 'Wembley nerves' from both sides, with a lot of wayward passing. Blackpool were the first to settle down, and in the first twenty minutes they generally succeeded in keeping the ball in the Newcastle half. Mortensen's header was cleared off the line by a defender, and Mudie failed to make the most of an opening provided by Matthews' clever dribble.

Matthews, in fact, stood head and shoulders above every other forward on the field, but in the first half the rest of the Blackpool forward-line seemed incapable of capitalizing on his brilliant wing-play.

Five minutes after the interval Milburn scored a dramatic goal to put Newcastle in front. Robledo's pass beat the offside trap and Milburn was away to tuck the ball past Farm from fifteen yards. Blackpool never recovered from the shock of going behind, and Milburn scored an even better goal five minutes later. Receiving a clever back-heel from Taylor, he fired in a terrific left-foot drive from twenty-five yards out which had Farm completely beaten.

Newcastle United: Fairbrother; Cowell, Corbett; Harvey, Brennan, Crowe; Walker, Taylor, Milburn, Robledo (G.), Mitchell
Blackpool: Farm; Shimwell, Garrett; Johnston, Hayward, Kelly; Matthews, Mudie, Mortensen, W. J. Slater, Perry
Referee: W. Ling (Cambridge)

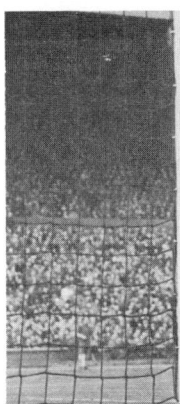

1951-2

First Round

Accrington S v Chester 1—2; Aylesbury Utd v Watford 0—5; Bangor C v Southport 2—2, 0—3; Barnstaple v Folkestone 2—2, 2—5; Barrow v Chesterfield 0—2; Blackhall Colliery Welfare v Workington 2—5; Blyth Spartans v Bishop Auckland 2—1; Bradford C v Carlisle Utd 6—1; Brighton & H Alb v Bristol C 1—2; Bristol R v Kettering T 3—0; Brush Sports v Weymouth 2—3; Colchester Utd v Port Vale 3—1; Crewe Alex v Lincoln C 2—4; Crystal Palace v Gillingham 0—1; Grimsby T v Darlington 4—0; Guildford C v Hereford Utd 4—1; Hartlepools Utd v Rhyl 2—0; Ilkeston v Rochdale 0—2; King's Lynn v Exeter C 1—3; Leyton v Chippenham T 3—0; Leyton Orient v Gorleston 2—2, 0—0, 5—4; Leytonstone v Shrewsbury T 2—0; Merthyr Tydfil v Ipswich T 2—2, 0—1; Millwall v Plymouth Arg 1—0; Nelson v Oldham Ath 0—4; Newport Co v Barry T 4—0; Norwich C v Northampton T 3—2; Rawmarsh Welfare v Buxton 1—4; Reading v Walsall 1—0; Scunthorpe Utd v Billingham Synthonia 5—0; Southend Utd v Bournemouth & Bos Ath 6—1; Stockport Co v Gateshead 2—2, 1—1, 1—2; Stockton v Mansfield T 1—1, 2—0; Swindon T v Bedford T 2—0; Tonbridge v Aldershot 0—0, 2—3; Torquay Utd v Bromley 3—2; Tranmere R v Goole T 4—2; Witton Alb v Gainsboro Tr 2—1; Wrexham v Halifax T 3—0; York C v Bradford PA 1—1, 1—1, 0—4

Second Round

Bradford PA v Bradford C 3—2; Bristol R v Weymouth 2—0; Buxton v Aldershot 4—3; Chester v Leyton 5—2; Colchester Utd v Bristol C 2—1; Gateshead v Guildford C 2—0; Gillingham v Rochdale 0—3; Ipswich T v Exeter C 4—0; Leytonstone v Newport Co 2—2, 0—3; Lincoln C v Grimsby T 3—1; Millwall v Scunthorpe Utd 0—0, 0—3; Norwich C v Chesterfield 3—1; Reading v Southport 1—1, 1—1, 2—0; Southend Utd v Oldham Ath 5—0; Stockton v Folkestone 2—1; Swindon T v Torquay Utd 3—3, 1—1, 3—1; Tranmere R v Blyth Spartans 1—1, 2—2, 5—1; Watford v Hartlepools Utd 1—2; Witton Alb v Workington 3—3, 0—1; Wrexham v Leyton Orient 1—1, 2—3

Third Round

NEWCASTLE UTD v Aston Villa 4—2; Scunthorpe Utd v Spurs 0—3; Reading v Swansea T 0—3; Rotherham Utd v Bury 2—1; Portsmouth v Lincoln C 4—0; Notts Co v Stockton 4—0; Doncaster R v Buxton 2—0; Middlesbro v Derby Co 2—2, 2—0; Nott'm Forest v Blackburn R 2—2, 0—2; Man Utd v Hull C 0—2; WBA v Bolton Wand 4—0; Ipswich T v Gateshead 2—2, 3—3, 1—2; Burnley v Hartlepools Utd 1—0; Leicester C v Coventry C 1—1, 1—4; Liverpool v Workington 1—0; Man C v Wolves 2—2, 1—4; Norwich C v ARSENAL 0—5; Barnsley v Colchester Utd 3—0; Leyton Orient v Everton 0—0, 3—1; Fulham v Birmingham C 0—1; Luton T v Charlton Ath 1—0; Brentford v QPR 3—1; Cardiff C v Swindon T 1—1, 0—1; Sunderland v Stoke C 0—0, 1—3; Chelsea v Chester 2—2, 3—2; Huddersfield T v Tranmere R 1—2; Rochdale v Leeds Utd 0—2; Bradford PA v Sheff Wed 2—1; Sheff Utd v Newport Co 2—0; W. Ham v Blackpool 2—1; Southend Utd v Southampton 3—0; Bristol R v PNE 2—0

Fourth Round

Spurs v NEWCASTLE UTD 0—3; Swansea T v Rotherham Utd 3—0; Notts Co v Portsmouth 1—3; Middlesbro v Doncaster R 1—4; Blackburn R v Hull C 2—0; Gateshead v WBA 0—2; Burnley v Coventry C 2—0; Liverpool v Wolves 2—1; ARSENAL v Barnsley 4—0; Birmingham C v Leyton Orient 0—1; Luton T v Brentford 2—2, 0—0, 3—2; Swindon T v Stoke C 1—1, 1—0; Chelsea v Tranmere R 4—0; Leeds Utd v Bradford PA 2—0; W. Ham v Sheff Utd 0—0, 2—4; Southend Utd v Bristol R 2—1

Fifth Round

Swansea T v NEWCASTLE UTD 0—1; Portsmouth v Doncaster R 4—0; Blackburn R v WBA 1—0; Burnley v Liverpool 2—0; Leyton Orient v ARSENAL 0—3; Luton T v Swindon T 3—1; Leeds Utd v Chelsea 1—1, 1—1, 1—5; Southend Utd v Sheff Utd 1—2

Sixth Round

Portsmouth v NEWCASTLE UTD 2—4; Blackburn R v Burnley 3—1; Luton T v ARSENAL 2—3; Sheff Utd v Chelsea 0—1

Semi-Final

NEWCASTLE UTD v Blackburn 0—0, 2—1; ARSENAL v Chelsea 1—1, 3—0

NEWCASTLE UNITED **1**
ARSENAL **0**

The luck had been on Arsenal's side in the earlier rounds but it deserted them at Wembley. Full-back Barnes was injured in the first half of the Final – wrenched ligaments behind a knee meant he could take no further part in the match – and Arsenal had to face the Newcastle attack with only ten men in a radically revised line-up.

Newcastle drove hard through the open spaces towards goal following Barnes' departure, but time and again they were foiled by the Arsenal half-back trio of Forbes, Daniel and Mercer. Once Milburn nearly scored for Newcastle with a header towards an open goal, but Lionel Smith was well positioned to clear off the line with Swindin beaten.

The eleven men of Newcastle attacked relentlessly after the change of ends and became more and more desperate as what appeared to be fairly easy chances went astray. Arsenal held out bravely until the eighty-fourth minute – certainly the sympathy of the crowd was with them – and then Robledo headed the goal that won the Cup.

Arsenal had almost achieved a miracle five minutes earlier when Lishman's header from Cox's corner kick struck the top of the Newcastle crossbar. But it was Newcastle's Cup, and they became the first team to win two seasons running since Blackburn Rovers back in the nineteenth century. There was glory for the losers this time, too.

Newcastle United: Simpson; Cowell, McMichael; Harvey, Brennan, Robledo (E.); Walker, Foulkes, Milburn, Robledo (G.), Mitchell
Arsenal: Swindin; Barnes, Smith (L.); Forbes, Daniel, Mercer; Cox, Logie, Holton, Lishman, Roper
Referee: A. Ellis (Halifax)

Robledo (second from right) nods the ball past Swindin.

1952–3

First Round
Aldershot v Millwall 0–0, 1–7; Bath C v Southend Utd 3–1; Beighton Miners' Welfare v Wrexham 0–3; Boston Utd v Oldham Ath 1–2; Bradford PA v Rochdale 2–1; Bradford C v Rhyl 4–0; Chester v Hartlepools Utd 0–1; Chesterfield v Workington 1–0; Coventry C v Bristol C 2–0; Crystal Palace v Reading 1–1, 3–1; Darlington v Grimsby T 2–3; Gainsboro Tr v Netherfield 1–1, 3–0; Gateshead v Crewe Alex 2–0; Grays' Ath v Llanelly 0–5; Guildford C v Gt Yarmouth 2–2, 0–1; Halifax T v Ashton Utd 1–1, 2–1; Hendon v Northampton T 0–0, 0–2; Horden Colliery Welfare v Accrington S 1–2; Ipswich T v Bournemouth & Bos Ath 2–2, 3–2; Kidderminster Harriers v Finchley 0–1; Leyton v Hereford Utd 0–0, 2–3; Leyton Orient v Bristol R 1–1, 0–1; Leytonstone v Watford 0–2; Newport Co v Walsall 2–1; North Shields v Stockport Co 3–6; Peterborough U v Torquay Utd 2–1; Port Vale v Exeter C 2–1; QPR v Shrewsbury T 2–2, 2–2, 1–4; Scarborough v Mansfield T 0–8; Scunthorpe Utd v Carlisle Utd 1–0; Selby T v Bishop Auckland 1–5; Southport v Bangor C 3–1; Swindon T v Newport (IoW) 5–0; Tunbridge v Norwich C 2–2, 0–1; Tranmere R v Ashington 8–1; Walthamstow Ave v Wimbledon 2–2, 3–0; Wellington T v Gillingham 1–1, 0–3; Weymouth v Colchester Utd 1–1, 0–4; Yeovil T v Brighton & H Alb 1–4; York C v Barrow 1–2

Second Round
Accrington S v Mansfield T 0–2; Barrow v Millwall 2–2, 1–4; Bishop Auckland v Coventry C 1–4; Bradford PA v Gateshead 1–2; Bradford C v Ipswich T 1–1, 1–5; Brighton & H Alb v Norwich C 2–0; Colchester Utd v Llanelly 3–2; Finchley v Crystal Palace 3–1; Gt Yarmouth v Wrexham 1–2; Grimsby T v Bath C 1–0; Halifax T v Southport 4–2; Hereford Utd v Scunthorpe Utd 0–0, 1–2; Newport Co v Gainsboro Tr 2–1; Peterborough Utd v Bristol R 0–1; Port Vale v Oldham Ath 0–3; Shrewsbury T v Chesterfield 0–0, 4–2; Stockport Co v Gillingham 3–1; Swindon T v Northampton T 2–0; Tranmere R v Hartlepools Utd 2–1; Walthamstow Ave v Watford 1–1, 2–1

Third Round
Sheff Wed v BLACKPOOL 1–2; Huddersfield T v Bristol R 2–0; Lincoln C v Southampton 1–1, 1–2; Shrewsbury T v Finchley 2–0; Arsenal v Doncaster R 4–0; Grimsby T v Bury 1–3; Portsmouth v Burnley 1–1, 1–3; Sunderland v Scunthorpe Utd 1–1, 2–1; Tranmere R v Spurs 1–1, 1–9; PNE v Wolves 5–2; Halifax T v Cardiff C 3–1; Stoke C v Wrexham 2–1; Oldham Ath v Birmingham C 1–3; Newport Co v Sheff Utd 1–4; Derby Co v Chelsea 4–4, 0–1; W. Ham v WBA 1–4; BOLTON WAND v Fulham 3–1; Leicester C v Notts Co 2–4; Luton T v Blackburn R 6–1; Man C v Swindon T 7–0; Gateshead v Liverpool 1–0; Hull C v Charlton Ath 3–1; Plymouth Arg v Coventry C 4–1; Barnsley v Brighton & H Alb 4–3; Everton v Ipswich T 3–2; Mansfield T v Nott'm Forest 0–1; Millwall v Man Utd 0–1; Walthamstow Ave v Stockport Co 2–1; Aston Villa v Middlesbro 3–1; Brentford v Leeds Utd 2–1; Rotherham Utd v Colchester Utd 2–2, 2–0; Newcastle Utd v Swansea T 3–0

Fourth Round
BLACKPOOL v Huddersfield T 1–0; Shrewsbury T v Southampton 1–4; Arsenal v Bury 6–2; Burnley v Sunderland 2–0; PNE v Spurs 2–2, 0–1; Halifax T v Stoke C 1–0; Sheff Utd v Birmingham C 1–1, 1–3; Chelsea v WBA 1–1, 0–0, 1–1, 4–0; BOLTON WAND v Notts Co 1–1, 2–2, 1–0; Man C v Luton T 1–1, 1–5; Hull C v Gateshead 1–2; Plymouth Arg v Barnsley 1–0; Everton v Nott'm Forest 4–1; Man Utd v Walthamstow Ave 1–1, 5–2; Aston Villa v Brentford 0–0, 2–1; Newcastle Utd v Rotherham Utd 1–3

Fifth Round
BLACKPOOL v Southampton 1–1, 2–1; Burnley v Arsenal 0–2; Halifax T v Spurs 0–3; Chelsea v Birmingham C 0–4; Luton T v BOLTON WAND 0–1; Plymouth Arg v Gateshead 0–1; Everton v Man Utd 2–1; Rotherham Utd v Aston Villa 1–3

Sixth Round
Arsenal v BLACKPOOL 1–2; Birmingham C v Spurs 1–1, 2–2, 0–1; Gateshead v BOLTON WAND 0–1; Aston Villa v Everton 0–1

Semi-Final
BLACKPOOL v Spurs 2–1; BOLTON WAND v Everton 4–3

BLACKPOOL **4**
BOLTON WANDERERS **3**

The 1953 Final has been dubbed the 'Matthews Final'. No one else could have rescued Blackpool from the plight they found themselves in ten minutes after the interval when the injured Bell headed home Holden's cross to put Bolton 3–1 up. At this Blackpool might have crumpled as they had done twice before at Wembley. Instead, Matthews, for whom the whole world crossed its fingers as he strove for the third (and perhaps the last?) time to gain a Cup-winners' medal, stepped forward to dominate the green stage.

The match had begun dramatically, with Lofthouse scoring for Bolton after only seventy-five seconds. Hassall deflected Mortensen's shot into the net to provide Blackpool with an equalizer, but within minutes Bolton were ahead again from Langton's cunning lob.

It was not until the last quarter of the match that Blackpool clicked into gear, and Matthews proved to be their inspiration. Twenty-two minutes from the end Mortensen met one of Matthews' spinning, curling crosses at the far post to make it 2–3.

Chances went begging until Mortensen scored direct from a free-kick three minutes from time. With only seconds left Matthews went inside the full-back, sprinted for the by-line, and in the last yard cut back a diagonal pass. Mortensen was too far forward, but Perry was on hand to shoot home inside the post.

Blackpool: Farm; Shimwell, Garrett; Fenton, Johnston, Robinson; Matthews, Taylor, Mortensen, Mudie, Perry
Bolton Wanderers: Hanson; Ball, Banks (R.); Wheeler, Barrass, Bell; Holden, Moir, Lofthouse, Hassall, Langton
Referee: M. Griffiths (Newport)

Langton's goal for Bolton

1953–4

First Round

Aldershot v Wellington T 5–3; Barnsley v York C 5–2; Bath C v Walsall 0–3; Blyth Spartans v Accrington S 0–1; Brighton & H Alb v Coventry C 5–1; Cambridge Utd v Newport Co 2–2, 2–1; Colchester Utd v Millwall 1–1, 0–4; Crewe Alex v Bradford C 0–0, 1–0; Darlington v Port Vale 1–3; Exeter C v Hereford Utd 1–1, 0–2; Finchley v Southend Utd 1–3; Gainsboro Tr v Chesterfield 1–4; Gateshead v Tranmere R 1–2; Gt Yarmouth v Crystal Palace 1–0; Grimsby T v Rochdale 2–0; Halifax T v Rhyl 0–0, 3–4; Hartlepools Utd v Mansfield T 1–1, 3–0; Harwich & Parkeston v Headington Utd 2–3; Hastings Utd v Guildford C 1–0; Hitchin T v Peterborough Utd 1–3; Horden Colliery Welfare v Wrexham 0–1; Ipswich T v Reading 4–1; Leyton Orient v Kettering T 3–0; Northampton T v Llanelly 3–0; Nuneaton Borough v Watford 3–0; QPR v Shrewsbury T 2–0; Scunthorpe Utd v Boston Utd 9–0; Selby T v Bradford PA 0–2; Southampton v Bournemouth & Bos Ath 1–1, 1–3; Southport v Carlisle Utd 1–0; Spennymoor Utd v Barrow 0–3; Stockport Co v Chester 4–2; Swindon T v Newport (IoW) 2–1; Torquay Utd v Bristol C 1–3; Walthamstow Ave v Gillingham 1–0; Weymouth v Bedford T 2–0; Wigan Ath v Scarborough 4–0; Witton Alb v Nelson 4–1; Workington v Ferryhill Ath 3–0; Yeovil T v Norwich C 0–2

Second Round

Accrington S v Tranmere R 2–2, 1–5; Barrow v Gt Yarmouth 5–2; Cambridge Utd v Bradford PA 1–2; Hastings Utd v Swindon T 4–1; Ipswich T v Walthamstow Ave 2–2, 1–0; Leyton Orient v Weymouth 4–0; Millwall v Headington Utd 3–3, 0–1; Northampton T v Hartlepools Utd 1–1, 0–1; Norwich C v Barnsley 2–1; Peterborough Utd v Aldershot 2–1; QPR v Nuneaton Borough 1–1, 2–1; Rhyl v Bristol C 0–3; Scunthorpe Utd v Bournemouth & Bos Ath 1–0; Southend Utd v Chesterfield 1–2; Southport v Port Vale 1–1, 0–2; Stockport Co v Workington 2–1; Walsall v Crewe Alex 3–0; Wigan Ath v Hereford Utd 4–1; Witton Alb v Grimsby T 1–1, 1–6; Wrexham v Brighton & H Alb 1–1, 1–1, 3–1

Third Round

WBA v Chelsea 1–0; Bristol C v Rotherham Utd 1–3; Newcastle Utd v Wigan Ath 2–2, 3–2; Burnley v Man Utd 5–3; Leeds Utd v Spurs 3–3, 0–1; Bradford PA v Man C 2–5; Brentford v Hull C 0–0, 2–2, 2–5; Bristol R v Blackburn R 0–1; QPR v Port Vale 0–1; Cardiff C v Peterborough Utd 3–1; Blackpool v Luton T 1–1, 0–0, 1–1, 2–0; W. Ham v Huddersfield T 4–0; Tranmere R v Leyton Orient 2–2, 1–4; Grimsby T v Fulham 5–5, 1–3; Sunderland v Doncaster R 0–2; Plymouth Arg v Nott'm Forest 2–0; Derby Co v PNE 0–2; Lincoln C v Walsall 1–1, 1–1, 2–1; Ipswich T v Oldham Ath 3–3, 1–0; Wolves v Birmingham C 1–2; Middlesbro v Leicester C 0–0, 2–3; Stoke C v Hartlepools Utd 6–2; Hastings Utd v Norwich C 3–3, 0–3; Arsenal v Aston Villa 5–1; Sheff Wed v Sheff Utd 1–1, 3–1; Chesterfield v Bury 2–0; Everton v Notts Co 2–1; Barrow v Swansea T 2–2, 2–4; Bolton Wand v Liverpool 1–0; Stockport Co v Headington Utd 0–0, 0–1; Portsmouth v Charlton Ath 3–3, 3–2; Wrexham v Scunthorpe Utd 3–3, 0–3

Fourth Round

WBA v Rotherham Utd 4–0; Burnley v Newcastle Utd 1–1, 0–1; Man C v Spurs 0–1; Blackburn R v Hull C 2–2, 1–2; Cardiff C v Port Vale 0–2; W. Ham v Blackpool 1–1, 1–3; Leyton Orient v Fulham 2–1; Plymouth Arg v Doncaster R 0–2; Lincoln C v PNE 0–2; Ipswich T v Birmingham C 1–0; Stoke C v Leicester C 0–0, 1–3; Arsenal v Norwich C 1–2; Sheff Wed v Chesterfield 0–0, 4–2; Everton v Swansea T 3–0; Headington Utd v Bolton Wand 2–4; Scunthorpe Utd v Portsmouth 1–1, 2–2, 0–4

Fifth Round

WBA v Newcastle Utd 3–2; Hull C v Spurs 1–1, 0–2; Port Vale v Blackpool 2–0; Leyton Orient v Doncaster R 3–1; PNE v Ipswich T 6–1; Norwich C v Leicester C 1–2; Sheff Wed v Everton 3–1; Bolton Wand v Portsmouth 0–0, 2–1

Sixth Round

WBA v Spurs 3–0; Leyton Orient v Port Vale 0–1; Leicester C v PNE 1–1, 2–2, 1–3; Sheff Wed v Bolton Wand 1–1, 2–0

Semi-Final

WBA v Port Vale 2–1; PNE v Sheff Wed 2–0

WEST BROMWICH ALBION **3**
PRESTON NORTH END **2**

The 1954 Final produced five goals and a grandstand finish, and yet the emphasis had been on defence and the teamwork had rarely been inspired.

The first two goals were in keeping with the match's fluctuating character. There seemed to be no danger in the twenty-first minute as Preston full-back Cunningham attempted to clear to Finney out on the wing, but then Lee intercepted the pass and set up an easy scoring chance for Allen. Preston equalized almost at once, with Morrison heading in from close range following a right-wing centre from Docherty.

Wayman had looked suspiciously offside as he received the ball thirty yards from the Albion goal early in the second half, but, in the absence of a signal from the referee, he ran on to dribble round Sanders and plant the ball in the net.

Albion's equalizer was another goal out of the ordinary. Barlow collided with Docherty in the penalty-area and Allen just squeezed his spot-kick past Thompson: 2–2. From that moment Albion seemed to take on extra stature. They mounted tremendous pressure in order to try to win the match in normal time, and, the referee's eye on his watch, Griffin slipped past Walton and drove the ball from a difficult angle just inside the far post.

West Bromwich Albion: Sanders; Kennedy, Millard; Dudley, Dugdale, Barlow; Griffin, Ryan, Allen, Nicholls, Lee
Preston North End: Thompson; Cunningham, Walton; Docherty, Marston, Forbes; Finney, Foster, Wayman, Baxter, Morrison
Referee: A. Luty (Leeds)

Allen shoots firmly past Thompson from the penalty-spot

1954–5

First Round
Accrington S v Cresswell Colliery 7–1; Aldershot v Chelmsford 3–1; Barnet v Southampton 1–4; Barnsley v Wigan Ath 3–2; Barnstaple v Bournemouth & Bos Ath 1–4; Barrow v Darlington 1–1, 1–2; Bishop Auckland v Kettering T 5–1; Boston Utd v Blyth Spartans 1–1, 4–5; Bradford PA v Southport 2–0; Bradford C v Mansfield T 3–1; Brentford v Nuneaton Borough 2–1; Brighton & H Alb v Tunbridge Wells 5–0; Bristol C v Southend Utd 1–2; Corby T v Watford 0–2; Crook T v Stanley 5–3; Dorchester v Bedford T 2–0; Frome v Leyton Orient 0–3; Gateshead v Chester 6–0; Gillingham v Newport Co 2–0; Grimsby T v Halifax T 2–1; Hartlepools Utd v Chesterfield 1–0; Hinckley v Newport (IoW) 4–3; Horden Colliery Welfare v Scunthorpe Utd 0–1; Hounslow T v Hastings Utd 2–4; Merthyr Tydfil v Wellington T 1–1, 6–1; Millwall v Exeter C 3–2; Netherfield v Wrexham 3–3, 0–4; Northampton T v Coventry C 0–1; Norwich C v Headington Utd 4–2; Oldham Ath v Crewe Alex 1–0; QPR v Walthamstow Ave 2–2, 2–2, 0–4; Reading v Colchester Utd 3–3, 2–1; Selby T v Rhyl 2–1; Stockport Co v Carlisle Utd 0–1; Swindon T v Crystal Palace 0–2; Torquay Utd v Cambridge Utd 4–0; Tranmere R v Rochdale 3–3, 0–1; Walsall v Shrewsbury T 5–2; Workington v Hyde 5–1; York C v Scarborough 3–2

Second Round
Blyth Spartans v Torquay Utd 1–3; Bournemouth & Bos Ath v Oldham Ath 1–0; Bradford PA v Southend Utd 2–3; Bradford C v Merthy Tydfil 7–1; Brentford v Crook T 4–1; Carlisle Utd v Watford 2–2, 1–4; Coventry C v Scunthorpe Utd 4–0; Crystal Palace v Bishop Auckland 2–4; Dorchester v York C 2–5; Gateshead v Barnsley 3–3, 1–0; Gillingham v Reading 1–1, 3–5; Grimsby T v Southampton 4–1; Hartlepools Utd v Aldershot 4–0; Leyton Orient v Workington 0–1; Millwall v Accrington S 3–2; Norwich C v Brighton & H Alb 0–0, 1–5; Rochdale v Hinckley 2–1; Selby T v Hastings Utd 0–2; Walthamstow Ave v Darlington 0–3; Wrexham v Walsall 1–2

Third Round
Plymouth Arg v NEWCASTLE UTD 0–1; Brentford v Bradford C 1–1, 2–2, 1–0; Sheff Utd v Nott'm Forest 1–3; Hartlepools Utd v Darlington 1–1, 2–2, 2–0; Huddersfield T v Coventry C 3–3, 2–1; Leeds Utd v Torquay Utd 2–2, 0–4; Lincoln C v Liverpool 1–1, 0–1; Everton v Southend Utd 3–1; Blackpool v York C 0–2; Ipswich T v Bishop Auckland 2–2, 0–3; Gateshead v Spurs 0–2; W. Ham v Port Vale 2–2, 1–3; Middlesbro v Notts Co 1–4; Sheff Wed v Hastings Utd 2–1; Chelsea v Walsall 2–0; Bristol R v Portsmouth 2–1; Derby Co v MAN C 1–3; Reading v Man Utd 1–1, 1–4; Luton T v Workington 5–0; Rotherham Utd v Leicester C 1–0; Hull C v Birmingham C 0–2; Bolton Wand v Millwall 3–1; Watford v Doncaster R 1–2; Brighton & H Alb v Aston Villa 2–2, 2–4; Sunderland v Burnley 1–0; Fulham v PNE 2–3; Blackburn R v Swansea T 0–2; Bury v Stoke C 1–1, 1–1, 3–3, 2–2, 2–3; Grimsby T v Wolves 2–5; Arsenal v Cardiff C 1–0; Rochdale v Charlton Ath 1–3; Bournemouth & Bos Ath v WBA 0–1

Fourth Round
NEWCASTLE UTD v Brentford 3–2; Hartlepools Utd v Nott'm Forest 1–1, 1–2; Torquay Utd v Huddersfield T 0–1; Everton v Liverpool 0–4; Bishop Auckland v York C 1–3; Spurs v Port Vale 4–2; Sheff Wed v Notts Co 1–1, 0–1; Bristol R v Chelsea 1–3; MAN C v Man Utd 2–0; Rotherham Utd v Luton T 1–5; Birmingham C v Bolton Wand 2–1; Doncaster R v Aston Villa 0–0, 2–2, 1–1, 0–0, 3–1; PNE v Sunderland 3–3, 0–2; Swansea T v Stoke C 3–1; Wolves v Arsenal 1–0; WBA v Charlton Ath 2–4

Fifth Round
Nott'm Forest v NEWCASTLE UTD 1–1, 2–2, 1–2; Liverpool v Huddersfield T 0–2; York C v Spurs 3–1; Notts Co v Chelsea 1–0; Luton T v MAN C 0–2; Birmingham C v Doncaster R 2–1; Swansea T v Sunderland 2–2, 0–1; Wolves v Charlton Ath 4–1

Sixth Round
Huddersfield v NEWCASTLE UTD 1–1, 0–2; Notts Co v York C 0–1; Birmingham C v MAN C 0–1; Sunderland v Wolves 2–0

Semi-Final
NEWCASTLE UTD v York C 1–1, 2–0; MAN C v Sunderland 1–0

NEWCASTLE UNITED **3**
MANCHESTER CITY **1**

Newcastle had the same dressing room as when they met Arsenal in 1952, plus the knowledge and confidence gained in two recent Final victories. There was another coincidence – City lost right back Meadows as the result of a twisted knee, in a way almost exactly paralleled in 1952 when Arsenal lost Barnes following his attempt to stop the very same player, Mitchell, in the very same corner of the field.

Milburn scored for Newcastle with a header from White's corner kick within a minute of the start. With City's 'Revie plan' operating so precisely and effectively, City played some great football in the twenty minutes after Meadows' untimely departure, and Johnstone even levelled the scores in the last minute of the half with a diving header.

Newcastle's counter move to City's plan had been for the defence to move upfield very quickly immediately Revie, well behind his own forwards, got the ball. City forwards found themselves in offside positions before the pass was made.

Meadows did not return, and it was not surprising that Newcastle, with the extra man, started the second half confidently. Within fifteen minutes they had scored twice. Mitchell cut in and shot from a narrow angle under Trautmann's dive, and then Mitchell's dazzle-dance took him past two City players and allowed him to lay on a fairly simple chance for Hannah.

Newcastle United: Simpson; Cowell, Batty; Scoular, Stokoe, Casey; White, Keeble, Milburn, Hannah, Mitchell
Manchester City: Trautmann; Meadows, Little; Barnes, Ewing, Paul; Spurdle, Hayes, Revie, Johnstone, Fagan
Referee: R. Leafe (Nottingham)

Little heads clear from the menacing Keeble

1955–6

First Round
Accrington S v Wrexham 3–1; Barrow v Crewe Alex 0–0, 3–2; Bedford T v Leyton 3–0; Bishop Auckland v Durham C 3–1; Boston Utd v Northwich Victoria 3–2; Bradford C v Oldham Ath 3–1; Brentford v March Town Utd 4–0; Brighton & H Alb v Newport Co 8–1; Chesterfield v Chester 1–0; Coventry C v Exeter C 0–1; Crook T v Derby Co 2–2, 1–5; Crystal Palace v Southampton 0–0, 0–2; Darlington v Carlisle Utd 0–0, 3–1; Easington Colliery Welfare v Tranmere R 0–2; Gillingham v Shrewsbury T 1–1, 1–4; Goole T v Halifax T 1–2; Halesowen v Hendon 2–4; Hartlepools Utd v Gateshead 3–0; Hastings Utd v Southall 6–1; Leyton Orient v Lovell's Ath 7–1; Mansfield T v Stockport Co 2–0; Margate v Walsall 2–2, 1–6; Netherfield v Grimsby T 1–5; Northampton T v Millwall 4–1; Norwich C v Dorchester T 4–0; Peterborough Utd v Ipswich T 3–1; Reading v Bournemouth & Bos Ath 1–0; Rhyl v Bradford PA 0–3; Rochdale v York C 0–1; Scunthorpe Utd v Shildon 3–0; Skegness T v Worksop T 0–4; Southend Utd v QPR 2–0; Southport v Ashton Utd 6–1; Swindon T v Hereford Utd 4–0; Torquay Utd v Colchester Utd 2–0; Watford v Ramsgate Ath 5–3; Weymouth v Salisbury 3–2; Workington v Scarborough 4–2; Wycombe Wand v Burton Alb 1–3; Yeovil T v Aldershot 1–1, 1–1, 0–3

Second Round
Bedford T v Watford 3–2; Bishop Auckland v Scunthorpe Utd 0–0, 0–2; Bradford PA v Workington 4–3; Bradford C v Worksop T 2–2, 0–1; Brighton & H Alb v Norwich C 1–2; Chesterfield v Hartlepools Utd 1–2; Darlington v Accrington S 0–1; Derby Co v Boston Utd 1–6; Exeter C v Hendon 6–2; Halifax T v Burton Alb 0–0, 0–1; Leyton Orient v Brentford 4–1; Northampton T v Hastings Utd 4–1; Reading v Aldershot 2–2, 0–3; Shrewsbury T v Torquay Utd 0–1; Southport v Grimsby T 0–0, 2–3; Swindon T v Peterborough Utd 1–1, 2–1; Tranmere R v Barrow 0–3; Walsall v Southampton 2–1; Weymouth v Southend Utd 0–1; York City v Mansfield T 2–1

Third Round
Torquay Utd v BIRMINGHAM C 1–7; Leyton Orient v Plymouth Arg 1–0; Wolves v WBA 1–2; Portsmouth v Grimsby T 3–1; Arsenal v Bedford T 2–2, 2–1; Aston Villa v Hull C 1–1, 2–1; Charlton Ath v Burton Alb 7–0; Swindon T v Worksop T 1–0; Sunderland v Norwich C 4–2; Swansea T v York C 1–2; Sheff Utd v Barrow 5–0; Bolton Wand v Huddersfield T 3–0; Sheff Wed v Newcastle Utd 1–3; Notts Co v Fulham 0–1; Exeter C v Stoke C 0–0, 0–3; Luton T v Leicester C 0–4; MAN C v Blackpool 2–1; Lincoln C v Southend Utd 2–3; Liverpool v Accrington S 2–0; Rotherham Utd v Scunthorpe Utd 1–1, 2–4; Everton v Bristol C 3–1; Walsall v Port Vale 0–1; Hartlepools Utd v Chelsea 0–1; Bury v Burnley 0–1; Spurs v Boston Utd 4–0; Bradford PA v Middlesbro 0–4; Doncaster R v Nott'm Forest 3–0; Bristol R v Man Utd 4–0; W. Ham v PNE 5–2; Leeds Utd v Cardiff C 1–2; Northampton T v Blackburn R 1–2; Aldershot v Barnsley 1–2

Fourth Round
Leyton Orient v BIRMINGHAM C 0–4; WBA v Portsmouth 2–0; Arsenal v Aston Villa 4–1; Charlton Ath v Swindon T 2–1; York C v Sunderland 0–0, 1–2; Bolton Wand v Sheff Utd 1–2; Fulham v Newcastle Utd 4–5; Leicester C v Stoke C 3–3, 1–2; Southend Utd v MAN C 0–1; Liverpool v Scunthorpe Utd 3–3, 2–1; Port Vale v Everton 2–3; Burnley v Chelsea 1–1, 1–1, 2–2, 0–0, 0–2; Spurs v Middlesbro 3–1; Bristol R v Doncaster R 1–1, 0–1; W. Ham v Cardiff C 2–1; Barnsley v Blackburn R 0–1

Fifth Round
WBA v BIRMINGHAM C 0–1; Charlton Ath v Arsenal 0–2; Sheff Utd v Sunderland 0–0, 0–1; Newcastle Utd v Stoke C 2–1; MAN C v Liverpool 0–0, 2–1; Everton v Chelsea 1–0; Doncaster R v Spurs 0–2; W. Ham v Blackburn R 0–0, 3–2

Sixth Round
Arsenal v BIRMINGHAM C 1–3; Newcastle Utd v Sunderland 0–2; MAN C v Everton 2–1; Spurs v W. Ham 3–3, 2–1

Semi-Final
BIRMINGHAM C v Sunderland 3–0; MAN C v Spurs 1–0

MANCHESTER CITY 3
BIRMINGHAM CITY 1

Birmingham were unable to produce the kind of football against Revie-inspired Manchester City that had carried them to Wembley, and could only hold their rivals by employing methods which resulted in their tiring visibly in the last half-hour. Manchester scored twice during this period to win the match.

Revie, a late inclusion for the injured Spurdle, was the key player as Manchester controlled the game with their 'Hungarian style' play, which involved keeping the ball on the ground and building up attacks in a slow and deliberate way.

Within three minutes of the start Revie began the move near his own penalty-area which led to the unmarked Hayes sweeping the ball past Merrick to put Manchester ahead. Birmingham's confidence was shaken, but they fought back to equalize in the fifteenth minute through Welsh international inside-forward Kinsey.

Both teams seemed to lose their touch immediately after half-time, but then, after an hour's play, Manchester regained their stride and suddenly went two goals ahead. Following a bout of interpassing on the right wing, Dyson was put clean through to score. Three minutes later Johnstone grabbed a third from Dyson's pass.

An unexpected chance for Birmingham occurred when Manchester's German goalkeeper Trautmann was badly injured making a typically heroic save at Murphy's feet. He played out the last fifteen minutes in great pain, and examination later revealed a broken neck.

Manchester City: Trautmann; Leivers, Little; Barnes, Ewing, Paul; Johnstone, Hayes, Revie, Dyson, Clarke
Birmingham City: Merrick; Hall, Green; Newman, Smith, Boyd; Astall, Kinsey, Brown, Murphy, Govan
Referee: A. Bond (London)

Trautmann is injured diving at Murphy's feet

1956–7

First Round
Accrington S v Morecambe 4–1; Bishop Auckland v Tranmere R 2–1; Boston Utd v Bradford PA 0–2; Bournemouth & Bos Ath v Burton Alb 8–0; Brentford v Guildford C 3–0; Brighton & H Alb v Millwall 1–1, 1–3; Carlisle Utd v Billingham Synthonia Recreation 6–1; Cheltenham T v Reading 1–2; Chester v Barrow 0–0, 1–3; Colchester Utd v Southend Utd 1–4; Crewe Alex v Wrexham 2–2, 1–2; Crystal Palace v Walthamstow Ave 2–0; Darlington v Evenwood T 7–2; Derby Co v Bradford C 2–1; Ely C v Torquay Utd 2–6; Exeter C v Plymouth Arg 0–2; Halifax T v Oldham Ath 2–3; Hartlepools Utd v Selby T 3–1; Hereford Utd v Aldershot 3–2; Hull C v Gateshead 4–0; Ilkeston T v Blyth Spartans 1–5; Ipswich T v Hastings Utd 4–0; Mansfield T v Workington 1–1, 1–2; Margate v Dunstable T 3–1; New Brighton v Stockport Co 3–3, 3–2; Newport (IoW) v Watford 0–6; Norwich C v Bedford T 2–4; QPR v Dorchester T 4–0; Rhyl v Scarborough 3–2; Scunthorpe Utd v Rochdale 1–0; Southampton v Northampton T 2–0; Southport v York C 0–0, 1–2; South Shields v Chesterfield 2–2, 0–4; Swindon T v Coventry C 2–1; Tooting & Mitcham v Bromsgrove 2–1; Walsall v Newport Co 0–1; Weymouth v Shrewsbury T 1–0; Wigan Ath v Goole T 1–2; Yeovil T v Peterborough Utd 1–3; Yiewsley v Gillingham 2–2, 0–2

Second Round
Accrington S v Oldham Ath 2–1; Blyth Spartans v Hartlepools Utd 0–1; Brentford v Crystal Palace 1–1, 2–3; Carlisle Utd v Darlington 2–1; Chesterfield v Barrow 4–1; Derby Co v New Brighton 1–3; Gillingham v Newport Co 1–2; Goole T v Workington 2–2, 1–0; Hereford Utd v Southend Utd 2–3; Hull C v York C 2–1; Millwall v Margate 4–0; Peterborough Utd v Bradford PA 3–0; Reading v Bedford T 1–0; Rhyl v Bishop Auckland 3–1; Scunthorpe Utd v Wrexham 0–0, 2–6; Southampton v Weymouth 3–2; Swindon T v Bournemouth & Bos Ath 0–1; Tooting & Mitcham v QPR 0–2; Torquay Utd v Plymouth Arg 1–0; Watford v Ipswich T 1–3

Third Round
Luton T v ASTON VILLA 2–2, 0–2; Middlesbro v Charlton Ath 1–1, 3–2; Bristol C v Rotherham Utd 4–1; Notts Co v Rhyl 1–3; Burnley v Chesterfield 7–0; New Brighton v Torquay Utd 2–1; Huddersfield T v Sheff Utd 0–0, 1–1, 2–1; Peterborough Utd v Lincoln C 2–2, 5–4; Arsenal v Stoke C 4–2; Newport Co v Southampton 3–3, 1–0; PNE v Sheff Wed 0–0, 2–2, 5–1; Hull C v Bristol R 3–4; Bolton W v Blackpool 2–3; Ipswich T v Fulham 2–3; Sunderland v QPR 4–0; Doncaster R v WBA 1–1, 0–2; Hartlepools Utd v MAN UTD 3–4; Wrexham v Reading 1–1, 2–1; Everton v Blackburn R 1–0; W. Ham v Grimsby T 5–3; Bournemouth & Bos Ath v Accrington S 2–0; Wolves v Swansea T 5–3; Spurs v Leicester C 2–0; Leyton Orient v Chelsea 0–2; Carlisle Utd v Birmingham C 3–3, 0–4; Southend Utd v Liverpool 2–1; Millwall v Crystal Palace 2–0; Newcastle Utd v Man C 1–1, 5–4; Barnsley v Port Vale 3–3, 1–0; Leeds Utd v Cardiff City 1–2; Bury v Portsmouth 1–3; Nott'm Forest v Goole T 6–0

Fourth Round
Middlesbro v ASTON VILLA 2–3; Bristol C v Rhyl 3–0; Burnley v New Brighton 9–0; Huddersfield T v Peterborough Utd 3–1; Newport Co v Arsenal 0–2; Bristol R v PNE 1–4; Blackpool v Fulham 6–2; WBA v Sunderland 4–2; Wrexham v MAN UTD 0–5; Everton v W. Ham 2–1; Wolves v Bournemouth & Bos Ath 0–1; Spurs v Chelsea 4–0; Southend Utd v Birmingham C 1–6; Millwall v Newcastle Utd 2–1; Cardiff C v Barnsley 0–1; Portsmouth v Nott'm Forest 1–3

Fifth Round
ASTON VILLA v Bristol C 2–1; Huddersfield T v Burnley 1–2; PNE v Arsenal 3–3, 1–2; Blackpool v WBA 0–0, 1–2; MAN UTD v Everton 1–0; Bournemouth & Bos Ath v Spurs 3–1; Millwall v Birmingham C 1–4; Barnsley v Nott'm Forest 1–2

Sixth Round
Burnley v ASTON VILLA 1–1, 0–2; WBA v Arsenal 2–2, 2–1; Bournemouth & Bos Ath v MAN UTD 1–2; Birmingham C v Nott'm Forest 0–0, 1–0

Semi-Final
ASTON VILLA v WBA 2–2, 1–0; MAN UTD v Birmingham C 2–0

ASTON VILLA **2**
MANCHESTER UNITED **1**

There can be no doubt that the injury suffered by United's goalkeeper Wood in an eighth minute collision with McParland materially affected this Final. It must remain a matter of opinion whether it affected the result.

Although on the defensive, the depleted United side never let their opponents dominate the game. Edwards was tough and uncompromising at centre-half, and Byrne proceeded to play a real captain's game at left-back. Villa, in fact, were reduced to long-range shots which Blanchflower, stand-in goalkeeper for Wood, fielded without too much trouble.

United still held the upper hand as the second half began, and when Wood returned to play on the right wing, their chances seemed even brighter.

But is was not to be. Smith slipped a pass to Dixon in the sixty-eighth minute, the Villa captain's centre drifted into the penalty-area, and McParland raced in to head a great goal. Five minutes later the irrepressible McParland scored again, making no mistake after Dixon's shot had crashed against the bar and bounced back straight to his feet.

United, League champions and unquestionably the season's outstanding team, were more dangerous when two goals down than at any other time in the match. The only reward for their efforts came in the eighty-third minute when Taylor headed over Sims and into the net from Edwards' corner. It was small consolation.

Aston Villa: Sims; Lynn, Aldis; Crowther, Dugdale, Saward; Smith, Sewell, Myerscough, Dixon, McParland
Manchester United: Wood; Foulkes, Byrne; Colman, Blanchflower (J.), Edwards; Berry, Whelan, Taylor (T.), Charlton, Pegg
Referee: F. Coultas (Hull)

Taylor heads a consolation goal for United

1957-8

First Round

Aldershot v Worcester C 0–0, 2–2, 3–2; Bath C v Exeter C 2–1; Bishop Auckland v Bury 0–0, 1–4; Boston Utd v Billingham Synthonia Recreation 5–2; Bradford C v Scarborough 6–0; Brighton & H Alb v Walsall 2–1; Carlisle Utd v Rhyl 5–1; Chester v Gateshead 4–3; Clapton v QPR 1–1, 1–3; Coventry C v Walthamstow Ave 1–0; Dorchester T v Wycombe Wand 3–2; Durham C v Spalding Utd 3–1; Gillingham v Gorleston 10–1; Guildford C v Yeovil T 2–2, 0–1; Hartlepools Utd v Prescot Cables 5–0; Hull C v Crewe Alex 2–1; Mansfield T v Halifax T 2–0; Margate v Crystal Palace 2–3; Millwall v Brentford 1–0; Newport (IoW) v Hereford Utd 0–3; Northampton T v Newport Co 3–0; Norwich C v Redhill 6–1; Oldham Ath v Bradford PA 2–0; Oswestry T v Bournemouth & Bos Ath 1–5; Peterborough Utd v Torquay Utd 3–3, 0–1; Plymouth Arg v Watford 6–2; Port Vale v Shrewsbury T 2–1; Reading v Swindon T 1–0; Rochdale v Darlington 0–2; Scunthorpe Utd v Goole T 2–1; Southport v Wigan Ath 1–2; South Shields v Frickley Colliery 3–2; Stockport Co v Barrow 2–1; Tranmere R v Witton Alb 2–1; Trowbridge T v Southend Utd 0–2; Walton & Hersham v Southampton 1–6; Wisbech T v Colchester Utd 1–0; Workington v Crook T 8–1; Wrexham v Accrington S 0–1; York C v Chesterfield 1–0

Second Round

Aldershot v Coventry C 4–1; Carlisle Utd v Accrington S 1–1, 2–3; Chester v Bradford C 3–3, 1–3; Crystal Palace v Southampton 1–0; Darlington v Boston Utd 5–3; Durham C v Tranmere R 0–3; Hereford Utd v QPR 6–1; Millwall v Gillingham 1–1, 1–6; Northampton T v Bournemouth & Bos Ath 4–1; Norwich C v Brighton & H Alb 1–1, 2–1; Oldham Ath v Workington 1–5; Plymouth Arg v Dorchester T 5–2; Port Vale v Hull C 2–2, 3–4; Reading v Wisbech T 2–1; Scunthorpe Utd v Bury 2–0; South Shields v York C 1–3; Stockport Co v Hartlepools Utd 2–1; Torquay Utd v Southend Utd 1–1, 1–2; Wigan Ath v Mansfield T 1–1, 1–3; Yeovil T v Bath C 2–0

Third Round

Rotherham Utd v Blackburn R 1–4; Sunderland v Everton 2–2, 1–3; Leyton Orient v Reading 1–0; Leeds Utd v Cardiff C 1–2; Liverpool v Southend Utd 1–1, 3–2; Northampton T v Arsenal 3–1; Plymouth Arg v Newcastle Utd 1–6; Scunthorpe Utd v Bradford C 1–0; Lincoln C v Wolves 0–1; Portsmouth v Aldershot 5–1; Norwich C v Darlington 1–2; Doncaster R v Chelsea 0–2; Stoke C v Aston Villa 1–1, 3–3, 2–0; Middlesbro v Derby Co 5–0; York C v Birmingham C 3–0; PNE v BOLTON WAND 0–3; Workington v MAN UTD 1–3; Crystal Palace v Ipswich T 0–1; Hull C v Barnsley 1–1, 2–0; Hereford Utd v Sheff Wed 0–3; WBA v Man C 5–1; Nott'm Forest v Gillingham 2–0; Spurs v Leicester C 4–0; Sheff Utd v Grimsby T 5–1; Bristol R v Mansfield T 5–0; Burnley v Swansea T 4–2; Notts Co v Tranmere R 2–0; Accrington S v Bristol C 2–2, 1–3; W. Ham v Blackpool 5–1; Stockport Co v Luton T 3–0; Huddersfield T v Charlton Ath 2–2, 0–1; Fulham v Yeovil T 4–0

Fourth Round

Everton v Blackburn R 1–2; Cardiff C v Leyton Orient 4–1; Liverpool v Northampton T 3–1; Newcastle Utd v Scunthorpe Utd 1–3; Wolves v Portsmouth 5–1; Chelsea v Darlington 3–3, 1–4; Stoke C v Middlesbro 3–1; York C v BOLTON WAND 0–0, 0–3; MAN UTD v Ipswich T 2–0; Sheff Wed v Hull C 4–3; WBA v Nott'm Forest 3–3, 5–1; Spurs v Sheff Utd 0–3; Bristol R v Burnley 2–2, 3–0; Notts Co v Bristol C 1–2; W. Ham v Stockport Co 3–2; Fulham v Charlton Ath 1–1, 2–0

Fifth Round

Cardiff C v Blackburn R 0–0, 1–2; Scunthorpe Utd v Liverpool 0–1; Wolves v Darlington 6–1; BOLTON WAND v Stoke C 3–1; MAN UTD v Sheff Wed 3–0; Sheff Utd v WBA 1–1, 1–4; Bristol C v Bristol R 3–4; W. Ham v Fulham 2–3

Sixth Round

Blackburn R v Liverpool 2–1; BOLTON WAND v Wolves 2–1; WBA v MAN UTD 2–2, 0–1; Fulham v Bristol R 3–1

Semi-Final

Blackburn R v BOLTON WAND 1–2; MAN UTD v Fulham 2–2, 5–3

BOLTON WANDERERS **2**
MANCHESTER UNITED **0**

Bolton won the Cup and ended a Wembley tradition – for the first time the previous year's beaten finalists had returned to Wembley and lost again. They were undoubtedly the better side on the day and their play was more imaginative, balanced, and carrying more punch than that of their opponents. Yet, for a tragic reason, this will always be Manchester United's Final. Three months earlier, with United already through to the fifth round, the team had been decimated by the Munich crash.

United had four crash survivors in their Wembley line-up and were first on the attack. It was Bolton, though, who snatched the lead after only two minutes, with Lofthouse's close-range effort.

The United defence held on as Bolton were quick to try to ram home their advantage. Gregg saved superbly from Lofthouse and Birch, and Cope was a tower of strength at centre-half. There was always a chance that one of Bobby Charlton's flashing shots would bring them level, though the rest of the United attack seemed more inclined to play across the field than down it.

Three minutes after Charlton had struck a post, the game was finally lost for United as Bolton scored a controversial second goal. From Stevens's hard shot, Gregg pushed the ball into the air, and Lofthouse moved forward to charge both goalkeeper and ball over the line.

Bolton Wanderers: Hopkinson; Hartle, Banks; Hennin, Higgins, Edwards; Birch, Stevens, Lofthouse, Parry, Holden
Manchester United: Gregg; Foulkes, Greaves; Goodwin, Cope, Crowther; Dawson, Taylor (E.), Charlton, Viollet, Webster
Referee: J. Sherlock (Sheffield)

Lofthouse puts Bolton into the lead after two minutes

1958-9

First Round
Accrington S v Workington 5–1; Ashford v Crystal Palace 0–1; Brentford v Exeter C 3–2; Bury v York C 0–0, 1–0; Buxton v Crook T 4–1; Chelmsford C v Worcester C 0–0, 1–3; Chester v Boston Utd 3–2; Chesterfield v Rhyl 3–0; Colchester Utd v Bath C 2–0; Crewe Alex v South Shields 2–2, 0–5; Denaby Utd v Oldham Ath 0–2; Doncaster R v Consett 5–0; Gateshead v Bradford PA 1–4; Guildford C v Hereford Utd 1–2; Hartlepools Utd v Rochdale 1–1, 3–3, 2–1; Headington Utd v Margate 3–2; Heanor T v Carlisle Utd 1–5; Hitchin T v Millwall 1–1, 1–2; Hull C v Stockport Co 0–1; King's Lynn v Merthyr 2–1; Mansfield T v Bradford C 3–4; Morecambe v Blyth Spartans 1–2; Newport (IoW) v Shrewsbury T 0–0, 0–5; Northampton T v Wycombe Wand 2–0; Norwich C v Ilford 3–1; Notts Co v Barrow 1–2; Peterborough Utd v Kettering T 2–2, 3–2; Plymouth Arg v Gillingham 2–2, 4–1; Southampton v Woking 4–1; Southend Utd v Yeovil T 0–0, 0–1; Southport v Halifax T 0–2; Swindon T v Aldershot 5–0; Tooting & Mitcham v Bournemouth & Bos Ath 3–1; Torquay Utd v Port Vale 1–0; Tranmere R v Bishop Auckland 8–1; Walsall v QPR 0–1; Watford v Reading 1–1, 2–0; Weymouth v Coventry C 2–5; Wisbech T v Newport Co 2–2, 1–4; Wrexham v Darlington 1–2

Second Round
Accrington S v Buxton 6–1; Barrow v Hartlepools Utd 2–0; Blyth Spartans v Stockport Co 3–4; Bradford PA v Bradford C 0–2; Brentford v King's Lynn 3–1; Carlisle Utd v Chesterfield 0–0, 0–1; Chester v Bury 1–1, 1–2; Colchester Utd v Yeovil T 1–1, 7–1; Coventry C v Plymouth Arg 1–3; Crystal Palace v Shrewsbury T 2–2, 2–2, 4–1; Halifax T v Darlington 1–1, 0–3; Hereford Utd v Newport Co 0–2; Oldham Ath v South Shields 2–0; Peterborough Utd v Headington Utd 4–2; QPR v Southampton 0–1; Swindon T v Norwich C 1–1, 0–1; Tooting & Mitcham v Northampton T 2–1; Torquay Utd v Watford 2–0; Tranmere R v Doncaster R 1–2; Worcester C v Millwall 5–2

Third Round
LUTON T v Leeds Utd 5–1; Leicester C v Lincoln C 2–2, 2–0; Stoke C v Oldham Ath 5–1; Ipswich T v Huddersfield T 1–0; Southampton v Blackpool 1–2; Doncaster R v Bristol C 0–2; Sheff Wed v WBA 0–2; Brentford v Barnsley 2–0; Colchester Utd v Chesterfield 2–0; Bury v Arsenal 0–1; Worcester C v Liverpool 2–1; Sheff Utd v Crystal Palace 2–0; Spurs v W. Ham 2–0; Newport Co v Torquay Utd 0–0, 1–0; Norwich C v Man Utd 3–0; Plymouth Arg v Cardiff C 0–3; Bristol R v Charlton Ath 0–4; Everton v Sunderland 4–0; Newcastle Utd v Chelsea 1–4; Aston Villa v Rotherham Utd 2–1; Blackburn R v Leyton Orient 4–2; Stockport Co v Burnley 1–3; Accrington S v Darlington 3–0; Portsmouth v Swansea T 3–1; Barrow v Wolves 2–4; Scunthorpe Utd v Bolton Wand 0–2; Derby Co v PNE 2–2, 2–4; Brighton & H Alb v Bradford C 0–2; Middlesbro v Birmingham C 0–1; Fulham v Peterborough Utd 0–0, 1–0; Grimsby T v Man C 2–2, 2–1; Tooting & Mitcham v NOTT'M FOREST 2–2, 0–3

Fourth Round
Leicester C v LUTON T 1–1, 1–4; Stoke C v Ipswich T 0–1; Bristol C v Blackpool 1–1, 0–1; WBA v Brentford 2–0; Colchester Utd v Arsenal 2–2, 0–4; Worcester C v Sheff Utd 0–2; Spurs v Newport Co 4–1; Norwich C v Cardiff C 3–2; Charlton Ath v Everton 2–2, 1–4; Chelsea v Aston Villa 1–2; Blackburn R v Burnley 1–2; Accrington S v Portsmouth 0–0, 1–4; Wolves v Bolton Wand 1–2; PNE v Bradford C 3–2; Birmingham C v Fulham 1–1, 3–2; NOTT'M FOREST v Grimsby T 4–1

Fifth Round
Ipswich T v LUTON T 2–5; Blackpool v WBA 3–1; Arsenal v Sheff Utd 2–2, 0–3; Spurs v Norwich C 1–1, 0–1; Everton v Aston Villa 1–4; Burnley v Portsmouth 1–0; Bolton Wand v PNE 2–2, 1–1, 1–0; Birmingham C v NOTT'M FOREST 1–1, 1–1, 0–5

Sixth Round
Blackpool v LUTON T 1–1, 0–1; Sheff Utd v Norwich C 1–1, 2–3; Aston Villa v Burnley 0–0, 2–0; NOTT'M FOREST v Bolton Wand 2–1

Semi-Final
LUTON T v Norwich C 1–1, 1–0; Aston Villa v NOTT'M FOREST 0–1

NOTTINGHAM FOREST **2**
LUTON TOWN **1**

Forest had come within an ace of losing to non-League Tooting & Mitcham in the third round of the competition, drawing after being two goals down, but there have probably never been more worthy Final winners. Reduced to ten men after Dwight's injury on the half-hour, they became the first side to win at Wembley with a depleted team. They were two goals up after fourteen minutes and had established a moral superiority that even the loss of Dwight could not affect.

Forest settled quickly into their best form, and it came as no surprise when they took the lead in the tenth minute. Imlach, out on the left, feinted to cut inside, then beat McNally on the outside before pulling the ball back for Dwight to shoot into the top corner. Four minutes later the scene was repeated as Imlach centred perfectly for the unmarked Wilson to head past Baynham.

As the weight of numbers took its effect in the second half, Luton came more and more into the game and played much better football. Hawkes' hard cross into the goalmouth in the sixty-second minute eluded several players before Pacey slammed the ball into the net to reduce Forest's lead.

In the last few minutes Forest were desperately kicking long balls upfield whenever possible, and, though Luton remained on the attack right up to the final whistle, the ten men stood firm.

Nottingham Forest: Thomson; Whare, McDonald; Whitefoot, McKinlay, Burkitt; Dwight, Quigley, Wilson, Gray, Imlach
Luton Town: Baynham; McNally, Hawkes; Groves, Owen, Pacey; Bingham, Brown, Morton, Cummins, Gregory
Referee: J. Clough (Bolton)

Dwight rockets a shot past Baynham

1959–60

First Round
Accrington S v Mansfield T 1–2; Barnsley v Bradford C 3–3, 1–2; Bath C v Millwall 3–1; Bedford T v Gillingham 0–4; Bradford PA v Scarborough 6–1; Brentford v Ashford 5–0; Burscough R v Crewe Alex 1–3; Bury v Hartlepools Utd 5–0; Cheltenham T v Watford 0–0, 0–3; Colchester Utd v QPR 2–3; Coventry C v Southampton 1–1, 1–5; Crook T v Matlock T 2–2, 1–0; Crystal Palace v Chelmsford C 5–1; Darlington v Prescot Cables 4–0; Doncaster R v Gainsboro Tr 3–3, 1–0; Dorchester T v Port Vale 1–2; Enfield T v Headington Utd 4–3; Exeter C v Barnstaple 4–0; Gateshead v Halifax T 3–4; Hastings Utd v Notts Co 1–2; Kettering T v Margate 1–1, 2–3; King's Lynn v Aldershot 3–1; Newport Co v Hereford Utd 4–2; Norwich C v Reading 1–1, 1–2; Peterborough Utd v Shrewsbury T 4–3; Rhyl v Grimsby T 1–2; Rochdale v Carlisle Utd 2–2, 3–1; Salisbury v Barnet 1–0; Shildon v Oldham Ath 1–1, 0–3; Southend Utd v Oswestry 6–0; Southport v Workington 2–2, 0–3; South Shields v Chesterfield 2–1; Swindon T v Walsall 2–3; Torquay Utd v Northampton T 7–1; Tranmere R v Chester 0–1; Walthamstow Ave v Bournemouth & Bos Ath 2–3; West Auckland T v Stockport Co 2–6; Wrexham v Blyth Spartans 2–1; Wycombe Wand v Wisbech T 4–2; York C v Barrow 3–1

Second Round
Bury v Oldham Ath 2–1; Crook T v York C 0–1; Doncaster R v Darlington 3–2; Enfield T v Bournemouth & Bos Ath 1–5; Exeter C v Brentford 3–1; Gillingham v Torquay Utd 2–2, 2–1; Grimsby T v Wrexham 2–3; Mansfield T v Chester 2–0; Margate v Crystal Palace 0–0, 0–3; Notts Co v Bath C 0–1; QPR v Port Vale 3–3, 1–2; Reading v King's Lynn 4–2; Rochdale v Bradford City 1–1, 1–2; Salisbury v Newport Co 0–1; Southampton v Southend Utd 3–0; South Shields v Bradford PA 1–5; Stockport Co v Crewe Alex 0–0, 0–2; Walsall v Peterborough Utd 2–3; Watford v Wycombe Wand 5–1; Workington v Halifax T 1–0

Third Round
Sunderland v BLACKBURN R 1–1, 1–4; Blackpool v Mansfield T 3–0; Crewe Alex v Workington 2–0; Newport Co v Spurs 0–4; Bradford C v Everton 3–0; Bournemouth & Bos Ath v York C 1–0; Gillingham v Swansea T 1–4; Lincoln C v Burnley 1–1, 0–2; Sheff Utd v Portsmouth 3–0; Nott'm Forest v Reading 1–0; Man C v Southampton 1–5; Watford v Birmingham C 2–1; Liverpool v Leyton Orient 2–1; Derby Co v Man Utd 2–4; Sheff Wed v Middlesbro 2–1; Ipswich T v Peterborough Utd 2–3; Scunthorpe Utd v Crystal Palace 1–0; Cardiff C v Port Vale 0–2; Chelsea v Bradford PA 5–1; Aston Villa v Leeds Utd 2–1; Bristol R v Doncaster R 0–0, 2–1; Stoke C v PNE 1–1, 1–3; Rotherham Utd v Arsenal 2–2, 1–1, 2–0; Bath C v Brighton & H Alb 0–1; Wrexham v Leicester C 1–2; Fulham v Hull C 5–0; WBA v Plymouth Arg 3–2; Bury v Bolton Wand 1–1, 2–4; Huddersfield T v W. Ham 1–1, 5–1; Exeter C v Luton T 1–2; Newcastle Utd v WOLVES 2–2, 2–4; Bristol C v Charlton Ath 2–3

Fourth Round
BLACKBURN R v Blackpool 1–1, 3–0; Crewe Alex v Spurs 2–2, 2–13; Bradford C v Bournemouth & Bos Ath 3–1; Swansea T v Burnley 0–0, 1–2; Sheff Utd v Nott'm Forest 3–0; Southampton v Watford 2–2, 0–1; Liverpool v Man Utd 1–3; Sheff Wed v Peterborough Utd 2–0; Scunthorpe Utd v Port Vale 0–1; Chelsea v Aston Villa 1–2; Bristol R v PNE 3–3, 1–5; Rotherham Utd v Brighton & H Alb 1–1, 1–1, 0–6; Leicester C v Fulham 2–1; WBA v Bolton Wand 2–0; Huddersfield T v Luton T 0–1; WOLVES v Charlton Ath 2–1

Fifth Round
Spurs v BLACKBURN R 1–3; Bradford C v Burnley 2–2, 0–5; Sheff Utd v Watford 3–2; Man Utd v Sheff Wed 0–1; Port Vale v Aston Villa 1–2; PNE v Brighton & H Alb 2–1; Leicester C v WBA 2–1; Luton T v WOLVES 1–4

Sixth Round
Burnley v BLACKBURN R 3–3, 0–2; Sheff Utd v Sheff Wed 0–2; Aston Villa v PNE 2–0; Leicester C v WOLVES 1–2

Semi-Final
BLACKBURN R v Sheff Wed 2–1; Aston Villa v WOLVES 0–1

WOLVERHAMPTON WANDERERS 3
BLACKBURN ROVERS 0

Wolves had high hopes of achieving the elusive League and Cup double until Burnley's victory at Manchester City on the Monday before the Final meant that they were concentrating solely on winning the Cup.

Wolves were on top at the start and took the lead four minutes before half-time when Rovers defender McGrath, trying to cut out Stobart's low cross into the goalmouth, only succeeded in deflecting the ball into his own net. Two minutes later tragedy struck when Rovers defender Whelan broke a leg in a harmless-looking tackle with Deeley.

At half-time, then, Wolves must have gone off knowing that, barring further accidents, the Cup was surely theirs. Despite their handicap, however, Rovers were far from prepared to accept defeat without a struggle.

As the combined effects of the heat and of playing with ten men began to tell on the Rovers team, Wolves almost inevitably went further ahead. In the sixty-seventh minute Horne beat the offside trap and had plenty of time in which to centre from the left to Deeley who scored with a first-time shot from near the penalty-spot.

The remainder of the match was dominated by Wolves. Flowers had a 'goal' disallowed for offside, and then Deeley followed up to score a third after Stobart's centre had come back off a post.

Wolverhampton Wanderers: Finlayson; Showell, Harris; Clamp, Slater, Flowers; Deeley, Stobart, Murray, Broadbent, Horne
Blackburn Rovers: Leyland; Bray, Whelan; Clayton, Woods, McGrath; Bimpson, Dobing, Dougan, Douglas, McLeod
Referee: K. Howley (Middlesbrough)

The ball sails into the net for Wolves' third goal

1960–1

First Round

Accrington S v Barrow 2–1; Aldershot v Notts Co 2–0; Ashford v Gillingham 1–2; Bangor C v Wrexham 1–0; Bishop Auckland v Bridlington 3–2; Bradford C v Scarborough 0–0, 3–1; Bridgwater T v Hereford Utd 3–0; Bristol C v Chichester 11–0; Chelmsford C v Port Vale 2–3; Chester v Carlisle Utd 0–1; Chesterfield v Doncaster R 3–3, 1–0; Clacton v Southend Utd 1–3; Colchester Utd v Maidenhead Utd 5–0; Crewe Alex v Rochdale 1–1, 2–1; Crystal Palace v Hitchin T 6–2; Darlington v Grimsby T 2–0; Dover v Peterborough Utd 1–4; Exeter C v Bournemouth & Bos Ath 1–1, 1–3; Gateshead v Barnsley 0–0, 0–2; Halifax T v Hartlepools Utd 5–1; Hendon v Oxford Utd 2–2, 2–3; Hull C v Sutton T 3–0; Loughborough v King's Lynn 0–0, 0–3; Mansfield T v Blyth Spartans 3–1; Northampton T v Hastings Utd 2–1; QPR v Walthamstow Ave 3–2; Reading v Millwall 6–2; Rhyl v Oldham Ath 0–1; Shrewsbury T v Newport Co 4–1; Southport v Macclesfield 7–2; Stockport Co v Workington 1–0; Swindon T v Bath C 2–2, 6–4; Sutton Utd v Romford 2–2, 0–5; Tranmere R v Bury 1–0; Walsall v Yeovil T 0–1; Watford v Brentford 2–2, 2–0; Weymouth v Torquay Utd 1–3; Worcester C v Coventry C 1–4; Wycombe Wand v Kettering T 1–2; York C v Bradford PA 0–0, 2–0

Second Round

Accrington S v Mansfield T 3–0; Aldershot v Colchester Utd 3–1; Bangor C v Southport 1–1, 1–3; Bournemouth & Bos Ath v Yeovil T 3–1; Bradford C v Barnsley 1–2; Chesterfield v Oldham Ath 4–4, 3–0; Crystal Palace v Watford 0–0, 0–1; Darlington v Hull C 1–1, 1–1, 0–0, 0–3; Gillingham v Southend Utd 3–2; Halifax T v Crewe Alex 2–2, 0–3; King's Lynn v Bristol C 2–2, 0–3; Oxford Utd v Bridgwater T 2–1; Port Vale v Carlisle Utd 2–1; QPR v Coventry C 1–2; Reading v Kettering T 4–2; Romford v Northampton T 1–5; Stockport Co v Bishop Auckland 2–0; Swindon T v Shrewsbury T 0–1; Torquay Utd v Peterborough Utd 1–3; Tranmere R v York C 1–1, 1–2

Third Round

LEICESTER C v Oxford Utd 3–1; Plymouth Arg v Bristol C 0–1; Nott'm Forest v Birmingham C 0–2; Rotherham Utd v Watford 1–0; Wolves v Huddersfield T 1–1, 1–2; Reading v Barnsley 1–1, 1–3; Luton T v Northampton T 4–0; Cardiff C v Man C 1–1, 0–0, 0–2; Newcastle Utd v Fulham 5–0; Stockport C v Southport 3–1; W. Ham v Stoke C 2–2, 0–1; Aldershot v Shrewsbury T 1–1, 2–2, 2–0; Everton v Sheff Utd 0–1; Lincoln C v WBA 3–1; Hull C v Bolton Wand 0–1; Chesterfield v Blackburn R 0–0, 0–3; Southampton v Ipswich T 7–1; Gillingham v Leyton Orient 2–6; Sheff Wed v Leeds Utd 2–0; Man Utd v Middlesbro 3–0; Brighton & H Alb v Derby Co 3–1; Burnley v Bournemouth & Bos Ath 1–0; Swansea T v Port Vale 3–0; PNE v Accrington S 1–1, 4–0; Scunthorpe Utd v Blackpool 6–2; York C v Norwich C 1–1, 0–1; Liverpool v Coventry C 3–2; Sunderland v Arsenal 2–1; Portsmouth v Peterborough Utd 1–2; Bristol R v Aston Villa 1–1, 0–4; Chelsea v Crewe Alex 1–2; SPURS v Charlton Ath 3–2

Fourth Round

LEICESTER C v Bristol C 5–1; Birmingham C v Rotherham Utd 4–0; Huddersfield T v Barnsley 1–1, 0–1; Luton T v Man C 3–1; Newcastle Utd v Stockport Co 4–0; Stoke C v Aldershot 0–0, 0–0, 3–0; Sheff Utd v Lincoln C 3–1; Bolton Wand v Blackburn R 3–3, 0–4; Southampton v Leyton Orient 0–1; Sheff Wed v Man Utd 1–1, 7–2; Brighton & H Alb v Burnley 3–3, 0–2; Swansea T v PNE 2–1; Scunthorpe Utd v Norwich C 1–4; Liverpool v Sunderland 0–2; Peterborough Utd v Aston Villa 1–1, 1–2; SPURS v Crewe Alex 5–1

Fifth Round

Birmingham C v LEICESTER C 1–1, 1–2; Barnsley v Luton T 1–0; Newcastle Utd v Stoke C 3–1; Sheff Utd v Blackburn R 2–1; Leyton Orient v Sheff Wed 0–2; Burnley v Swansea T 4–0; Norwich C v Sunderland 0–1; Aston Villa v SPURS 0–2

Sixth Round

LEICESTER C v Barnsley 0–0, 2–1; Newcastle Utd v Sheff Utd 1–3; Sheff Wed v Burnley 0–0, 0–2; Sunderland v SPURS 1–1, 0–5

Semi-Final

LEICESTER C v Sheff Utd 0–0, 0–0, 2–0; Burnley v SPURS 0–3

TOTTENHAM HOTSPUR **2**
LEICESTER CITY **0**

Tottenham had made certain of the League championship on 17 April, nineteen days before the Cup Final, defeating their closest rivals Sheffield Wednesday 2–1 at White Hart Lane. But could 'Super Spurs' land the League and Cup double?

Despite an early injury to right-back Chalmers – another victim of the famous 'Wembley hoodoo' – Leicester City's rearranged side held their own successfully for forty-five minutes against a Tottenham team hardly recognizable as the one which had attracted over two and a half million fans in a season of sparkling displays. But if Tottenham were disappointing, judged by their own standards, their opponents never really looked like scoring.

The vital first goal was scored by the hard-working Bobby Smith. With about twenty-five minutes of the match remaining, he dashed into a vacant space to receive a pass in the inside-right position and hammered in a powerful drive on the half-turn. Seven minutes later, White intercepted a square pass on the half-way line, quickly moved the ball to Smith, and Dyson joyfully raced in to head the far post centre firmly past Banks to make the result, and the 'double', quite certain.

Tottenham Hotspur: Brown; Baker, Henry; Blanchflower, Norman, Mackay; Jones, White, Smith, Allen, Dyson
Leicester City: Banks; Chalmers, Norman; McLintock, King, Appleton; Riley, Walsh, McIlmoyle, Keyworth, Cheeseborough
Referee: J. Kelly (Chorley)

Dyson (out of picture) heads past Banks from Smith's cross

1961–2

First Round
Aldershot v Tunbridge Wells Utd 3–1; Barry T v QPR 1–1, 0–7; Bournemouth & Bos Ath v Margate 0–3; Bradford PA v Port Vale 0–1; Bradford C v York C 1–0; Brentford v Oxford Utd 3–0; Bridgwater T v Weston-super-Mare 0–0, 1–0; Brierley Hill v Grantham 3–0; Bristol C v Hereford Utd 1–1, 5–2; Chelmsford C v King's Lynn 1–2; Chester v Ashington 4–1; Coventry C v Gillingham 2–0; Crewe Alex v Lincoln C 2–0; Crystal Palace v Portsmouth 3–0; Darlington v Carlisle Utd 0–4; Doncaster R v Chesterfield 0–4; Exeter C v Dartford 3–3, 1–2; Hartlepools Utd v Blyth Spartans 5–1; Hull C v Rhyl 5–0; Mansfield T v Grimsby T 3–2; Morecambe v South Shields 2–1; Northampton T v Millwall 2–0; Notts Co v Yeovil T 4–2; Oldham Ath v Shildon 5–2; Peterborough Utd v Colchester Utd 3–3, 2–2, 3–0; Reading v Newport Co 1–1, 0–1; Rochdale v Halifax T 2–0; Shrewsbury T v Banbury Utd 7–1; Southend Utd v Watford 0–2; Southport v Northwich Victoria 1–0; Stockport Co v Accrington S 0–1; Swindon T v Kettering T 2–2, 0–3; Torquay Utd v Harwich & Parkeston 5–1; Tranmere R v Gateshead 2–3; Walthamstow Ave v Romford 2–3; West Auckland T v Barnsley 3–3, 0–2; Weymouth v Barnet 1–0; Workington v Worksop 2–0; Wrexham v Barrow 3–2; Wycombe Wand v Ashford 0–0, 0–3

Second Round
Aldershot v Brentford 2–2, 0–2; Ashford v QPR 0–3; Barnsley v Carlisle Utd 1–2; Bridgwater T v Crystal Palace 0–3; Bristol C v Dartford 8–2; Chester v Morecambe 0–1; Chesterfield v Oldham Ath 2–2, 2–4; Coventry C v King's Lynn 1–2; Crewe Alex v Port Vale 1–1, 0–3; Gateshead v Workington 0–2; Hartlepools Utd v Accrington S 2–1; Hull C v Bradford C 0–2; Margate v Notts Co 1–1, 1–3; Northampton T v Kettering T 3–0; Rochdale v Wrexham 1–2; Romford v Watford 1–3; Shrewsbury T v Brierley Hill 3–0; Southport v Mansfield T 4–2; Torquay Utd v Peterborough Utd 1–4; Weymouth v Newport Co 1–0

Third Round
BURNLEY v QPR 6–1; Brentford v Leyton Orient 1–1, 1–2; Everton v King's Lynn 4–0; Notts Co v Man City 0–1; Newcastle Utd v Peterborough Utd 0–1; Bury v Sheff Utd 0–0, 2–2, 0–2; Norwich C v Wrexham 3–1; Ipswich T v Luton T 1–1, 1–1, 5–1; Fulham v Hartlepools Utd 3–1; Bristol C v Walsall 0–0, 1–4; Southampton v Sunderland 2–2, 0–3; Port Vale v Northampton T 3–1; Leicester C v Stoke C 1–1, 2–5; Brighton & H Alb v Blackburn R 0–3; Southport v Shrewsbury T 1–3; Middlesbro v Cardiff C 1–0; Bristol R v Oldham Ath 1–1, 0–2; Liverpool v Chelsea 4–3; PNE v Watford 3–2; Morecambe v Weymouth 0–1; Man Utd v Bolton Wand 2–1; Arsenal v Bradford C 3–0; Workington v Nott'm Forest 1–2; Sheff Wed v Swansea T 1–0; Aston Villa v Crystal Palace 4–3; Huddersfield T v Rotherham Utd 4–3; Charlton Ath v Scunthorpe Utd 1–0; Leeds Utd v Derby Co 2–2, 1–3; Wolves v Carlisle Utd 3–1; Blackpool v WBA 0–0, 1–2; Plymouth Arg v W. Ham 3–0; Birmingham C v SPURS 3–3, 2–4

Fourth Round
BURNLEY v Leyton Orient 1–1, 1–0; Everton v Man C 2–0; Peterborough Utd v Sheff Utd 1–3; Norwich C v Ipswich T 1–1, 2–1; Fulham v Walsall 2–2, 2–0; Sunderland v Port Vale 0–0, 1–3; Stoke C v Blackburn R 0–1; Shrewsbury T v Middlesbro 2–2, 1–5; Oldham Ath v Liverpool 1–2; PNE v Weymouth 2–0; Man Utd v Arsenal 1–0; Nott'm Forest v Sheff Wed 0–2; Aston Villa v Huddersfield T 2–1; Charlton Ath v Derby Co 2–1; Wolves v WBA 1–2; Plymouth v SPURS 1–5

Fifth Round
BURNLEY v Everton 3–1; Sheff Utd v Norwich C 3–1; Fulham v Port Vale 1–0; Blackburn R v Middlesbro 2–1; Liverpool v PNE 0–0, 0–0, 0–1; Man Utd v Sheff Wed 0–0, 2–0; Aston Villa v Charlton Ath 2–1; WBA v SPURS 2–4;

Sixth Round
Sheff Utd v BURNLEY 0–1; Fulham v Blackburn R 2–2, 1–0; PNE v Man Utd 0–0, 1–2; SPURS v Aston Villa 2–0

Semi-Final
BURNLEY v Fulham 1–1, 2–1; Man Utd v SPURS 1–3

TOTTENHAM HOTSPUR **3**
BURNLEY **1**

The 'Chessboard Final' of 1962 was a mixture of patience and artistry, rather than fire and passion, and some thought the match strangely flat and lacking in excitement.

No team had lost a Wembley Final after winning there a year earlier, and Burnley's hopes of forcing Spurs to become the first side to do so took a jolt as early as the third minute, when Greaves scored.

Tottenham kept their lead to the interval, but Burnley were level a few minutes later. Pointer swept the ball out to Harris on the left and Robson diverted his centre between Spurs goalkeeper Brown and a post – the one hundredth goal to be scored in a Wembley Final.

For a fatal moment Burnley allowed themselves a moment of relaxation. Within a minute they were behind again as Smith turned on White's centre and thumped his shot past Blacklaw. Burnley quickly recovered from this blow to their morale, and they were soon setting up good attacks again. Robson's 'goal' was disallowed for offside, Harris drilled in a shot straight at Brown and then Robson's header missed by a fraction.

Ten minutes from time Spurs ended the doubts. Smith appeared to foul Blacklaw as they went up for White's lob into the middle, and when Medwin hit the loose ball goalwards, Burnley centre-half Cummings handled on the line. Blanchflower sent Blacklaw the wrong way with the spot-kick.

Tottenham Hotspur: Brown; Baker, Henry; Blanchflower, Norman, Mackay; Medwin, White, Smith, Greaves, Jones
Burnley: Blacklaw; Angus, Elder; Adamson, Cummings, Miller; Connelly, McIlroy, Pointer, Robson, Harris
Referee: J. Finney (Hereford)

Skipper Blanchflower sends Blacklaw the wrong way with his spot-kick

1962–3

First Round
Aldershot v Brentford 1–0; Andover v Gillingham 0–1; Barnsley v Rhyl 4–0; Bedford T v Cambridge Utd 2–1; Blyth Spartans v Morecambe 2–1; Boston Utd v King's Lynn 1–2; Bristol C v Wellington T 4–2; Bristol R v Port Vale 0–2; Buxton v Barrow 2–2, 1–3; Carlisle Utd v Hartlepools Utd 2–1; Chelmsford C v Shrewsbury T 2–6; Cheltenham T v Enfield 3–6; Chester v Tranmere R 0–2; Chesterfield v Stockport Co 4–1; Coventry C v Bournemouth & Bos Ath 1–0; Crewe Alex v Scarborough 1–1, 3–2; Crystal Palace v Hereford Utd 2–0; Falmouth v Oxford Utd 1–2; Gateshead v Wigan Ath 2–1; Gravesend & Northfleet v Exeter C 3–2; Halifax T v Bradford PA 1–0; Hinckley Ath v Sittingbourne 3–0; Hounslow v Mansfield T 3–3, 2–9; Hull C v Crook T 5–4; Lincoln C v Darlington 1–1, 2–1; Maidenhead Utd v Wycombe Wand 0–3; Millwall v Margate 3–1; Northampton T v Torquay Utd 1–2; North Shields v Workington 2–2, 2–7; Notts Co v Peterborough Utd 0–3; Oldham Ath v Bradford C 2–5; QPR v Newport Co 3–2; Southend Utd v Brighton & H Alb 2–1; Southport v Wrexham 1–1, 2–3; South Shields v Doncaster R 0–0, 1–2; Swindon T v Reading 4–2; Watford v Poole T 2–2, 2–1; Wimbledon v Colchester Utd 2–1; Yeovil T v Dartford 3–2; York C v Rochdale 0–0, 2–1

Second Round
Barnsley v Chesterfield 2–1; Blyth Spartans v Carlisle Utd 0–2; Bradford C v Gateshead 3–2; Bristol C v Wimbledon 2–1; Crystal Palace v Mansfield T 2–2, 2–7; Doncaster R v Tranmere R 1–4; Gillingham v Bedford T 3–0; Gravesend & Northfleet v Wycombe Wand 3–1; Hull C v Workington 2–0; King's Lynn v Oxford Utd 1–2; Lincoln C v Halifax T 1–0; Millwall v Coventry C 0–0, 1–2; Peterborough Utd v Enfield 1–0; Port Vale v Aldershot 2–0; QPR v Hinckley Ath 7–2; Shrewsbury T v Torquay Utd 2–1; Southend Utd v Watford 0–2; Wrexham v Barrow 5–2; Yeovil T v Swindon T 0–2; York C v Crewe Alex 2–1

Third Round
Grimsby T v LEICESTER C 1–3; Mansfield T v Ipswich T 2–3; Leyton Orient v Hull C 1–1, 2–0; Derby Co v Peterborough Utd 2–0; Walsall v Man C 0–1; Birmingham C v Bury 3–3; 0–2; Norwich C v Blackpool 1–1, 3–1; Bradford C v Newcastle Utd 1–6; Arsenal v Oxford Utd 5–1; Shrewsbury T v Sheff Wed 1–1, 1–2; Spurs v Burnley 0–3; Wrexham v Liverpool 0–3; W. Ham v Fulham 0–0, 2–1; Swansea T v QPR 2–0; Luton T v Swindon T 0–2; Barnsley v Everton 0–3; Plymouth Arg v WBA 1–5; Nott'm Forest v Wolves 4–3; Blackburn R v Middlesbro 1–1, 1–3; Leeds Utd v Stoke C 3–1; Southampton v York C 5–0; Watford v Rotherham Utd 2–0; Gillingham v Port Vale 2–4; Sheff Utd v Bolton Wand 3–1; Portsmouth v Scunthorpe Utd 1–1, 2–1; Lincoln C v Coventry C 1–5; Carlisle Utd v Gravesend & Northfleet 0–1; PNE v Sunderland 1–4; Charlton Ath v Cardiff C 1–0; Tranmere R v Chelsea 2–2, 1–3; Bristol C v Aston Villa 1–1, 2–3; MAN UTD v Huddersfield T 5–0

Fourth Round
LEICESTER C v Ipswich T 3–1; Leyton Orient v Derby Co 3–0; Man C v Bury 1–0; Norwich C v Newcastle Utd 5–0; Arsenal v Sheff Wed 2–0; Burnley v Liverpool 1–1, 1–2; W. Ham v Swansea T 1–0; Swindon T v Everton 1–5; WBA v Nott'm Forest 0–0, 1–2; Middlesbro v Leeds Utd 0–2; Southampton v Watford 3–1; Port Vale v Sheff Utd 1–2; Portsmouth v Coventry C 1–1, 2–2, 1–2; Gravesend & Northfleet v Sunderland 1–1, 2–5; Charlton Ath v Chelsea 0–3; MAN UTD v Aston Villa 1–0

Fifth Round
Leyton Orient v LEICESTER C 0–1; Man C v Norwich C 1–2; Arsenal v Liverpool 1–2; W. Ham v Everton 1–0; Nott'm Forest v Leeds Utd 3–0; Southampton v Sheff Utd 1–0; Coventry C v Sunderland 2–1; MAN UTD v Chelsea 2–1

Sixth Round
Norwich C v LEICESTER C 0–2; Liverpool v W. Ham 1–0; Nott'm Forest v Southampton 1–1, 3–3, 0–5; Coventry C v MAN UTD 1–3

Semi-Final
LEICESTER C v Liverpool 1–0; Southampton v MAN UTD 0–1

MANCHESTER UNITED **3**
LEICESTER CITY **1**

United came to Wembley in the season of 'The Big Freeze' – the Final took place three weeks later than scheduled – with a narrow escape from relegation just behind them. On the day, and for the great occasion, they at last found their touch.

The new United team had been assembled at astronomical cost and was the most expensive team to play in a Final, with more than £300,000 having been spent on six men.

The first goal came on the half-hour. Crerand squared the ball to Law, and Law, completely in control, swung away towards the right, and then turned sharply back to hook the ball in. The goal merely confirmed United's superiority, and from then on they had time and space and played with commanding ease. United's Scottish centre-forward, David Herd, netted twice in the second half and, for Leicester, Keyworth scored a courageous goal when they were 2–0 down, diving to head the ball only a foot from the ground.

Herd's father, Alec, had played for Manchester City in the Finals of 1933 and 1934, and the pair had had a few games together for Stockport County in the early 1950s. Herd junior was on hand to score after Charlton's effort had been too hard for Banks to hold, and then, with only five minutes remaining, he banged in his second and United's third after Banks had dropped Giles' centre.

Manchester United: Gaskell; Dunne, Cantwell; Crerand, Foulkes, Setters; Giles, Quixall, Herd, Law, Charlton
Leicester City: Banks; Sjoberg, Norman; McLintock, King, Appleton; Riley, Cross, Keyworth, Gibson, Stringfellow
Referee: K. Aston (Ilford)

Herd follows up to score United's second

1963-4

First Round

Altrincham v Wrexham 0–0, 0–3; Barnsley v Stockport Co 1–0; Barrow v Bangor C 3–2; Bexley Utd v Wimbledon 1–5; Bournemouth & Bos Ath v Bristol R 1–3; Bradford PA v Heanor T 3–1; Bradford C v Port Vale 1–2; Brentford v Margate 2–2, 2–0; Bridgwater T v Luton T 0–3; Brighton & H Alb v Colchester Utd 0–1; Cambridge Utd v Chelmsford C 0–1; Chester v Blyth Spartans 3–2; Corby T v Bristol C 1–3; Crook T v Chesterfield 1–2; Crystal Palace v Harwich & Parkeston 8–2; Darlington v Gateshead 1–4; Doncaster R v Tranmere R 3–0; Exeter C v Shrewsbury T 2–1; Hartlepools Utd v Lincoln C 0–1; Hereford Utd v Newport Co 1–1, 0–4; Hull C v Crewe Alex 2–2, 3–0; Kettering T v Millwall 1–1, 3–2; Maidenhead Utd v Bath C 0–2; Netherfield v Loughborough Utd 6–1; Notts Co v Frickley Colliery 2–1; Oldham Ath v Mansfield T 3–2; Oxford Utd v Folkestone T 2–0; Peterborough Utd v Watford 1–1, 1–2; QPR v Gillingham 4–1; Reading v Enfield 2–2, 4–2; Rochdale v Chorley 2–1; Southport v Walsall 2–1; Sutton Utd v Aldershot 0–4; Tooting & Mitcham v Gravesend & Northfleet 1–2; Torquay Utd v Barnet 6–2; Trowbridge T v Coventry C 1–6; Weymouth v Bedford T 1–1, 0–1; Workington v Halifax T 4–1; Yeovil T v Southend Utd 1–0; York C v Carlisle Utd 2–5

Second Round

Barnsley v Rochdale 3–1; Brentford v Gravesend & Northfleet 1–0; Carlisle Utd v Gateshead 4–3; Chelmsford C v Bedford T 0–1; Chester v Barrow 0–2; Colchester Utd v QPR 0–1; Coventry C v Bristol R 1–2; Doncaster R v Notts Co 1–1, 2–1; Exeter C v Bristol C 0–2; Lincoln C v Southport 2–0; Luton T v Reading 2–1; Netherfield v Chesterfield 1–1, 1–4; Newport Co v Watford 2–0; Oldham Ath v Bradford PA 2–0; Oxford Utd v Kettering T 2–1; Port Vale v Workington 2–1; Torquay Utd v Aldershot 2–3; Wimbledon v Bath C 2–2, 0–4; Wrexham v Hull C 0–2; Yeovil T v Crystal Palace 3–1

Third Round

W. HAM v Charlton Ath 3–0; Leicester C v Leyton Orient 2–3; Aston Villa v Aldershot 0–0, 1–2; Swindon T v Man C 2–1; Burnley v Rotherham Utd 1–1, 3–2; Newport Co v Sheff Wed 3–2; Spurs v Chelsea 1–1, 0–2; Plymouth Arg v Huddersfield T 0–1; Sunderland v Northampton T 2–0; Doncaster R v Bristol C 2–2, 0–2; Cardiff C v Leeds Utd 0–1; Hull C v Everton 1–1, 1–2; Scunthorpe Utd v Barnsley 2–2, 2–3; Yeovil T v Bury 0–2; Southampton v Man Utd 2–3; Bristol R v Norwich C 2–1; Ipswich T v Oldham Ath 6–3; Stoke C v Portsmouth 4–1; Lincoln C v Sheff Utd 0–4; Swansea T v Barrow 4–1; WBA v Blackpool 2–2, 1–0; Arsenal v Wolves 2–1; Liverpool v Derby Co 5–0; Birmingham C v Port Vale 1–2; Oxford Utd v Chesterfield 1–0; Brentford v Middlesbro 2–1; Blackburn R v Grimsby T 4–0; Fulham v Luton T 4–1; Newcastle Utd v Bedford T 1–2; Carlisle Utd v QPR 2–0; Bath C v Bolton Wand 1–1, 0–3; Nott'm Forest v PNE 0–0, 0–1

Fourth Round

Leyton Orient v W. HAM 1–1, 0–3; Aldershot v Swindon T 1–2; Burnley v Newport Co 2–1; Chelsea v Huddersfield T 1–2; Sunderland v Bristol C 6–1; Leeds Utd v Everton 1–1, 0–2; Barnsley v Bury 2–1; Man Utd v Bristol R 4–1; Ipswich T v Stoke C 1–1, 0–1; Sheff Utd v Swansea T 1–1, 0–4; WBA v Arsenal 3–3, 0–2; Liverpool v Port Vale 0–0, 2–1; Oxford Utd v Brentford 2–2, 2–1; Blackburn R v Fulham 2–0; Bedford T v Carlisle Utd 0–3; Bolton Wand v PNE 2–2, 1–2

Fifth Round

Swindon T v W. HAM 1–3; Burnley v Huddersfield T 3–0; Sunderland v Everton 3–1; Barnsley v Man Utd 0–4; Stoke C v Swansea T 2–2, 0–2; Arsenal v Liverpool 0–1; Oxford Utd v Blackburn R 3–1; PNE v Carlisle Utd 1–0

Sixth Round

W. HAM v Burnley 3–2; Man Utd v Sunderland 3–3, 2–2, 5–1; Liverpool v Swansea T 1–2; Oxford Utd v PNE 1–2

Semi-Final

W. HAM v Man Utd 3–1; Swansea T v PNE 1–2

WEST HAM UNITED **3**
PRESTON NORTH END **2**

Defeat, after being level or in front for all but ninety seconds of the match: that was Preston's fate in the 1964 Final. These Second Division outsiders had moved into the game with all the confidence of tradition and injured pride, and may ultimately be regarded as one of Wembley's unluckiest losers in a great Final.

Preston were ahead in nine minutes. Standen failed to hold Dawson's low shot and Holden ran the ball in.

In the 1954 Final Preston had wiped out a West Bromwich goal within a minute. History repeated itself ten years later, but with a change in the order, as the 'Hammers' winger Sissons became the youngest scorer in a Final when he hit home an angled shot a minute later.

Dawson lurched forward to score with a powerful header from Wilson's corner, to put Preston into the lead again five minutes from half-time. They held it for twelve minutes until Hurst got his head to Brabrook's corner and the ball rolled over the line after hitting both crossbar and prostrate goalkeeper.

The scores were even now, but as the second half developed West Ham strengthened. It was as late as two minutes into injury time when they finally clinched it. Boyce ran in unchallenged to head Brabrook's lofted cross from the right firmly past Kelly's left hand and thereby crown a fine afternoon's work.

West Ham United: Standen; Bond, Burkett; Bovington, Brown, Moore; Brabrook, Boyce, Byrne, Hurst, Sissons
Preston North End; Kelly; Ross, Smith; Lawton, Singleton, Kendall; Wilson, Ashworth, Dawson, Spavin, Holden
Referee: A. Holland (Barnsley)

Boyce ecstatic after scoring West Ham's last gasp winner

1964–5

First Round
Barnet v Cambridge Utd 2–1; Barrow v Grimsby T 1–1, 2–2, 0–2; Bournemouth & Bos Ath v Gravesend & Northfleet 7–0; Bradford PA v Doncaster R 2–3; Bristol C v Brighton & H Alb 1–0; Canterbury C v Torquay Utd 0–6; Chester v Crewe Alex 5–0; Chesterfield v South Shields 2–0; Colchester Utd v Bideford 3–3, 2–1; Corby T v Hartlepools Utd 1–3; Crook T v Carlisle Utd 1–0; Dartford v Aldershot 1–1, 0–1; Exeter C v Hayes 1–0; Guildford C v Gillingham 2–2, 0–1; Halifax T v South Liverpool 2–2, 2–4; Kidderminster Harriers v Hull C 1–4; King's Lynn v Shrewsbury T 0–1; Luton T v Southend Utd 1–0; Macclesfield T v Wrexham 1–2; Millwall v Kettering T 2–0; Netherfield v Barnsley 1–3; Newport Co v Spalding Utd 5–3; Notts Co v Chelmsford C 2–0; Oldham Ath v Hereford Utd 4–0; Oxford Utd v Mansfield T 0–1; Peterborough Utd v Salisbury 5–1; Port Vale v Hendon 2–1; QPR v Bath C 2–0; Reading v Watford 3–1; Romford v Enfield 0–0, 0–0, 2–4; Scarborough v Bradford C 1–0; Scunthorpe Utd v Darlington 1–2; Southport v Annfield Plain 6–1; Stockport Co v Wigan Ath 2–1; Tranmere R v Lincoln C 0–0, 0–1; Walsall v Bristol R 0–2; Welton R v Weymouth 1–1, 3–4; Wisbech T v Brentford 0–2; Workington v Rochdale 2–0; York C v Bangor C 5–1

Second Round
Aldershot v Reading 1–3; Barnsley v Chester 2–5; Bournemouth & Bos Ath v Bristol C 0–3; Brentford v Notts Co 4–0; Bristol R v Weymouth 4–1; Chesterfield v York C 2–1; Crook T v Oldham Ath 0–1; Doncaster R v Scarborough 0–0, 2–1; Enfield v Barnet 4–4, 0–3; Exeter C v Shrewsbury T 1–2; Hartlepools Utd v Darlington 0–0, 1–4; Hull C v Lincoln C 1–1, 1–3; Luton T v Gillingham 1–0; Millwall v Port Vale 4–0; Newport Co v Mansfield T 3–0; QPR v Peterborough Utd 3–3, 1–2; South Liverpool v Workington 0–2; Stockport Co v Grimsby T 0–0, 1–0; Torquay Utd v Colchester Utd 2–0; Wrexham v Southport 2–3

Third Round
WBA v LIVERPOOL 1–2; Bristol R v Stockport Co 0–0, 2–3; Bolton Wand v Workington 4–1; Barnet v PNE 2–3; Leicester C v Blackburn R 2–2, 2–1; Plymouth Arg v Derby Co 4–2; Middlesbro v Oldham Ath 6–2; Cardiff C v Charlton Ath 1–2; Chelsea v Northampton T 4–1; W. Ham v Birmingham C 4–2; Torquay Utd v Spurs 3–3, 1–5; Swindon T v Ipswich T 1–2; Chesterfield v Peterborough Utd 0–3; Darlington v Arsenal 0–2; Swansea T v Newcastle Utd 1–0; Doncaster R v Huddersfield T 0–1; Portsmouth v Wolves 0–0, 2–3; Rotherham Utd v Lincoln C 5–1; Bristol C v Sheff Utd 1–1, 0–3; Aston Villa v Coventry C 3–0; Stoke C v Blackpool 4–1; Man Utd v Chester 2–1; Reading v Newport Co 2–2, 1–0; Burnley v Brentford 1–1, 2–0; Southampton v Leyton Orient 3–1; Crystal Palace v Bury 5–1; Luton T v Sunderland 0–3; Nott'm Forest v Norwich C 1–0; Fulham v Millwall 3–3, 0–2; Man C v Shrewsbury T 1–1, 1–3; Everton v Sheff Wed 2–2, 3–0; LEEDS UTD v Southport 3–0

Fourth Round
LIVERPOOL v Stockport Co 1–1, 2–0; PNE v Bolton Wand 1–2; Leicester C v Plymouth Arg 5–0; Charlton Ath v Middlesbro 1–1, 1–2; W. Ham v Chelsea 0–1; Spurs v Ipswich T 5–0; Peterborough Utd v Arsenal 2–1; Swansea T v Huddersfield T 1–0; Wolves v Rotherham Utd 2–2, 3–0; Sheff Utd v Aston Villa 0–2; Stoke C v Man Utd 0–0, 0–1; Reading v Burnley 1–1, 0–1; Southampton v Crystal Palace 1–2; Sunderland v Nott'm Forest 1–3; Millwall v Shrewsbury T 1–2; LEEDS UTD v Everton 1–1, 2–1

Fifth Round
Bolton Wand v LIVERPOOL 0–1; Middlesbro v Leicester C 0–3; Chelsea v Spurs 1–0; Peterborough Utd v Swansea T 0–0, 2–0; Aston Villa v Wolves 1–1, 0–0, 1–3; Man Utd v Burnley 2–1; Crystal Palace v Nott'm Forest 3–1; LEEDS UTD v Shrewsbury T 2–0

Sixth Round
Leicester C v LIVERPOOL 0–0, 0–1; Chelsea v Peterborough Utd 5–1; Wolves v Man Utd 3–5; Crystal Palace v LEEDS UTD 0–3

Semi-Final
LIVERPOOL v Chelsea 2–0; Man Utd v LEEDS UTD 0–0, 0–1

LIVERPOOL **2**
LEEDS UNITED **1**

'Ee-ay-addio, we won the Cup!' The twentieth post-war Final, though not a classic, was a remarkable emotional experience and probably the noisiest and most passionate Final of them all. The game ran to extra time – the first Final to do so since 1947 – and the additional period was played out in an atmosphere of great tension and drama before Liverpool got their deserved victory.

Defensively Leeds were excellent, but there was a lack of invention in their attack. The Collins–Bremner midfield machine for once failed to function, their passes down the middle invariably mastered by Yeats and Smith.

Liverpool, on the other hand, were always forcing their way forward, with St John and Hunt in particular showing tremendous bursts of energy. Every raid looked full of danger, but Leeds survived.

Three minutes into extra time Liverpool at last got a goal. Left-back Byrne, who had played most of the match with a broken collar-bone, took the ball to the by-line and crossed for Hunt, stooping low, to nod home. But they quickly lost the advantage when Leeds equalized with what was virtually their only shot of the game. Charlton headed the ball down and Bremner slashed a half-volley into the top corner.

Then Liverpool contrived to score again, St John diving to head in Callaghan's low centre from the right, to give the match a fitting result.

Liverpool: Lawrence; Lawler, Byrne; Strong, Yeats, Stevenson; Callaghan, Hunt, St John, Smith, Thompson
Leeds United: Sprake; Reaney, Bell; Bremner, Charlton, Hunter; Giles, Storrie, Peacock, Collins, Johanneson
Referee: W. Clements (West Bromwich)

St John meets Callaghan's centre to head past Reaney on the line

1965–6

First Round
Aldershot v Wellingborough T 2–1; Altrincham v Scarborough 6–0; Barrow v Grimsby T 1–2;
Barnet v Dartford 0–2; Bath v Newport Co 2–0; Bournemouth & Bos Ath v Weymouth 0–0, 4–1;
Bradford PA v Hull C 2–3; Brentford v Yeovil T 2–1; Brighton & H Alb v Wisbech T 10–1;
Chesterfield v Chester 0–2; Colchester Utd v QPR 3–3, 0–4; Corby T v Burton Alb 6–3;
Corinthian Casuals v Watford 1–5; Crewe Alex v Scunthorpe Utd 3–0; Darlington v Bradford C 3–2;
Doncaster R v Wigan Ath 2–2, 1–3; Exeter C v Bedford T 1–2; Fleetwood v Rochdale 2–2, 0–5;
Gateshead v Crook T 4–2; Gillingham v Folkestone T 1–2; Grantham v Hendon 4–1; Guildford C v
Wycombe Wand 2–2, 1–0; Hartlepools Utd v Workington 3–1; Leytonstone v Hereford Utd 0–1;
Lincoln C v Barnsley 1–3; Mansfield T v Oldham Ath 1–3; Millwall v Wealdstone 3–1; Oxford Utd v
Port Vale 2–2, 2–3; Peterborough Utd v Kidderminster Harriers 2–1; Reading v Bristol R 3–2;
Romford v Luton T 1–1, 0–1; Shrewsbury T v Torquay Utd 2–1; Southend Utd v Notts Co 3–1;
Southport v Halifax T 2–0; South Shields v York C 3–1; Swindon T v Merthyr Tydfil T 5–1;
Tranmere R v Stockport Co 0–1; Walsall v Swansea T 6–3; Wimbledon v Gravesend & Northfleet
4–1; Wrexham v South Liverpool 4–1

Second Round
Aldershot v Walsall 0–2; Barnsley v Grimsby T 1–1, 0–2; Bournemouth & Bos Ath v Bath C 5–3;
Brighton & H Alb v Bedford T 1–1, 1–2; Chester v Wigan Ath 2–1; Corby T v Luton T 2–2, 1–0;
Crewe Alex v South Shields 3–1; Darlington v Oldham Ath 0–1; Gateshead v Hull C 0–4; Grantham
v Swindon T 1–6; Hartlepools Utd v Wrexham 2–0; Hereford Utd v Millwall 1–0; Port Vale v
Dartford 1–0; QPR v Guildford C 3–0; Reading v Brentford 5–0; Rochdale v Altrincham 1–3;
Shrewsbury T v Peterborough Utd 3–2; Southend Utd v Watford 2–1; Southport v Stockport Co
3–3, 2–0; Wimbledon v Folkestone T 0–1

Third Round
EVERTON v Sunderland 3–0; Bedford T v Hereford Utd 2–1; Swindon T v Coventry C 1–2;
Folkestone T v Crewe Alex 1–5; Blackpool v Man C 1–1, 1–3; Grimsby T v Portsmouth 0–0, 3–1;
Birmingham C v Bristol C 3–2; Aston Villa v Leicester C 1–2; Derby Co v Man Utd 2–5;
Rotherham Utd v Southend Utd 3–2; Wolves v Altrincham 5–0; Sheff Utd v Fulham 3–1;
Bolton Wand v WBA 3–0; Charlton Ath v PNE 2–3; Spurs v Middlesbro 4–0;
Bournemouth & Bos Ath v Burnley 1–1, 0–7; Liverpool v Chelsea 1–2; Leeds Utd v Bury 6–0;
QPR v Shrewsbury T 0–0, 0–1; Carlisle Utd v Crystal Palace 3–0; Hull C v Southampton 1–0;
Northampton T v Nott'm Forest 1–2; Southport v Ipswich T 0–0, 3–2; Cardiff C v Port Vale 2–1;
Leyton Orient v Norwich C 1–3; Stoke C v Walsall 0–2; Oldham Ath v W. Ham 2–2, 1–2;
Blackburn R v Arsenal 3–0; Plymouth Arg v Corby T 6–0; Huddersfield v Hartlepools Utd 3–1;
Chester v Newcastle Utd 1–3; Reading v SHEFF WED 2–3

Fourth Round
Bedford T v EVERTON 0–3; Crewe Alex v Coventry C 1–1, 1–4; Man C v Grimsby T 2–0;
Birmingham C v Leicester C 1–2; Man Utd v Rotherham Utd 0–0, 1–0; Wolves v Sheff Utd 3–0;
Bolton Wand v PNE 1–1, 2–3; Spurs v Burnley 4–3; Chelsea v Leeds Utd 1–0; Shrewsbury T v
Carlisle Utd 0–0, 1–1, 4–3; Hull C v Nott'm Forest 2–0; Southport v Cardiff C 2–0; Norwich C v
Walsall 3–2; W. Ham v Blackburn R 3–3, 1–4; Plymouth Arg v Huddersfield T 0–2; Newcastle Utd v
SHEFF WED 1–2

Fifth Round
EVERTON v Coventry C 3–0; Man C v Leicester C 2–2, 1–0; Wolves v Man Utd 2–4; PNE v Spurs
2–1; Chelsea v Shrewsbury T 3–2; Hull C v Southport 2–0; Norwich C v Blackburn R 2–2, 2–3;
Huddersfield T v SHEFF WED 1–2

Sixth Round
Man C v EVERTON 0–0, 0–0, 0–2; PNE v Man Utd 1–1, 1–3; Chelsea v Hull C 2–2, 3–1;
Blackburn R v SHEFF WED 1–2

Semi-Final
EVERTON v Man Utd 1–0; Chelsea v SHEFF WED 0–2

EVERTON **3**
SHEFFIELD WEDNESDAY **2**

This Final will be remembered, along with the 'Matthews Final' of 1953, for a dramatic recovery by an apparently beaten team. In a match of extremes of elation and disappointment, and an exciting contrast of styles, Everton scored three times in sixteen minutes to win 3–2 after being two goals in arrears with two-thirds of the game gone.

Wednesday, underrated in advance, dictated the tempo in the first half and had the boost of an early goal. McCalliog's slightly mistimed shot from Ford's square pass was deflected past West into the net after only four minutes.

Everton might have had a penalty when Springett seemed to bring down Young, and just after half-time Springett made a superb one-handed save from the same player's hard, knee-high shot.

Five minutes later Wednesday were two up through Ford, and they were now calmly and authoritatively in control. Then a young Cornishman, Trebilcock, playing in only his second Cup match, changed the pattern of the game with a brace of goals inside five minutes. Now, with the scores level, it was the Everton style that seemed more appropriate to the occasion.

Wednesday half-back Young failed to control a bouncing ball in midfield, and immediately Temple was racing away towards goal with the ball at his feet, swerving slightly before driving the ball past Springett as he came out.

Everton: West; Wright, Wilson; Gabriel, Labone, Harris; Scott, Trebilcock, Young, Harvey, Temple
Sheffield Wednesday: Springett; Smith, Megson; Eustace, Ellis, Young; Pugh, Fantham, McCalliog, Ford, Quinn
Referee: J. K. Taylor (Wolverhampton)

Springett dives too late to prevent Trebilcock's shot from going in

1966–7

First Round
Aldershot v Torquay Utd 2–1; Ashford v Cambridge C 4–1; Barnsley v Southport 3–1; Bath C v Sutton Utd 1–0; Bishop Auckland v Blyth Spartans 1–1, 0–0, 3–3, 4–1; Bournemouth & Bos Ath v Welton R 3–0; Bradford PA v Witton Alb 3–2; Bradford C v Port Vale 1–2; Brentford v Chelmsford C 1–0; Chester v Middlesbro 2–5; Crewe Alex v Grimsby T 1–1, 1–0; Darlington v Stockport Co 0–0, 1–1, 4–2; Enfield v Chesham Utd 6–0; Exeter C v Luton T 1–1, 0–2; Folkestone T v Swansea T 2–2, 2–7; Gainsboro Tr v Colchester Utd 0–1; Gillingham v Tamworth 4–1; Grantham v Wimbledon 2–1; Halifax T v Doncaster R 2–2, 3–1; Hendon v Reading 1–3; Horsham v Swindon T 0–3; Leyton Orient v Lowestoft 2–1; Lincoln C v Scunthorpe Utd 3–4; Mansfield T v Bangor C 4–1; Newport Co v Brighton & Hove Alb 1–2; Oldham Ath v Notts Co 3–1; Oxford C v Bristol R 2–2, 0–4; Peterborough Utd v Hereford Utd 4–1; QPR v Poole T 3–2; Rochdale v Barrow 1–3; South Shields v Workington 1–4; Shrewsbury T v Hartlepools Utd 5–2; Tranmere R v Wigan Ath 1–1, 1–0; Walsall v St Neots T 2–0; Watford v Southend Utd 1–0; Wealdstone v Nuneaton Borough 0–2; Wrexham v Chesterfield 3–2; Wycombe Wand v Bedford T 1–1, 3–3, 1–1, 2–3; Yeovil T v Oxford Utd 1–3; York C v Morecambe 0–0, 1–1, 1–0

Second Round
Aldershot v Reading 1–0; Barnsley v Port Vale 1–1, 3–0; Barrow v Tranmere R 2–1; Bath C v Brighton & H Alb 0–5; Bishop Auckland v Halifax T 0–0, 0–7; Bradford PA v Workington 3–0; Bristol R v Luton T 3–2; Colchester Utd v Peterborough Utd 0–3; Crewe Alex v Darlington 2–1; Enfield v Watford 2–4; Grantham v Oldham Ath 0–4; Leyton Orient v Brentford 0–0, 1–3; Mansfield T v Scunthorpe Utd 2–1; Middlesbro v York C 1–1, 0–0, 4–1; Nuneaton Borough v Swansea T 2–0; Oxford Utd v Bedford T 1–1, 0–1; QPR v Bournemouth & Bos Ath 2–0; Shrewsbury T v Wrexham 5–1; Swindon T v Ashford 5–0; Walsall v Gillingham 3–1

Third Round
Huddersfield T v CHELSEA 1–2; Aldershot v Brighton & H Alb 0–0, 1–3; Bradford PA v Fulham 1–3; Charlton Ath v Sheff Utd 0–1; Man Utd v Stoke C 2–0; Norwich C v Derby Co 3–0; Sheff Wed v QPR 3–0; Mansfield T v Middlesbro 2–0; Sunderland v Brentford 5–2; Bedford T v Peterborough Utd 2–6; Leeds Utd v Crystal Palace 3–0; Northampton T v WBA 1–3; Barnsley v Cardiff C 1–1, 1–2; Man C v Leicester C 2–1; Ipswich T v Shrewsbury T 4–1; Blackburn R v Carlisle Utd 1–2; Nott'm Forest v Plymouth Arg 2–1; Coventry C v Newcastle Utd 3–4; W. Ham v Swindon T 3–3, 1–3; Bury v Walsall 2–0; Oldham Ath v Wolves 2–2, 1–4; Burnley v Everton 0–0, 1–2; Watford v Liverpool 0–0, 1–3; PNE v Aston Villa 0–1; Nuneaton Borough v Rotherham Utd 1–1, 0–1; Birmingham C v Blackpool 2–1; Bolton Wand v Crewe Alex 1–0; Bristol R v Arsenal 0–3; Halifax T v Bristol C 1–1, 1–4; Barrow v Southampton 2–2, 0–3; Hull C v Portsmouth 1–1, 2–2, 1–3; Millwall v SPURS 0–0, 0–1

Fourth Round
Brighton & H Alb v CHELSEA 1–1, 0–4; Fulham v Sheff Utd 1–1, 1–3; Man Utd v Norwich C 1–2; Sheff Wed v Mansfield T 4–0; Sunderland v Peterborough Utd 7–1; Leeds Utd v WBA 5–0; Cardiff C v Man C 1–1, 1–3; Ipswich T v Carlisle Utd 2–0; Nott'm Forest v Newcastle Utd 3–0; Swindon T v Bury 2–1; Wolves v Everton 1–1, 1–3; Liverpool v Aston Villa 1–0; Rotherham Utd v Birmingham C 0–0, 1–2; Bolton Wand v Arsenal 0–0, 0–3; Bristol C v Southampton 1–0; SPURS v Portsmouth 3–1

Fifth Round
CHELSEA v Sheff Utd 2–0; Norwich C v Sheff Wed 1–3; Sunderland v Leeds Utd 1–1, 1–1, 1–2; Man C v Ipswich T 1–1, 3–0; Nott'm Forest v Swindon T 0–0, 1–1, 3–0; Everton v Liverpool 1–0; Birmingham C v Arsenal 1–0; SPURS v Bristol C 2–0

Sixth Round
CHELSEA v Sheff Wed 1–0; Leeds Utd v Man C 1–0; Nott'm Forest v Everton 3–2; Birmingham C v SPURS 0–0, 0–6

Semi-Final
CHELSEA v Leeds Utd 1–0; Nott'm Forest v SPURS 1–2

TOTTENHAM HOTSPUR **2**
CHELSEA **1**

Tottenham won the first all-London Final more easily than the 2—1 score suggests. The two sides matched each other in fitness, but Tottenham's greater skill and their ability to muster more men in attack prevailed over Chelsea's admirable energy and persistence.

There were a few startling moments before the first goal came, just before half-time. Robertson's powerful left-foot volley in the fourteenth minute was turned expertly round the post by Bonetti, and a similar Robertson effort shortly afterwards just cleared the bar. For Chelsea, Cooke's fine shot at the end of a superb dodging run was punched over by Jennings.

Then, on half-time, Tottenham scored. It was a case of third time lucky for Robertson, their Scottish international right-winger, as he cracked the ball, again left-footed, low past Bonetti's right hand after Harris had got in the way of Mullery's pile-driver from outside the area.

While still never reaching their peaks, the Tottenham players remained markedly superior in the second half, and they effectively clinched the Cup with a second goal after sixty-eight minutes. Robertson helped on Mackay's long throw-in from the left, and Saul, pivoting quickly and instinctively, hooked the ball in.

The pace dropped as Tottenham casually began to roll their passes, working in neat squares and triangles. With five minutes to go Tambling headed a goal for Chelsea, but they had left it too late to save the match.

Tottenham Hotspur: Jennings; Kinnear, Knowles; Mullery, England, Mackay; Robertson, Greaves, Gilzean, Venables, Saul. Sub: Jones
Chelsea: Bonetti; Harris (A.), McCreadie; Hollins, Hinton, Harris (R.); Cooke, Baldwin, Hateley, Tambling, Boyle. Sub: Kirkup
Referee: K. Dagnall (Bolton)

Greaves and Venables signal Robertson's goal for Spurs

1967–8

First Round
Arnold v Bristol R 0–3; Barrow v Oldham Ath 2–0; Bournemouth & Bos Ath v Northampton T 2–0; Bradford C v Wrexham 7–1; Brentford v Guildford C 2–2, 1–2; Brighton & H Alb v Southend Utd 1–0; Chelmsford C v Oxford Utd 3–3, 3–3, 1–0; Chesterfield v Barnsley 2–0; Corby T v Boston Utd 0–3; Dagenham v Tonbridge 1–0; Goole T v Spennymoor Utd 0–0, 1–3; Grantham v Altrincham 0–3; Grimsby T v Bradford PA 1–1, 1–4; Halifax T v Crewe Alex 3–2; Hartlepools Utd v Bury 2–3; Hereford Utd v Barnet 3–2; Leytonstone v Walsall 0–1; Lowestoft T v Watford 0–1; Newport Co v Gillingham 3–0; Nuneaton Borough v Exeter C 0–0, 0–0, 0–1; Peterborough Utd v Falmouth 5–2; Oxford C v Luton T 1–2; Port Vale v Chester 1–2; Reading v Aldershot 6–2; Runcorn v Notts Co 1–0; Ryhope CW v Workington 0–1; Scunthorpe Utd v Skelmersdale Utd 2–0; Shrewsbury T v Darlington 3–0; Southport v Lincoln C 3–1; Stockport Co v Macclesfield T 1–1, 1–2; Swansea T v Enfield 2–0; Swindon T v Salisbury 4–0; Torquay Utd v Colchester Utd 1–1, 1–2; Tow Law T v Mansfield T 5–1; Tranmere R v Rochdale 5–1; Walthamstow Ave v Kidderminster Harriers 2–1; Weymouth v Leyton Orient 0–2; Wimbledon v Romford 3–0; Yeovil T v Margate 1–3; York C v Doncaster R 0–1

Second Round
Altrincham v Barrow 1–2; Boston Utd v Leyton Orient 1–1, 1–2; Bradford PA v Tranmere R 2–3; Bradford C v Bury 2–3; Chelmsford C v Colchester Utd 0–2; Chester v Chesterfield 0–1; Doncaster R v Workington 1–1, 2–1; Exeter C v Walsall 1–3; Guildford C v Newport Co 0–1; Halifax T v Scunthorpe Utd 1–0; Macclesfield T v Spennymoor Utd 2–0; Margate v Peterborough Utd 0–4; Reading v Dagenham 1–1, 1–0; Southport v Runcorn 4–2; Swansea T v Brighton & H Alb 2–1; Swindon T v Lincoln C 3–2; Tow Law T v Shrewsbury T 1–1, 2–6; Walthamstow Ave v Bournemouth & Bos Ath 1–3; Watford v Hereford Utd 3–0; Wimbledon v Bristol R 0–4

Third Round
Southport v EVERTON 0–1; Newcastle Utd v Carlisle Utd 0–1; Coventry C v Charlton Ath 3–0; Tranmere R v Huddersfield T 2–1; Aston Villa v Millwall 3–0; Rotherham Utd v Wolves 1–0; Man C v Reading 0–0, 7–0; Barrow v Leicester C 1–2; Leeds Utd v Derby Co 2–0; Nott'm Forest v Bolton Wand 4–2; Middlesbro v Hull C 1–1, 2–2, 1–0; Bristol C v Bristol R 0–0, 2–1; Stoke C v Cardiff C 4–1; Burnley v W. Ham 1–3; Watford v Sheff Utd 0–1; Blackpool v Chesterfield 2–1; Doncaster R v Swansea T 0–2; Shrewsbury T v Arsenal 1–1, 0–2; Halifax T v Birmingham C 2–4; Leyton Orient v Bury 1–0; Sheff Wed v Plymouth Arg 3–0; Swindon T v Blackburn R 1–0; Chelsea v Ipswich T 3–0; Norwich C v Sunderland 1–1, 1–0; Man Utd v Spurs 2–2, 0–1; QPR v PNE 1–3; Walsall v Crystal Palace 1–1, 2–1; Bournemouth & Bos Ath v Liverpool 0–0, 1–4; Fulham v Macclesfield T 4–2; Peterborough Utd v Portsmouth 0–1; Southampton v Newport Co 1–1, 3–2; Colchester Utd v WBA 1–1, 0–4

Fourth Round
Carlisle Utd v EVERTON 0–2; Coventry C v Tranmere R 1–1, 0–2; Aston Villa v Rotherham Utd 0–1; Man C v Leicester C 0–0, 3–4; Leeds Utd v Nott'm Forest 2–1; Middlesbro v Bristol C 1–1, 1–2; Stoke C v W. Ham 0–3; Sheff Utd v Blackpool 2–1; Swansea T v Arsenal 0–1; Birmingham C v Leyton Orient 3–0; Sheff Wed v Swindon T 2–1; Chelsea v Norwich C 1–0; Spurs v PNE 3–1; Walsall v Liverpool 0–0, 2–5; Fulham v Portsmouth 0–0, 0–1; WBA v Southampton 1–1, 3–2

Fifth Round
EVERTON v Tranmere R 2–0; Rotherham Utd v Leicester C 1–1, 0–2; Leeds Utd v Bristol C 2–0; W. Ham v Sheff Utd 1–2; Arsenal v Birmingham C 1–1, 1–2; Sheff Wed v Chelsea 2–2, 0–2; Spurs v Liverpool 1–1, 1–2; Portsmouth v WBA 1–2

Sixth Round
Leicester C v EVERTON 1–3; Leeds Utd v Sheff Utd 1–0; Birmingham C v Chelsea 1–0; WBA v Liverpool 0–0, 1–1, 2–1

Semi-Final
EVERTON v Leeds Utd 1–0; Birmingham C v WBA 0–2

WEST BROMWICH ALBION **1**
EVERTON **0**

Through the first ninety minutes of this match Everton were the better organized and showed more aggression, but Albion took their chance in extra time and a Final dominated by cautious defence was settled by Astle's ninety-third minute goal.

In a depressing first half littered with trips, body-checks and sliding tackles, there were still moments of tension. Lovett was too slow to take advantage of a chance in front of the Everton goal, Husband's hasty shot for Everton went just wide and the tireless Ball set up shots for Kendall and Morrissey which almost counted.

Everton's best period came in the middle of the second half. Kaye was forced to head Royle's effort off the line with Osborne beaten, and Ball got in the way when Royle might have scored with a header. Albion's defence held out, and they improvised some swift counter-attacks.

Everton had their great chance with five minutes to go, but Husband, standing unmarked only six yards out, headed Morrissey's centre over the top.

An Astle double-strike in the first period of extra time won the match for Albion. His first attempt, right-footed, rebounded from Harvey, and he hit a second shot instantly and precisely with his left foot into the top corner. Astle had scored in every round, and Albion had equalled Newcastle's record of appearing in ten Finals.

West Bromwich Albion: Osborne; Fraser, Williams; Brown, Talbut, Kaye; Lovett, Collard, Astle, Hope, Clark. Sub: Clarke
Everton: West; Wright, Wilson; Kendall, Labone, Harvey; Husband, Ball, Royle, Hurst, Morrissey. Sub: Kenyon
Referee: L. Callaghan (Merthyr Tydfil)

Astle (No 9) slams the ball high into the net

1968–9

First Round
Altrincham v Crewe Alex 0–1; Bangor C v Morecambe 2–3; Barnet v Brentwood T 1–1, 0–1; Barnsley v Rochdale 0–0, 1–0; Bilston v Halifax T 1–3; Bradford C v Chester 1–2; Brentford v Woking 2–0; Brighton & H Alb v Kidderminster Harriers 2–2, 1–0; Bristol R v Peterborough Utd 3–1; Bury T v Bournemouth & Bos Ath 0–0, 0–3; Canterbury C v Swindon T 0–1; Cheltenham T v Watford 0–4; Chesterfield v Skelmersdale Utd 2–0; Colchester Utd v Chesham Utd 5–0; Darlington v Grimsby T 2–0; Dartford v Aldershot 3–1; Doncaster R v Notts Co 1–0; Exeter C v Newport Co 0–0, 3–1; Goole T v Barrow 1–3; Grantham v Chelmsford C 2–1; Hartlepool Utd v Rotherham Utd 1–1, 0–3; Hereford Utd v Torquay Utd 0–0, 2–4; Leytonstone v Walsall 0–1; Luton T v Ware 6–1; Macclesfield T v Lincoln C 1–3; Mansfield T v Tow Law T 4–1; Northampton T v Margate 3–1; Orient v Gillingham 1–1, 0–2; Oxford C v Swansea T 2–3; Reading v Plymouth Arg 1–0; Shrewsbury T v Port Vale 1–1, 1–3; Southend Utd v King's Lynn 9–0; South Shields v York C 0–6; Stockport Co v Bradford PA 3–0; Tranmere R v Southport 0–1; Waterlooville v Kettering T 1–2; Wealdstone v St Albans C 1–1, 0–1; Weymouth v Yeovil T 2–1; Workington v Scunthorpe Utd 2–0; Wrexham v Oldham Ath 4–2

Second Round
Bournemouth & Bos Ath v Bristol R 0–0, 0–1; Brighton & H Alb v Northampton T 1–2; Chester v Lincoln C 1–1, 1–2; Chesterfield v Wrexham 2–1; Colchester Utd v Exeter C 0–1; Darlington v Barnsley 0–0, 0–1; Doncaster R v Southport 2–1; Grantham v Swindon T 0–2; Halifax T v Crewe Alex 1–1, 3–1; Kettering T v Dartford 5–0; Luton T v Gillingham 3–1; Port Vale v Workington 0–0, 2–1; Reading v Torquay Utd 0–0, 2–1; Rotherham Utd v Mansfield T 2–2, 0–1; St Albans C v Walsall 1–1, 1–3; Southend Utd v Brentwood T 10–1; Stockport Co v Barrow 2–0; Watford v Brentford 1–0; Weymouth v Swansea T 1–1, 0–2; York C v Morecambe 2–0

Third Round
MAN C v Luton T 1–0; Newcastle Utd v Reading 4–0; Blackburn R v Stockport Co 2–0; Portsmouth v Chesterfield 3–0; Walsall v Spurs 0–1; Hull C v Wolves 1–3; Oxford Utd v Southampton 1–1, 0–2; Aston Villa v QPR 2–1; Sheff Wed v Leeds Utd 1–1, 3–1; Birmingham C v Lincoln C 2–1; Exeter C v Man Utd 1–3; Watford v Port Vale 2–0; Everton v Ipswich T 2–1; Coventry C v Blackpool 3–1; Bolton Wand v Northampton T 2–1; Bristol R v Kettering T 1–1, 2–1; PNE v Nott'm Forest 3–0; Chelsea v Carlisle Utd 2–0; York C v Stoke C 0–2; Swansea T v Halifax T 0–1; Sunderland v Fulham 1–4; WBA v Norwich C 3–0; Cardiff C v Arsenal 0–0, 0–2; Charlton Ath v Crystal Palace 0–0, 2–0; Mansfield T v Sheffield Utd 2–1; Swindon T v Southend Utd 0–2; Bury v Huddersfield T 1–2; W. Ham v Bristol C 3–2; Liverpool v Doncaster R 2–0; Burnley v Derby Co 3–1; Middlesbro v Millwall 1–1, 0–1; Barnsley v LEICESTER C 1–1, 1–2

Fourth Round
Newcastle Utd v MAN C 0–0, 0–2; Blackburn R v Portsmouth 4–0; Spurs v Wolves 2–1; Southampton v Aston Villa 2–2, 1–2; Sheff Wed v Birmingham C 2–2, 1–2; Man Utd v Watford 1–1, 2–0; Everton v Coventry C 2–0; Bolton Wand v Bristol R 1–2; PNE v Chelsea 0–0, 1–2; Stoke C v Halifax T 1–1, 3–0; Fulham v WBA 1–2; Arsenal v Charlton Ath 2–0; Mansfield T v Southend Utd 2–1; Huddersfield T v W. Ham 0–2; Liverpool v Burnley 2–1; Millwall v LEICESTER C 0–1

Fifth Round
Blackburn R v MAN C 1–4; Spurs v Aston Villa 3–2; Birmingham C v Man Utd 2–2, 2–6; Everton v Bristol R 1–0; Chelsea v Stoke C 3–2; WBA v Arsenal 1–0; Mansfield T v W. Ham 3–0; LEICESTER C v Liverpool 0–0, 1–0

Sixth Round
MAN C v Spurs 1–0; Man Utd v Everton 0–1; Chelsea v WBA 1–2; Mansfield T v LEICESTER C 0–1

Semi-Final
MAN C v Everton 1–0; WBA v LEICESTER C 0–1

MANCHESTER CITY **1**
LEICESTER CITY **0**

Manchester City lived up to their reputation for skilful attacking football, Leicester rose above the standard implied by their twenty-first position in the First Division, and between them they produced an open and exciting Final. Both sides took risks and missed chances, and the match was settled by a single goal scored by Manchester City's Neil Young in the first half.

Poor Leicester – it was their third Final of the decade and they lost all three. But Manchester's narrow win was well-deserved because they were the better organized, their attacks built from depth, and they relied less on the ability of outstanding individuals.

Clarke had an outstanding game for Leicester and came close to scoring in his first characteristic burst. After a fast dribble along the eighteen-yard line he let go a hard drive to the top right-hand corner for Dowd to tip it spectacularly round the post.

Sliding desperately in towards goal, Leicester full-back Rodrigues sliced wide from two yards out. Three minutes later Manchester scored. Summerbee survived tackles from Nish and Woollett by the dead-ball line on the right and sent a low, firm pass back to Young, who shot high into the net past Shilton from near the penalty-spot. Leicester continued to look dangerous in attack after the break, but the equalizer wouldn't come.

Manchester City: Dowd; Book, Pardoe; Doyle, Booth, Oakes; Summerbee, Bell, Lee, Young, Coleman. Sub: Connor
Leicester City: Shilton; Rodrigues, Nish; Roberts, Woollett, Cross; Fern, Gibson, Lochhead, Clarke, Glover. Sub: Manley
Referee: G. McCabe (Sheffield)

Young's shot beats Shilton's dive

1969–70

First Round
Alfreton T v Barrow 1–1, 0–0, 2–2, 0–2; Bangor C v Kirkby T 6–0; Bournemouth & Bos Ath v Luton T 1–1, 1–3; Bradford C v Grimsby T 2–1; Brentford v Plymouth Arg 0–0, 0–2; Brentwood T v Reading 1–0; Brighton & H Alb v Enfield 2–1; Bury v Mansfield T 2–2, 0–2; Chelmsford C v Hereford Utd 1–2; Cheltenham T v Oxford C 0–2; Dagenham v Sutton Utd 0–1; Darlington v Barnsley 0–0, 0–2; Doncaster R v Crewe Alex 1–1, 1–0; Exeter C v Fulham 2–0; Falmouth v Peterborough Utd 1–4; Halifax T v Chester 3–-3, 0–1; Hartlepool Utd v North Shields 3–0; Hendon v Carshalton Ath 5–3; Hillingdon Borough v Wimbledon 2–0; Kettering T v Swansea T 0–2; Lincoln C v Southport 2–0; Macclesfield T v Scunthorpe Utd 1–1, 2–4; Margate v Aldershot 2–7; Newport Co v Colchester Utd 2–1; Northampton T v Weymouth 0–0, 3–1; Notts Co v Rotherham Utd 0–3; Oldham Ath v Grantham 3–1; Southend Utd v Gillingham 0–0, 0–2; South Shields v Bradford PA 2–1; Spennymoor Utd v Wrexham 1–4; Stockport Co v Mossley 1–1, 1–0; Tamworth v Torquay Utd 2–1; Telford Utd v Bristol R 0–3; Tranmere R v Chesterfield 3–0; Walton & Hersham v Barnet 0–1; Walsall v Orient 0–0, 2–0; Wigan Ath v Port Vale 1–1, 2–2, 0–1; Workington v Rochdale 2–1; Yeovil T v Shrewsbury T 2–3; York C v Whitby T 2–0

Second Round
Aldershot v Bristol R 3–1; Bangor C v York C 0–0, 0–2; Barnet v Sutton Utd 0–2; Barnsley v Barrow 3–0; Bradford C v Lincoln C 3–0; Brighton & H Alb v Walsall 1–1, 1–1, 1–2; Chester v Doncaster R 1–1, 2–0; Gillingham v Tamworth 6–0; Hartlepool Utd v Wrexham 0–1; Hendon v Brentwood T 0–2; Hillingdon Borough v Luton T 2–1; Newport Co v Hereford Utd 2–1; Northampton T v Exeter C 1–1, 0–0, 2–1; Oxford C v Swansea T 1–5; Peterborough Utd v Plymouth Arg 2–0; Port Vale v Tranmere R 2–2, 1–3; Rotherham Utd v Workington 3–0; Shrewsbury T v Mansfield T 1–2; South Shields v Oldham Ath 0–0, 2–1; Stockport Co v Scunthorpe Utd 0–0, 0–4

Third Round
CHELSEA v Birmingham C 3–0; Burnley v Wolves 3–0; Bradford C v Spurs 2–2, 0–5; Crystal Palace v Walsall 2–0; Aston Villa v Charlton Ath 1–1, 0–1; QPR v South Shields 4–1; PNE v Derby Co 1–1, 1–4; Sheff Utd v Everton 2–1; Bolton Wand v Watford 1–2; Oxford Utd v Stoke C 0–0, 2–3; Gillingham v Newport Co 1–0; Rotherham Utd v Peterborough Utd 0–1; Coventry C v Liverpool 1–1, 0–3; Norwich C v Wrexham 1–2; Southampton v Newcastle Utd 3–0; Leicester C v Sunderland 1–0; Portsmouth v Tranmere R 1–2; Brentwood T v Northampton T 0–1; Ipswich T v Man Utd 0–1; Hull C v Man C 0–1; Nott'm Forest v Carlisle Utd 0–0, 1–2; Huddersfield T v Aldershot 1–1, 1–3; Middlesbro v W. Ham 2–1; York C v Cardiff C 1–1, 1–1, 3–1; Blackburn R v Swindon T 0–4; Chester v Bristol C 2–1; Sheff Wed v WBA 2–1; Scunthorpe Utd v Millwall 2–1; Arsenal v Blackpool 1–1, 2–3; Mansfield T v Barnsley 3–2; Hillingdon Borough v Sutton Utd 0–0, 1–4; LEEDS UTD v Swansea T 2–1

Fourth Round
CHELSEA v Burnley 2–2, 3–1; Spurs v Crystal Palace 0–0, 0–1; Charlton Ath v QPR 2–3; Derby Co v Sheff Utd 3–0; Watford v Stoke C 1–0; Gillingham v Peterborough Utd 5–1; Liverpool v Wrexham 3–1; Southampton v Leicester C 1–1, 2–4; Tranmere R v Northampton T 0–0, 1–2; Man Utd v Man C 3–0; Carlisle Utd v Aldershot 2–2, 4–1; Middlesbro v York C 4–1; Swindon T v Chester 4–2; Sheff Wed v Scunthorpe Utd 1–2; Blackpool v Mansfield T 0–2; Sutton Utd v LEEDS UTD 0–6

Fifth Round
Crystal Palace v CHELSEA 1–4; QPR v Derby Co 1–0; Watford v Gillingham 2–1; Liverpool v Leicester C 0–0, 2–0; Northampton T v Man Utd 2–8; Carlisle Utd v Middlesbro 1–2; Swindon T v Scunthorpe Utd 3–1; LEEDS UTD v Mansfield T 2–0

Sixth Round
QPR v CHELSEA 2–4; Watford v Liverpool 1–0; Middlesbro v Man Utd 1–1, 1–2; Swindon T v LEEDS UTD 0–2

Semi-Final
CHELSEA v Watford 5–1; Man Utd v LEEDS UTD 0–0, 0–0, 0–1

Third-Place Final
Man Utd v Watford 2–0 (at Highbury)

CHELSEA **2**
LEEDS UNITED **1** (after a 2–2 draw)

A Wembley Final ended all-square for the first time as Chelsea and Leeds fought out a 2–2 draw after extra time.

Leeds were superior in organization and team skill, but Chelsea would never admit the possibility of defeat, and their eventual victory after four hours' football was a triumph of spirit and determination.

The Wembley pitch was in poor condition – wet, patchy and sanded – and when Jack Charlton's downward header after fifteen minutes failed to bounce, McCreadie kicked over it, and the ball rolled over the line.

Houseman's ordinary-looking shot from twenty yards went through Sprake's arms for a Chelsea equalizer just before half-time. Jones' eighty-fourth minute goal would have been a killing blow to most teams, but in two minutes Hutchinson headed Chelsea level again.

The replay at Old Trafford was a less distinguished affair but again marked by long periods of domination by Leeds. For all of the first half – during which Clarke had beaten three men in a swerving run and put Jones through to score – and for a good part of the second, Leeds were quicker to the ball, covered better and passed more accurately. Twelve minutes from time Chelsea, incredibly, equalized again through Osgood.

Chelsea went ahead for the first time in the first period of extra time, Webb heading through from Hutchinson's long throw, and the Londoners held on to win.

Chelsea: Bonetti; Webb, McCreadie; Hollins, Dempsey, Harris; Baldwin, Houseman, Osgood, Hutchinson, Cooke. Sub: Hinton
Leeds United: Sprake (Harvey in replay); Madeley, Cooper; Bremner, Charlton, Hunter; Lorimer, Clarke, Jones, Giles, Gray. Sub: Bates

Sprake allows Houseman's speculative shot to slip through his hands

1970–1

First Round

Bradford C v Macclesfield T 3–2; Gt Harwood v Rotherham Utd 2–6; Lincoln C v Barrow 2–1; Grimsby T v Bury 0–1; Grantham v Stockport Co 2–1; Scarborough v Workington 2–3; Barnsley v Bradford PA 1–0; Mansfield T v Wrexham 2–0; PNE v Chester 1–1, 0–1; Chesterfield v Halifax T 2–0; Southport v Boston Utd 0–2; Tamworth v York C 0–0, 0–5; Rhyl v Hartlepool Utd 1–0; Crewe Alex v Doncaster R 0–0, 3–1; Darlington v Bangor C 5–1; South Shields v Wigan Ath 1–1, 0–2; Rochdale v Oldham Ath 2–0; Notts Co v Port Vale 1–0; Tranmere R v Scunthorpe Utd 1–1, 0–0, 0–1; Peterborough Utd v Wimbledon 3–1; Fulham v Bristol R 1–2; Dagenham v Margate 2–0; Yeovil T v Aveley 1–0; Brighton & H Alb v Cheltenham T 4–0; Colchester Utd v Ringmer 3–0; Swansea C v Exeter C 4–1; Hereford Utd v Northampton T 2–2, 2–1; Walsall v Plymouth Arg 3–0; Torquay Utd v Aston Villa 3–1; Crawley T v Chelmsford C 1–1, 1–6; Oxford C v Bournemouth & Bos Ath 1–1, 1–8; Southend Utd v Weymouth 7–0; Minehead v Shrewsbury T 1–2; Enfield v Cambridge Utd 0–1; Hendon v Aldershot 0–2; Wycombe Wand v Slough T 1–1, 0–1; Brentford v Gillingham 2–1; Walton & Hersham v Telford Utd 2–5; Barnet v Newport Co 6–1; Reading v Bishop's Stortford 6–1

Second Round

Rhyl v Barnsley 0–0, 1–1, 2–0; Lincoln C v Bradford C 2–2, 2–2, 4–1; Chester v Crewe Alex 1–0; Grantham v Rotherham Utd 1–4; Wigan Ath v Peterborough Utd 2–1; Boston Utd v York C 1–2; Bury v Notts Co 1–1, 0–3; Chesterfield v Workington 0–0, 2–3; Scunthorpe Utd v Mansfield T 3–0; Darlington v Rochdale 0–2; Hereford Utd v Brighton & H Alb 1–2; Chelmsford C v Torquay Utd 0–1; Southend Utd v Dagenham 1–0; Shrewsbury T v Reading 2–2, 0–1; Slough T v Barnet 0–1; Aldershot v Bristol R 1–1, 3–1; Swansea C v Telford Utd 6–2; Bournemouth & Bos Ath v Yeovil T 0–1; Colchester Utd v Cambridge Utd 3–0; Brentford v Walsall 1–0

Third Round

Yeovil T v ARSENAL 0–3; Portsmouth v Sheff Utd 2–0; Crystal Palace v Chelsea 2–2, 0–2; Man C v Wigan Ath 1–0; Leicester C v Notts Co 2–0; Torquay Utd v Lincoln C 4–3; Oxford Utd v Burnley 3–0; Watford v Reading 5–0; Hull C v Charlton Ath 3–0; Blackpool v W. Ham 4–0; Cardiff C v Brighton & H Alb 1–0; Workington v Brentford 0–1; Stoke C v Millwall 2–1; Huddersfield T v Birmingham C 1–1, 2–0; WBA v Scunthorpe Utd 0–0, 3–1; Newcastle Utd v Ipswich T 1–1, 1–2; Everton v Blackburn R 2–0; Man Utd v Middlesbro 0–0, 1–2; Chester v Derby Co 1–2; Wolves v Norwich C 5–1; Rochdale v Coventry C 2–1; Barnet v Colchester Utd 0–1; Rotherham Utd v Leeds Utd 0–0, 2–3; QPR v Swindon T 1–2; Southend Utd v Carlisle Utd 0–3; Spurs v Sheff Wed 4–1; Nott'm Forest v Luton T 1–1, 4–3; Sunderland v Orient 0–3; York C v Bolton Wand 2–0; Southampton v Bristol C 3–0; Swansea C v Rhyl 6–1; LIVERPOOL v Aldershot 1–0

Fourth Round

Portsmouth v ARSENAL 1–1, 2–3; Chelsea v Man C 0–3; Leicester C v Torquay Utd 3–0; Oxford Utd v Watford 1–1, 2–1; Hull C v Blackpool 2–0; Cardiff C v Brentford 0–2; Stoke C v Huddersfield T 3–3, 0–0, 1–0; WBA v Ipswich T 1–1, 0–3; Everton v Middlesbro 3–0; Derby Co v Wolves 2–1; Rochdale v Colchester Utd 3–3, 0–5; Leeds Utd v Swindon T 4–0; Carlisle Utd v Spurs 2–3; Nott'm Forest v Orient 1–1, 1–0; York C v Southampton 3–3, 2–3; LIVERPOOL v Swansea C 3–0

Fifth Round

Man C v ARSENAL 1–2; Leicester C v Oxford Utd 1–1, 3–1; Hull C v Brentford 2–1; Stoke C v Ipswich T 0–0, 1–0; Everton v Derby Co 1–0; Colchester Utd v Leeds Utd 3–2; Spurs v Nott'm Forest 2–1; LIVERPOOL v Southampton 1–0

Sixth Round

Leicester C v ARSENAL 0–0, 0–1; Hull C v Stoke C 2–3; Everton v Colchester Utd 5–0; LIVERPOOL v Spurs 0–0, 1–0

Semi-Final

ARSENAL v Stoke C 2–2, 2–0; Everton v LIVERPOOL 1–2

Third Place Final

Stoke C v Everton 3–2 (at Crystal Palace)

ARSENAL **2**
LIVERPOOL **1**

Arsenal won the Cup deservedly in their triumphal 'double' season, but, having made and missed chances in the first ninety minutes, found themselves forced to fight against the shock of being a goal down in extra time to a brave and skilful Liverpool team.

Liverpool spent most of the first half well up in their opponents' half, but rarely did they prompt Wilson in the Arsenal goal to sharp action, and Arsenal, counter-punching, looked more dangerous on the break.

Three times in the second half Arsenal went close to settling the matter within the ninety minutes. Kennedy flicked Radford's pass wide from five yards and Graham first headed against the bar and then had another header blocked on the line by Lindsay.

Liverpool scored two minutes into extra time, Heighway surprisingly beating Wilson at the near post, and that, it seemed, must be the end of Arsenal's 'double' hopes.

After Wilson's critical one-handed save from Hall's volley, Arsenal found the heart to fight back, and, with eleven minutes of extra time gone, they drew level. Radford's overhead kick into the Liverpool goalmouth was rolled gently goalwards by substitute Kelly, and Graham appeared to run the ball over the line. The goal was later credited to Kelly.

Now the scene was set for George's magnificent winner – an unstoppable twenty-five yard drive, shoulder-high, to Clemence's right.

Arsenal: Wilson; Rice, McNab; Storey, McLintock, Simpson; Armstrong, Graham, Radford, Kennedy, George. Sub: Kelly
Liverpool: Clemence; Lawler, Lindsay; Smith, Lloyd, Hughes; Callaghan, Evans, Heighway, Toshack, Hall. Sub: Thompson
Referee: N. Burtenshaw (Gorleston)

Kelly (third from left) squeezes home Arsenal's equalizer in extra time

1971–2

First Round
Barrow v Darlington 0–2; Bolton Wand v Bangor C 3–0; Chesterfield v Oldham Ath 3–0; Crewe Alex v Blyth Spartans 0–1; Hartlepool Utd v Scarborough 6–1; Frickley Colliery v Rotherham Utd 2–2, 0–4; Ellesmere Port T v Boston Utd 0–3; Lincoln C v Bury 1–2; Blackburn R v Port Vale 1–1, 1–3; Wigan Ath v Halifax T 2–1; Southport v Workington 1–3; South Shields v Scunthorpe Utd 3–3, 3–2; Rochdale v Barnsley 1–3; Rossendale Utd v Altrincham 1–0; Chester v Mansfield T 1–1, 3–4; Doncaster R v Stockport Co 1–2; Wrexham v Bradford C 5–1; York C v Grimsby T 4–2; Skelmersdale Utd v Tranmere R 0–4; Basingstoke T v Northampton T 1–5; Enfield v Maidenhead Utd 2–0; Crawley T v Exeter C 0–0, 0–2; AFC Bournemouth v Margate 11–0; Colchester Utd v Shrewsbury T 1–4; Redditch Utd v Peterborough Utd 1–1, 0–6; Swansea C v Brentford 1–1, 3–2; Witney T v Romford 0–3; Notts Co v Newport Co 6–0; King's Lynn v Hereford Utd 0–0, 0–1; Kettering T v Barnet 2–4; Gillingham v Plymouth Arg 3–2; Walsall v Dagenham 4–1; Aldershot v Alvechurch 4–2; Cambridge Utd v Weymouth 2–1; Bridgwater T v Reading 0–3; Torquay Utd v Nuneaton Borough 1–0; Guildford C v Dover 0–0, 2–0; Southend Utd v Aston Villa 1–0; Brighton & H Alb v Hillingdon Borough 7–1; Bristol R v Telford Utd 3–0

Second Round
Boston Utd v Hartlepool Utd 2–1; Rotherham Utd v York C 1–1, 3–2; Barnsley v Chesterfield 0–0, 0–1; Port Vale v Darlington 1–0; Workington v Bury 1–3; South Shields v Notts Co 1–3; Mansfield T v Tranmere R 2–2, 2–4; Blyth Spartans v Stockport Co 1–0; Wrexham v Wigan Ath 4–0; Rossendale Utd v Bolton Wand 1–4; Brighton & H Alb v Walsall 1–1, 1–2; Barnet v Torquay Utd 1–4; Peterborough Utd v Enfield 4–0; Hereford Utd v Northampton T 0–0, 2–2, 2–1; Shrewsbury T v Guildford C 2–1; Bristol R v Cambridge Utd 3–0; Swansea C v Exeter C 0–0, 1–0; Romford v Gillingham 0–1; Reading v Aldershot 1–0; AFC Bournemouth v Southend Utd 2–0

Third Round
LEEDS UTD v Bristol R 4–1; Oxford Utd v Liverpool 0–3; Sheff Utd v Cardiff C 1–3; Sunderland v Sheff Wed 3–0; Crystal Palace v Everton 2–2, 2–3; Walsall v AFC Bournemouth 1–0; Spurs v Carlisle Utd 1–1, 3–1; Bury v Rotherham Utd 1–1, 1–2; Birmingham C v Port Vale 3–0; Peterborough Utd v Ipswich T 0–2; Boston Utd v Portsmouth 0–1; Swansea C v Gillingham 1–0; Burnley v Huddersfield T 0–1; QPR v Fulham 1–1, 1–2; Newcastle Utd v Hereford Utd 2–2, 1–2; W. Ham v Luton T 2–1; PNE v Bristol C 4–2; Southampton v Man Utd 1–1, 1–4; Millwall v Nott'm Forest 3–1; Man C v Middlesbro 1–1, 0–1; Charlton Ath v Tranmere R 0–0, 2–4; Stoke C v Chesterfield 2–1; WBA v Coventry C 1–2; Norwich C v Hull C 0–3; Wolves v Leicester C 1–1, 0–2; Orient v Wrexham 3–0; Blackpool v Chelsea 0–1; Bolton Wand v Torquay Utd 2–1; Derby Co v Shrewsbury T 2–0; Watford v Notts Co 1–4; Blyth Spartans v Reading 2–2, 1–6; Swindon T v ARSENAL 0–2

Fourth Round
Liverpool v LEEDS UTD 0–0, 0–2; Cardiff C v Sunderland 1–1, 1–1, 3–1; Everton v Walsall 2–1; Spurs v Rotherham Utd 2–0; Birmingham C v Ipswich T 1–0; Portsmouth v Swansea C 2–0; Huddersfield T v Fulham 3–0; Hereford Utd v W. Ham 0–0, 1–3; PNE v Man Utd 0–2; Millwall v Middlesbro 2–2, 1–2; Tranmere R v Stoke C 2–2, 0–2; Coventry C v Hull C 0–1; Leicester C v Orient 0–2; Chelsea v Bolton Wand 3–0; Derby Co v Notts Co 6–0; Reading v ARSENAL 1–2

Fifth Round
Cardiff C v LEEDS UTD 0–2; Everton v Spurs 0–2; Birmingham C v Portsmouth 3–1; Huddersfield T v W. Ham 4–2; Man Utd v Middlesbro 0–0, 3–0; Stoke C v Hull C 4–1; Orient v Chelsea 3–2; Derby C v ARSENAL 2–2, 0–0, 0–1

Sixth Round
LEEDS UTD v Spurs 2–1; Birmingham C v Huddersfield T 3–1; Man Utd v Stoke C 1–1, 1–2; Orient v ARSENAL 0–1

Semi-Final
LEEDS UTD v Birmingham C 3–0; Stoke C v ARSENAL 1–1, 1–2

LEEDS UNITED **1**
ARSENAL **0**

Leeds United beat Arsenal by the only goal of the match and thereby frustrated the Londoners' ambition to become the third club to return as Cup-holders and win again for the second successive year, as Newcastle had done in 1952 and Tottenham in 1962.

Leeds were the better team all through. Their back four had no trouble in mastering the Arsenal attacks and obliterating the threat posed by strikers George and Radford. By contrast, the Leeds front runners, Jones and Clarke, continually harassed the Arsenal defence.

The Jones–Clarke combination produced a goal in the fifty-third minute. Jones sent across a hard, shoulder-high centre and 'Sniffer' Clarke headed powerfully past Barnett's left hand from fifteen yards.

A match that often fell below the highest level began badly with a foul by Clarke on Ball in the first five seconds and the first of four bookings – McNab for bringing down Lorimer – as early as the second minute. Neither side played consistently up to their capabilities, yet both had their moments. George's fierce volley cannoned back off the bar for Arsenal, and both Clarke and Lorimer struck the woodwork for Leeds.

Leeds' jubilation at the end was tempered by a last-minute injury to Jones, who fell awkwardly near the touch-line and had to be helped up the steps to receive his winners' medal.

Leeds United: Harvey; Reaney, Madeley; Bremner, Charlton, Hunter; Lorimer, Clarke, Jones, Giles, Gray. Sub: Bates
Arsenal: Barnett; Rice, McNab; Storey, McLintock, Simpson; Armstrong, Ball, George, Radford, Graham. Sub: Kennedy
Referee: D. W. Smith (Stonehouse)

Clarke's header is on its way into the net

1972–3

First Round
Doncaster R v Bury 3–1; South Liverpool v Tranmere R 0–2; Hartlepool Utd v Scunthorpe Utd 0–0, 0–0, 1–2; Stockport Co v Workington 1–0; Spennymoor Utd v Shrewsbury T 1–1, 1–3; Chesterfield v Rhyl 4–2; Altrincham v Notts Co 0–1; Port Vale v Southport 2–1; Rochdale v Bangor C 1–2; Boston Utd v Lancaster C 1–2; Bolton Wand v Chester 1–1, 1–0; Crewe Alex v Stafford Rangers 1–0; Darlington v Wrexham 1–1, 0–5; Lincoln C v Blackburn R 2–2, 1–4; Barnsley v Halifax T 1–1, 1–2; Bradford C v Grantham 3–0; Oldham Ath v Scarborough 1–1, 1–2; Grimsby T v Wigan Ath 2–1; York C v Mansfield T 2–1; Rotherham Utd v South Shields 4–0; Yeovil T v Brentford 2–1; Margate v Swansea C 1–0; Peterborough Utd v Northampton T 1–0; Banbury Utd v Barnet 0–2; Walton & Hersham v Exeter C 2–1; Tonbridge v Charlton Ath 0–5; Walsall v Kettering T 3–3, 2–1; Newport Co v Alton T 5–1; Hayes v Bristol R 1–0; Watford v Guildford C 4–2; Torquay Utd v Hereford Utd 3–0; Barnstaple T v Bilston 0–2; AFC Bournemouth v Cambridge Utd 5–1; Colchester Utd v Bognor Regis T 6–0; Southend Utd v Aldershot 0–2; Enfield v Bishop's Stortford 1–1, 0–1; Telford Utd v Nuneaton Borough 3–2; Chelmsford C v Hillingdon Borough 2–0; Plymouth Arg v Hendon 1–0; Gillingham v Reading 1–2

Second Round
Bolton Wand v Shrewsbury T 3–0; Grimsby T v Chesterfield 2–2, 1–0; Blackburn R v Crewe Alex 0–1; Rotherham Utd v Stockport Co 0–1; Scarborough v Doncaster R 1–2; Port Vale v Wrexham 1–0; Bradford C v Tranmere R 2–1; Bangor C v York C 2–3; Notts Co v Lancaster C 2–1; Scunthorpe Utd v Halifax T 3–2; Barnet v Bilston 1–1, 1–0; Walsall v Charlton Ath 1–2; AFC Bournemouth v Colchester Utd 0–0, 2–0; Walton & Hersham v Margate 0–1; Reading v Hayes 0–0, 1–0; Watford v Aldershot 2–0; Chelmsford C v Telford Utd 5–0; Yeovil T v Plymouth Arg 0–2; Torquay Utd v Newport Co 0–1; Bishop's Stortford v Peterborough U 2–2, 1–3

Third Round
Notts Co v SUNDERLAND 1–1, 0–2; Reading v Doncaster R 2–0; Burnley v Liverpool 0–0, 0–3; Man C v Stoke C 3–2; Charlton Ath v Bolton Wand 1–1, 0–4; Scunthorpe Utd v Cardiff C 2–3; Newcastle Utd v AFC Bournemouth 2–0; Luton T v Crewe Alex 2–0; Sheff Wed v Fulham 2–0; Crystal Palace v Southampton 2–0; Brighton & H Alb v Chelsea 0–2; Chelmsford C v Ipswich T 1–3; Carlisle Utd v Huddersfield T 2–2, 1–0; Watford v Sheff Utd 0–1; Arsenal v Leicester C 2–2, 2–1; Bradford C v Blackpool 2–1; Wolves v Man Utd 1–0; Portsmouth v Bristol C 1–1, 1–4; Everton v Aston Villa 3–2; Millwall v Newport Co 3–0; Orient v Coventry C 1–4; Grimsby T v PNE 0–0, 1–0; Stockport Co v Hull C 0–0, 0–2; Port Vale v W. Ham 0–1; Peterborough Utd v Derby Co 0–1; Margate v Spurs 0–6; York C v Oxford Utd 0–1; QPR v Barnet 0–0, 3–0; WBA v Nott'm Forest 1–1, 0–0, 3–1; Swindon T v Birmingham C 2–0; Plymouth Arg v Middlesbro 1–0; Norwich C v LEEDS UTD 1–1, 1–1, 0–5

Fourth Round
SUNDERLAND v Reading 1–1, 3–1; Liverpool v Man C 0–0, 0–2; Bolton Wand v Cardiff C 2–2, 1–1, 1–0; Newcastle Utd v Luton T 0–2; Sheff Wed v Crystal Palace 1–1, 1–1, 3–2; Chelsea v Ipswich T 2–0; Carlisle Utd v Sheff Utd 2–1; Arsenal v Bradford C 2–0; Wolves v Bristol C 1–0; Everton v Millwall 0–2; Coventry C v Grimsby T 1–0; Hull C v W. Ham 1–0; Derby Co v Spurs 1–1, 5–3; Oxford Utd v QPR 0–2; WBA v Swindon T 2–0; LEEDS UTD v Plymouth Arg 2–1

Fifth Round
Man C v SUNDERLAND 2–2, 1–3; Bolton Wand v Luton T 0–1; Sheff Wed v Chelsea 1–2; Carlisle Utd v Arsenal 1–2; Wolves v Millwall 1–0; Coventry C v Hull C 3–0; Derby Co v QPR 4–2; LEEDS UTD v WBA 2–0

Sixth Round
SUNDERLAND v Luton T 2–0; Chelsea v Arsenal 2–2, 1–2; Wolves v Coventry C 2–0; Derby Co v LEEDS UTD 0–1

Semi-Final
SUNDERLAND v Arsenal 2–1; Wolves v LEEDS UTD 0–1

SUNDERLAND **1**
LEEDS UNITED **0**

Leeds United, a team boasting ten internationals, and experienced in the conflicts of First Division and European competition, came to Wembley in 1973 as Cup-holders for their third Final in four years. Sunderland came from the Second Division, and when their new manager Bob Stokoe took over during the season, they were third from bottom. No Second Division side had won the Cup for more than forty years, and very few people outside Sunderland gave them any chance of winning.

Leeds had their chances, and might have been ahead before Porterfield scored the goal that won the Cup for Sunderland, on the half-hour from Hughes's corner. As one would have expected, Leeds fought back with a determined assault just before half-time and with increasingly desperate power through the second half.

The turning point of the match came in the seventieth minute, when Sunderland goalkeeper Jim Montgomery dived to palm away a header across goal from Cherry – straight into the path of Lorimer, one of the most powerful and accurate shots in the game. Lorimer blasted the ball goal-wards, but Montgomery, miraculously, managed to divert the ball on to the underside of the bar. It bounced clear.

There were more anxious moments for Sunderland, but they held out. More than that, Halom almost made it 2–0 in the last seconds, forcing a brilliant save from Harvey.

Sunderland: Montgomery; Malone, Guthrie; Horswill, Watson, Pitt; Kerr, Hughes, Halom, Porterfield, Tueart. Sub: Young
Leeds United: Harvey; Reaney, Cherry; Bremner, Madeley, Hunter; Lorimer, Clarke, Jones, Giles, Gray (E.). Sub: Yorath
Referee: K. Burns (Stourbridge)

Montgomery about to make a miraculous save from Lorimer

1973–4

First Round
Crewe Alex v Scarborough 0–0, 1–2; Chesterfield v Barnsley 0–0, 1–2; Bradford C v Workington 2–0; Runcorn v Grimsby T 0–1; Rochdale v South Shields 2–0; Stockport Co v Port Vale 0–1; Huddersfield T v Wigan Ath 2–0; Alfreton T v Blyth Spartans 0–0, 1–2; Altrincham v Hartlepool Utd 2–0; Formby v Oldham Ath 0–2; York C v Mansfield T 0–0, 3–5; Rotherham Utd v Southport 2–1; Chester v Telford Utd 1–0; Halifax T v Frickley Coll 6–1; Tranmere R v Bury 2–1; Willington v Blackburn R 0–0, 1–6; Doncaster R v Lincoln C 1–0; Scunthorpe Utd v Darlington 1–0; Wrexham v Shrewsbury T 1–1, 1–0; King's Lynn v Wimbledon 1–0; Wycombe Wand v Newport Co 3–1; Walsall v Swansea C 1–0; Hitchin T v Guildford C 1–1, 4–1; Plymouth Arg v Brentford 2–1; Weymouth v Merthyr Tydfil 0–1; AFC Bournemouth v Charlton Ath 1–0; Hillingdon Borough v Grantham 0–4; Reading v Slough T 3–0; Banbury Utd v Northampton T 0–2, 2–3; Hereford Utd v Torquay Utd 3–1; Dagenham v Aldershot 0–4; Exeter C v Alvechurch 0–1; Cambridge Utd v Gillingham 3–2; Boston Utd v Hayes 0–0, 2–1; Colchester Utd v Peterborough Utd 2–3; Watford v Chelmsford C 1–0; Bideford v Bristol R 0–2; Hendon v Leytonstone 3–0; Southend Utd v Boreham Wood 3–0; Walton & Hersham v Brighton & H Alb 0–0, 4–0

Second Round
Halifax T v Oldham Ath 0–1; Grantham v Rochdale 1–1, 5–3; Port Vale v Scarborough 2–1; Barnsley v Bradford C 1–1, 1–2; Chester v Huddersfield T 3–2; Mansfield T v Scunthorpe Utd 1–1, 0–1; Blackburn R v Altrincham 0–0, 2–0; Grimsby T v Blyth Spartans 1–1, 2–0; Doncaster R v Tranmere R 3–0; Wrexham v Rotherham Utd 3–0; Northampton T v Bristol R 1–2; Wycombe Wand v Peterborough Utd 1–3; Aldershot v Cambridge Utd 1–2; Hereford Utd v Walton & Hersham 3–0; Boston Utd v Hitchin T 1–0; Alvechurch v King's Lynn 6–1; Merthyr Tydfil v Hendon 0–3; Watford v AFC Bournemouth 0–1; Plymouth Arg v Walsall 1–0; Southend Utd v Reading 2–0

Third Round
LIVERPOOL v Doncaster R 2–2, 2–0; Carlisle Utd v Sunderland 0–0, 1–0; Man Utd v Plymouth Arg 1–0; Ipswich T v Sheff Utd 3–2; W. Ham v Hereford Utd 1–1, 1–2; Bristol C v Hull C 1–1, 1–0; Peterborough Utd v Southend Utd 3–1; Wolves v Leeds Utd 1–1, 0–1; Sheff Wed v Coventry C 0–0, 1–3; Derby Co v Boston Utd 0–0, 6–1; Chelsea v QPR 0–0, 0–1; Birmingham C v Cardiff C 5–2; Port Vale v Luton T 1–1, 2–4; Bradford C v Alvechurch 4–2; Fulham v PNE 1–0; Leicester C v Spurs 1–0; Cambridge Utd v Oldham Ath 2–2, 3–3, 1–2; Grimsby T v Burnley 0–2; Norwich C v Arsenal 0–1; Aston Villa v Chester 3–1; Southampton v Blackpool 2–1; Bolton Wand v Stoke C 3–2; Crystal Palace v Wrexham 0–2; Grantham v Middlesbro 0–2; Nott'm Forest v Bristol R 4–3; Oxford Utd v Man C 2–5; Portsmouth v Swindon T 3–3, 1–0; Orient v AFC Bournemouth 2–1; Everton v Blackburn R 3–0; WBA v Notts Co 4–0; Millwall v Scunthorpe Utd 1–1, 0–1; NEWCASTLE UTD v Hendon 1–1, 4–0

Fourth Round
LIVERPOOL v Carlisle Utd 0–0, 2–0; Man Utd v Ipswich T 0–1; Hereford Utd v Bristol C 0–1; Peterborough Utd v Leeds Utd 1–4; Coventry C v Derby Co 0–0, 1–0; QPR v Birmingham C 2–0; Luton T v Bradford C 3–0; Fulham v Leicester C 1–1, 1–2; Oldham Ath v Burnley 1–4; Arsenal v Aston Villa 1–1, 0–2; Southampton v Bolton Wand 3–3, 2–0; Wrexham v Middlesbro 1–0; Nott'm Forest v Man C 4–1; Portsmouth v Orient 0–0, 1–1, 2–0; Everton v WBA 0–0, 0–1; NEWCASTLE UTD v Scunthorpe Utd 1–1, 3–0

Fifth Round
LIVERPOOL v Ipswich T 2–0; Bristol C v Leeds Utd 1–1, 1–0; Coventry C v QPR 0–0, 2–3; Luton T v Leicester C 0–4; Burnley v Aston Villa 1–0; Southampton v Wrexham 0–1; Nott'm Forest v Portsmouth 1–0; WBA v NEWCASTLE UTD 0–3

Sixth Round
Bristol C v LIVERPOOL 0–1; QPR v Leicester C 0–2; Burnley v Wrexham 1–0; NEWCASTLE UTD v Nott'm Forest 4–3, 0–0, 1–0 (FA ordered replay. Both replays at Goodison Park)

Semi-Final
LIVERPOOL v Leicester C 0–0, 3–1; Burnley v NEWCASTLE UTD 0–2

LIVERPOOL **3**
NEWCASTLE UNITED **0**

At half-time, with no goals scored, this was theoretically still a match either side might have won – but this was an illusion. Liverpool, composed and well organized, had been steadily tightening their grip.

Newcastle had moments of promise in the first half. In midfield, McDermott played with skill and determination, Smith was at his jinking best and Hibbitt showed excellent positioning and passing.

But Newcastle were disappointing in attack. Tudor's early enthusiasm seemed to fall away after some early frustrations, and MacDonald, the flamboyant 'Supermac', was handled coolly by the Liverpool defence and caused them few problems.

Liverpool's first sharp attacks before half-time were a foretaste of their liberation and Newcastle's destruction in the second half. Lindsay's fifty-first minute 'goal' looked perfect but was disallowed. Seven minutes later Smith centred from the right, Hall dummied, and Keegan drove the ball high past McFaul. That one counted.

There was a little left now of Newcastle, and Liverpool were running wild. From Toshack's back-header, Heighway gathered the ball, rounded Moncur and shot just inside McFaul's right-hand post.

The game was over, but there was still one goal to come. The build-up involved eleven uninterrupted passes, and the last, Smith's from near the deadball-line, found its way to Keegan in front of goal: 3–0.

Liverpool: Clemence; Smith, Lindsay; Thompson, Cormack, Hughes; Keegan, Hall, Heighway, Toshack, Callaghan. Sub: Lawler
Newcastle United: McFaul; Clark, Kennedy; McDermott, Howard, Moncur; Smith, Cassidy, MacDonald, Tudor, Hibbitt. Sub: Gibb
Referee: G. C. Kew (Amersham)

Keegan (No 7) turns away after scoring Liverpool's third

1974–5

First Round
Crewe Alex v Gateshead Utd 2–2, 0–1; Matlock T v Blackburn R 1–4; Hartlepool Utd v Bradford C 1–0; Stockport Co v Stafford Rangers 0–0, 0–1; Farsley Celtic v Tranmere R 0–2; Mansfield T v Wrexham 3–1; Rochdale v Marine 0–0, 2–1; Blyth Spartans v PNE 1–1, 1–5; Bury v Southport 4–2; Chesterfield v Boston Utd 3–1; Oswestry T v Doncaster R 1–3; Bishop Auckland v Morecambe 5–0; Grimsby T v Huddersfield T 1–0; Barnsley v Halifax T 1–2; Shrewsbury T v Wigan Ath 1–1, 1–2; Darlington v Workington 1–0; Rotherham Utd v Chester 1–0; Port Vale v Lincoln C 2–2, 0–2; Scunthorpe Utd v Altrincham 1–1, 1–3; Hereford Utd v Gillingham 1–0; Wimbledon v Bath C 1–0; AP Leamington v Southend Utd 1–2; Romford v Ilford 0–2; Wycombe Wand v Cheltenham T 3–1; Hitchin T v Cambridge Utd 0–0, 0–3; Torquay Utd v Northampton T 0–1; Ashford T v Walsall 1–3; Slough T v Brentford 1–4; Swindon T v Reading 4–0; Bishop's Stortford v Leatherhead 0–0, 0–2; Tooting and Mitcham v Crystal Palace 1–2; Exeter C v Newport Co 1–2; Swansea C v Kettering T 1–1, 1–3; Brighton & H Alb v Aldershot 3–1; Chelmsford C v Charlton Ath 0–1; Nuneaton Borough v Maidstone Utd 2–2, 0–2; AFC Bournemouth v Southwick 5–0; Dartford v Plymouth Arg 2–3; Peterborough Utd v Weymouth 0–0, 3–3, 3–0; Watford v Colchester Utd 0–1

Second Round
Chesterfield v Doncaster R 1–0; Rotherham Utd v Northampton T 2–1; Grimsby T v Bury 1–1, 1–2; Hartlepool Utd v Lincoln C 0–0, 0–1; Stafford Rangers v Halifax T 2–1; Altrincham v Gateshead Utd 3–0; Bishop Auckland v PNE 0–2; Wigan Ath v Mansfield T 1–1, 1–3; Blackburn R v Darlington 1–0; Rochdale v Tranmere R 1–1, 0–1; Cambridge Utd v Hereford Utd 2–0; Leatherhead v Colchester Utd 1–0; Brighton & H Alb v Brentford 1–0; Ilford v Southend Utd 0–2; Wimbledon v Kettering T 2–0; Plymouth Arg v Crystal Palace 2–1; Swindon T v Maidstone Utd 3–1; Newport Co v Walsall 1–3; Peterborough Utd v Charlton Ath 3–0; Wycombe Wand v AFC Bournemouth 0–0, 2–1

Third Round
Southampton v W. HAM 1–2; Swindon T v Lincoln C 2–0; Southend v QPR 2–2, 0–2; Notts Co v Portsmouth 3–1; Coventry C v Norwich C 2–0; Arsenal v York C 1–1, 3–1; Leicester C v Oxford Utd 3–1; Brighton & H Alb v Leatherhead 0–1; Wolves v Ipswich T 1–2; Liverpool v Stoke C 2–0; Oldham Ath v Aston Villa 0–3; Sheff Utd v Bristol C 2–0; Orient v Derby Co 2–2, 1–2; Blackburn R v Bristol R 1–2; Leeds Utd v Cardiff C 4–1; Burnley v Wimbledon 0–1; Chelsea v Sheff Wed 3–2; Luton T v Birmingham C 0–1; Man Utd v Walsall 0–0, 2–3; Man C v Newcastle Utd 0–2; Stafford Rangers v Rotherham Utd 0–0, 2–0; Peterborough Utd v Tranmere R 1–0; Wycombe Wand v Middlesbro 0–0, 0–1; Sunderland v Chesterfield 2–0; Bury v Millwall 2–2, 1–1, 2–0; Mansfield T v Cambridge Utd 1–0; PNE v Carlisle Utd 0–1; Bolton Wand v WBA 0–0, 0–4; Plymouth Arg v Blackpool 2–0; Everton v Altrincham 1–1, 2–0; Nott'm Forest v Spurs 1–1, 1–0; FULHAM v Hull C 1–1, 2–2, 1–0

Fourth Round
W. HAM v Swindon T 1–1, 2–1; QPR v Notts Co 3–0; Coventry C v Arsenal 1–1, 0–3; Leatherhead v Leicester C 2–3; Ipswich T v Liverpool 1–0; Aston Villa v Sheff Utd 4–1; Derby Co v Bristol R 2–0; Leeds Utd v Wimbledon 0–0, 1–0; Chelsea v Birmingham C 0–1; Walsall v Newcastle Utd 1–0; Stafford Rangers v Peterborough Utd 1–2; Middlesbro v Sunderland 3–1; Bury v Mansfield T 1–2; Carlisle Utd v WBA 3–2; Plymouth Arg v Everton 1–3; FULHAM v Nott'm Forest 0–0, 1–1, 1–1, 2–1

Fifth Round
W. HAM v QPR 2–1; Arsenal v Leicester C 0–0, 1–1, 1–0; Ipswich T v Aston Villa 3–2; Derby Co v Leeds Utd 0–1; Birmingham C v Walsall 2–1; Peterborough Utd v Middlesbro 1–1, 0–2; Mansfield T v Carlisle Utd 0–1; Everton v FULHAM 1–2

Sixth Round
Arsenal v W. HAM 0–2; Ipswich T v Leeds Utd 0–0, 1–1, 0–0, 3–2; Birmingham C v Middlesbro 1–0; Carlisle Utd v FULHAM 0–1

Semi-Final
W. HAM v Ipswich T 0–0, 2–1; Birmingham C v FULHAM 1–1, 0–1

WEST HAM UNITED **2**
FULHAM **0**

The Hammers won only thirteen of their forty-two League games during the 1974–5 season, while Fulham averaged exactly one point per match in the Second Division. Yet, such is the fickleness of Cup fortune that, against all the odds, two moderate sides fought their way to the Final.

It was a Final abounding in personalities. Alec Stock and Ron Greenwood had already tasted Cup success at Wembley as managers, and Fulham could boast two ex-England captains in Mullery and Moore.

Fulham looked to be the better side in a dull first half, with the ball rarely in either penalty-area except when defenders passed nervously back to their goalkeepers. Lacey went close with powerful headers from Conway's corner kick and Mullery's free-kick. At the other end Brooking's cracking volley from thirty-five yards soared high over the bar.

West Ham slowly but surely increased the pressure after the interval, and made the vital breakthrough on the hour. Mellor parried Jennings' awkwardly swerving shot and the rebound was gratefully slammed home from six yards by Alan Taylor.

West Ham scored an almost identical goal four minutes later. Mellor failed to make a clean catch from Paddon's hard shot and Taylor again put the ball in.

In a most sporting Final, intelligently refereed by Pat Partridge, neither trainer set foot on the pitch.

West Ham United: Day; McDowell, Lampard; Bonds, Taylor (T.), Lock; Jennings, Paddon, Taylor (A.), Brooking, Holland. Sub: Gould
Fulham: Mellor; Cutbush, Fraser; Mullery, Lacey, Moore; Mitchell, Conway, Busby, Slough, Barrett. Sub: Lloyd
Referee: P. Partridge (Bishop Auckland)

Taylor celebrates his second goal for Hammers

1975–6

First Round

Wigan Ath v Matlock T 4–1; PNE v Scunthorpe Utd 2–1; Sheff Wed v Macclesfield T 3–1; Bury v Doncaster R 4–2; Bradford C v Chesterfield 1–0; Rotherham Utd v Crewe Alex 2–1; Workington v Rochdale 1–1, 1–2; Darlington v Chester 0–0, 0–2; Spennymoor Utd v Southport 4–1; Halifax T v Altrincham 3–1; Rossendale Utd v Shrewsbury T 0–1; Hartlepool Utd v Stockport Co 3–0; Scarborough v Morecambe 2–0; Grantham v Port Vale 2–2, 1–4; Peterborough Utd v Winsford Utd 4–1; Mansfield T v Wrexham 1–1, 1–1, 2–1; AP Leamington v Stafford Rangers 2–3; Marine v Barnsley 3–1; Walsall v Huddersfield T 0–1; Grimsby T v Gateshead Utd 1–3; Boston Utd v Lincoln C 0–1; Coventry Sporting v Tranmere R 2–0; Sutton Utd v AFC Bournemouth 1–1, 0–1; Crystal Palace v Walton & Hersham 1–0; Aldershot v Wealdstone 4–3; Nuneaton Borough v Wimbledon 0–1; Yeovil T v Millwall 1–1, 2–2, 0–1; Colchester Utd v Dover 3–3, 1–4; Weymouth v Gillingham 0–2; Watford v Brighton & H Alb 0–3; Brentford v Northampton T 2–0; Hereford Utd v Torquay Utd 2–0; Wycombe Wand v Bedford T 0–0, 2–2, 2–1; Cardiff C v Exeter C 6–2; Southend Utd v Swansea C 2–0; Dartford v Bishop's Stortford 1–4; Leatherhead v Cambridge Utd 2–0; Newport Co v Swindon T 2–2, 0–3; Romford v Tooting & Mitcham 0–1; Hendon v Reading 1–0

Second Round

Mansfield T v Lincoln C 1–2; Huddersfield T v Port Vale 2–1; Marine v Hartlepool Utd 1–1, 3–6; Stafford Rangers v Halifax T 1–3; Coventry Sporting v Peterborough Utd 0–4; Shrewsbury T v Chester 3–1; Bury v Spennymoor Utd 3–0; Scarborough v PNE 3–2; Gateshead Utd v Rochdale 1–1, 1–3; Sheff Wed v Wigan Ath 2–0; Rotherham Utd v Bradford C 0–3; Southend Utd v Dover 4–1; Cardiff C v Wycombe Wand 1–0; Wimbledon v Brentford 0–2; Gillingham v Brighton & H Alb 0–1; Millwall v Crystal Palace 1–1, 1–2; Aldershot v Bishop's Stortford 2–0; AFC Bournemouth v Hereford Utd 2–2, 0–2; Leatherhead v Tooting & Mitcham 0–0, 1–2; Hendon v Swindon T 0–1

Third Round

SOUTHAMPTON v Aston Villa 1–1, 2–1; Blackpool v Burnley 1–0; WBA V Carlisle Utd 3–1; Aldershot v Lincoln C 1–2; Norwich C v Rochdale 1–1, 0–0, 2–1; Luton T v Blackburn R 2–0; Shrewsbury T v Bradford C 1–2; Swindon T v Tooting & Mitcham 2–2, 1–2; Spurs v Stoke C 1–1, 1–2; Man C v Hartlepool Utd 6–0; Sunderland v Oldham Ath 2–0; Hull C v Plymouth Arg 1–1, 4–1; York C v Hereford Utd 2–1; Chelsea v Bristol R 1–1, 1–0; Notts Co v Leeds Utd 0–1; Scarborough v Crystal Palace 1–2; Derby Co v Everton 2–1; W. Ham v Liverpool 0–2; Southend Utd v Brighton & H Alb 2–1; Orient v Cardiff C 0–1; Fulham v Huddersfield T 2–3; Brentford v Bolton Wand 0–0, 0–2; Coventry C v Bristol C 2–1; QPR v Newcastle Utd 0–0, 1–2; Ipswich T v Halifax T 3–1; Wolves v Arsenal 3–0; Charlton Ath v Sheff Wed 2–1; Portsmouth v Birmingham C 1–1, 1–0; Leicester C v Sheff Utd 3–0; Middlesbro v Bury 0–0, 2–3; Nott'm Forest v Peterborough Utd 0–0, 0–1; MAN UTD v Oxford Utd 2–1

Fourth Round

SOUTHAMPTON v Blackpool 3–1; WBA v Lincoln C 3–2; Norwich C v Luton T 2–0; Bradford C v Tooting & Mitcham 3–1; Stoke C v Man C 1–0; Sunderland v Hull C 1–0; York C v Chelsea 0–2; Leeds Utd v Crystal Palace 0–1; Derby Co v Liverpool 1–0; Southend Utd v Cardiff C 2–0; Huddersfield T v Bolton Wand 0–1; Coventry C v Newcastle Utd 1–1, 0–5; Ipswich T v Wolves 0–0, 0–1; Charlton Ath v Portsmouth 1–1, 3–0; Leicester C v Bury 1–0; MAN UTD v Peterborough Utd 3–1

Fifth Round

WBA v SOUTHAMPTON 1–1, 0–4; Norwich C v Bradford C 1–2; Stoke C v Sunderland 0–0, 1–2; Chelsea v Crystal Palace 2–3; Derby Co v Southend Utd 1–0; Bolton Wand v Newcastle Utd 3–3, 0–0, 1–2; Wolves v Charlton Ath 3–0; Leicester C v MAN UTD 1–2

Sixth Round

Bradford C v SOUTHAMPTON 0–1; Sunderland v Crystal Palace 0–1; Derby Co v Newcastle Utd 4–2; MAN UTD v Wolves 1–1, 3–2

Semi-Final

SOUTHAMPTON v Crystal Palace 2–0; Derby Co v MAN UTD 0–2

SOUTHAMPTON **1**
MANCHESTER UNITED **0**

Southampton, the Second Division underdogs, beat Manchester United, who finished the season third in the First Division, with an eighty-third minute goal by outside-left Bobby Stokes.

From the beginning United played fast, clever football with neat movements sometimes involving six players as the ball was manoeuvred from defence to attack. Southampton, on the other hand, possessed few skilled ball players and relied on long passes up to their twin strike force of Channon and Osgood.

Pearson and Daly missed two golden opportunities to score in the first fifteen minutes, and then Turner brilliantly caught the ball as Hill attempted to lob it over him and denied United what might well have been the vital goal of the whole match.

That save inspired Southampton and the underdogs began to function with increasing conviction. Determined defence kept out United's attacks and Channon then showed his England form as he dashed through the centre and forced Stepney to streak out of his goal to bravely smother his close-range shot.

United had dreadful luck when Macari headed on Coppell's corner and McIlroy headed against the top of a post. Then, with seven minutes to go, Stokes ran on to McCalliog's gem of a through-pass and shot across Stepney into the far corner. Stokes may have been offside, but the TV playback suggested that he wasn't.

Southampton: Turner; Rodrigues, Peach; Holmes, Blyth, Steele; Gilchrist, Channon, Osgood, McCalliog, Stokes. Sub: Fisher
Manchester United: Stepney; Forsyth, Houston; Daly, Greenhoff, Buchan; Coppell, McIlroy, Pearson, Macari, Hill. Sub: McCreery
Referee: C. Thomas (Treorchy)

Stokes shoots past Stepney

1976–7

First Round

Huddersfield T v Mansfield T 0–0, 1–2; Crook T v Nuneaton Borough 1–4; Rotherham Utd v Altrincham 5–0; Droylsden v Grimsby T 0–0, 3–5; Barnsley v Boston Utd 3–1; Rochdale v Northwich Vic 1–1, 0–0, 1–2; Barrow v Goole T 0–2; Scarborough v Darlington 0–0, 1–4; Scunthorpe Utd v Chesterfield 1–2; Walsall v Bradford C 0–0, 2–0; Bury v Workington 6–0; Lincoln C v Morecambe 1–0; Doncaster R v Shrewsbury T 2–2, 3–4; Chester v Hartlepool Utd 1–0; Matlock T v Wigan Ath 2–0; Dudley T v York C 1–1, 1–4; Stafford Rangers v Halifax T 0–0, 0–1; Wrexham v Gateshead Utd 6–0; Tranmere R v Peterborough Utd 0–4; Sheff Wed v Stockport Co 2–0; Southport v Port Vale 1–2; Crewe Alex v PNE 1–1, 2–2, 0–3; Waterlooville v Wycombe Wand 1–2; Aldershot v Portsmouth 1–1, 1–2; Brentford v Chesham Utd 2–0; Reading v Wealdstone 1–0; Gillingham v Watford 0–1; Torquay Utd v Hillingdon Borough 1–2; Swansea C v Minehead 0–1; Tooting & Mitcham Utd v Dartford 4–2; Weymouth v Hitchin T 1–1, 2–2, 3–3, 1–3; AFC Bournemouth v Newport Co 0–0, 0–3; Brighton & H Alb v Crystal Palace 2–2, 1–1, 0–1; Cambridge Utd v Colchester Utd 1–1, 0–2; Wimbledon v Woking 1–0; Swindon T v Bromley 7–0; Exeter C v Southend Utd 1–1, 1–2; Leatherhead v Northampton T 2–0; Enfield v Harwich & Parkeston 0–0, 3–0; Kettering T v Oxford Utd 1–1, 1–0

Seond Round

Bury v Shrewsbury T 0–0, 1–2; Chesterfield v Walsall 1–1, 0–0, 0–1; Darlington v Sheff Wed 1–0; Port Vale v Barnsley 3–0; Northwich Vic v Peterborough Utd 4–0; Wrexham v Goole T 1–1, 1–0; Halifax T v PNE 1–0; Mansfield T v Matlock T 2–5; Lincoln C v Nuneaton Borough 6–0; Rotherham Utd v York C 0–0, 1–1, 2–1; Grimsby T v Chester 0–1; Hillingdon Borough v Watford 2–3; Leatherhead v Wimbledon 1–3; Colchester Utd v Brentford 3–2; Southend Utd v Newport Co 3–0; Portsmouth v Minehead 2–1; Kettering T v Tooting & Mitcham Utd 1–0; Wycombe Wand v Reading 1–2; Hitchin T v Swindon T 1–1, 1–3; Enfield v Crystal Palace 0–4

Third Round

MAN UTD v Walsall 1–0; QPR v Shrewsbury T 2–1; Nott'm Forest v Bristol R 1–1, 1–1, 6–0; Southampton v Chelsea 1–1, 3–0; Leicester C v Aston Villa 0–1; W. Ham v Bolton Wand 2–1; Hull C v Port Vale 1–1, 1–3; Burnley v Lincoln C 2–2, 1–0; Ipswich T v Bristol C 4–1; Wolves v Rotherham Utd 3–2; Southend Utd v Chester 0–4; Halifax T v Luton T 0–1; Birmingham C v Portsmouth 1–0; Leeds Utd v Norwich C 5–2; Sheff Utd v Newcastle Utd 0–0, 1–3; Man C v WBA 1–1, 1–0; Cardiff C v Spurs 1–0; Sunderland v Wrexham 2–2, 0–1; Fulham v Swindon T 3–3, 0–5; Everton v Stoke C 2–0; Kettering T v Colchester Utd 2–3; Blackpool v Derby Co 0–0, 2–3; Charlton Ath v Blackburn R 1–1, 0–2; Darlington v Orient 2–2, 0–0, 0–3; Wimbledon v Middlesbro 0–0, 0–1; Hereford Utd v Reading 1–0; Notts Co v Arsenal 0–1; Coventry C v Millwall 1–0; Northwich Vic v Watford 3–2; Oldham Ath v Plymouth Arg 3–0; Carlisle Utd v Matlock T 5–1; LIVERPOOL v Crystal Palace 0–0, 3–2

Fourth Round

MAN UTD v QPR 1–0; Nott'm Forest v Southampton 3–3, 1–2; Aston Villa v W. Ham 3–0; Port Vale v Burnley 2–1; Ipswich T v Wolves 2–2, 0–1; Chester v Luton T 1–0; Birmingham C v Leeds Utd 1–2; Newcastle Utd v Man C 1–3; Cardiff C v Wrexham 3–2; Swindon T v Everton 2–2, 1–2; Colchester Utd v Derby Co 1–1, 0–1; Blackburn R v Orient 3–0; Middlesbro v Hereford Utd 4–0; Arsenal v Coventry C 3–1; Northwich Vic v Oldham Ath 1–3; LIVERPOOL v Carlisle Utd 3–0

Fifth Round

Southampton v MAN UTD 2–2, 1–2; Aston Villa v Port Vale 3–0; Wolves v Chester 1–0; Leeds Utd v Man C 1–0; Cardiff C v Everton 1–2; Derby Co v Blackburn R 3–1; Middlesbro v Arsenal 4–1; LIVERPOOL v Oldham Ath 3–1

Sixth Round

MAN UTD v Aston Villa 2–1; Wolves v Leeds Utd 0–1; Everton v Derby Co 2–0; LIVERPOOL v Middlesbro 2–0

Semi-Final

MAN UTD v Leeds Utd 2–1; Everton v LIVERPOOL 2–2, 0–3

MANCHESTER UNITED **2**
LIVERPOOL **1**

The proverbial 'luck of the draw' has such an influence on the competition that it is only on rare occasions that the two teams which are, by common consent, the best in the country are able to meet in the Final.

United were determined not to repeat their mediocre display against Southampton in the 1976 Final, while Liverpool came to Wembley with every hope of achieving a thrilling hat-trick of successes – League Championship, FA Cup and European Cup.

Liverpool seemed to be the complete team, with neat flicks and pushes alternating with long sweeping passes out to the wings. For all their midfield pressure, Liverpool rarely looked like scoring in the first half, which finished goalless, though Stepney had been forced to make an unorthodox save with his foot from Kennedy's goalbound header.

The skills of the first half were replaced by the thrills of the second. Within five minutes Greenhoff had flicked McIlroy's pass over Hughes to give Pearson the opportunity to shoot past Clemence – a real body-blow to Liverpool.

Yet, like true champions, Liverpool bounced back with an equalizer only two minutes later. Jones advanced down the left and centred to the edge of the penalty-area, where Case swivelled to hit a magnificent half-volley high into the net to Stepney's left.

An untidy-looking goal three minutes later won the match for United. Macari's shot, going wide, struck Greenhoff's side and looped into the net.

Manchester United: Stepney; Nicholl, Albiston; McIlroy, Greenhoff (B.), Buchan; Coppell, Greenhoff (J.), Pearson, Macari, Hill. Sub: McCreery
Liverpool: Clemence; Neal, Jones; Smith, Kennedy, Hughes; Keegan, Case, Heighway, Johnson, McDermott. Sub: Callaghan
Referee: R. Matthewson (Bolton)

Pearson appears to be nudged in the back by Hughes

1977–8

First Round

Chesterfield v Halifax T 1–0; Wigan Ath v York C 1–0; Workington v Grimsby T 0–2;
Chester v Darlington 4–1; Scarborough v Rochdale 4–2; Tranmere R v Hartlepool Utd 1–1, 1–3;
Blyth Spartans v Burscough 1–0; Barnsley v Huddersfield T 1–0; Rotherham Utd v Mossley 3–0;
Spennymoor Utd v Goole T 3–1; Southport v Runcorn 2–2, 0–1; PNE v Lincoln C 3–2; Sheff Wed v
Bury 1–0; Doncaster R v Shrewsbury T 0–1; Stockport Co v Scunthorpe Utd 3–0; Arnold v Port Vale
0–0, 2–5; Wrexham v Burton Alb 2–0; Carlisle Utd v Stafford Rangers 2–0; Bradford C v
Crewe Alex 0–1; Nuneaton Borough v Oxford Utd 2–0; Wealdstone v Hereford Utd 0–0, 3–2;
Gillingham v Weymouth 1–1, 1–0; Tooting & Mitcham Utd v Northampton T 1–2; Barnet v
Peterborough Utd 1–2; Lowestoft T v Cambridge Utd 0–2; Walsall v Dagenham 1–0; Minehead v
Wycombe Wand 2–0; Brentford v Folkestone & Shepway 2–0; Reading v Aldershot 3–1;
Torquay Utd v Southend Utd 1–2; Bath C v Plymouth Arg 0–0, 0–2; Enfield v Wimbledon 3–0;
Portsmouth v Bideford 3–1; AP Leamington v Enderby T 6–1; Colchester Utd v
AFC Bournemouth 1–1, 0–0, 4–1; Tilbury v Kettering T 2–2, 3–2; Boreham Wood v Swindon T
0–0, 0–2; Newport Co v Exeter C 1–1, 2–4; Leatherhead v Swansea C 0–0, 1–2; Watford v
Hendon 2–0

Second Round

Wigan Ath v Sheff Wed 1–0; Grimsby T v Barnsley 2–0; Shrewsbury T v Stockport Co 1–1, 2–1;
Crewe Alex v Scarborough 0–0, 0–2; Carlisle Utd v Chester 3–1; Blyth Spartans v Chesterfield
1–0; Hartlepool Utd v Runcorn 4–2; Walsall v Port Vale 1–1, 3–1; Rotherham Utd v
Spennymoor Utd 6–0; PNE v Wrexham 0–2; Gillingham v Peterborough Utd 1–1, 0–2;
AP Leamington v Southend Utd 0–0, 0–4; Wealdstone v Reading 2–1; Nuneaton Borough v Tilbury
1–2; Swindon T v Brentford 2–1; Plymouth Arg v Cambridge Utd 1–0; Minehead v Exeter C 0–3;
Portsmouth v Swansea C 2–2, 1–2; Northampton T v Enfield 0–2; Watford v Colchester Utd 2–0

Third Round

Cardiff C v IPSWICH T 0–2; Hartlepool Utd v Crystal Palace 2–1; Sunderland v Bristol R v 0–1;
Grimsby T v Southampton 0–0, 0–0, 1–4; Rotherham Utd v Millwall 1–1, 0–2; Luton T v
Oldham Ath 1–1, 2–1; Brighton & H Alb v Scarborough 3–0; Charlton Ath v Notts Co 0–2; Derby Co
v Southend Utd 3–2; Birmingham C v Wigan Ath 4–0; Carlisle Utd v Man Utd 1–1, 2–4; WBA v
Blackpool 4–1; Nott'm Forest v Swindon T 4–1; Leeds Utd v Man City 1–2; W. Ham v Watford 1–0;
QPR v Wealdstone 4–0; Middlesbro v Coventry C 3–0; Everton v Aston Villa 4–1; Spurs v
Bolton Wand 2–2, 1–2; Mansfield T v Plymouth Arg 1–0; Orient v Norwich C 1–1, 1–0;
Blackburn R v Shrewsbury T 2–1; Chelsea v Liverpool 4–2; Burnley v Fulham 1–0;
Peterborough Utd v Newcastle Utd 1–1, 0–2; Bristol C v Wrexham 4–4, 0–3; Stoke C v Tilbury
4–0; Blyth Spartans v Enfield 1–0; Walsall v Swansea C 4–1; Hull C v Leicester C 0–1; Exeter C v
Wolves 2–2, 1–3; Sheff Utd v ARSENAL 0–5

Fourth Round

IPSWICH T v Hartlepool Utd 4–1; Bristol R v Southampton 2–0; Millwall v Luton T 4–0;
Brighton & H Alb v Notts Co 1–2; Derby Co v Birmingham C 2–1; Man Utd v WBA 1–1, 2–3;
Nott'm Forest v Man C 2–1; W. Ham v QPR 1–1, 1–6; Middlesbro v Everton 3–2; Bolton Wand v
Mansfield T 1–0; Orient v Blackburn R 3–1; Chelsea v Burnley 6–2; Newcastle Utd v Wrexham
2–2, 1–4; Stoke C v Blyth Spartans 2–3; Walsall v Leicester C 1–0; ARSENAL v Wolves 2–1

Fifth Round

Bristol R v IPSWICH T 2–2, 0–3; Millwall v Notts Co 2–1; Derby Co v WBA 2–3;
QPR v Nott'm Forest 1–1, 1–1, 1–3; Middlesbro v Bolton Wand 2–0; Orient v Chelsea 0–0, 2–1;
Wrexham v Blyth Spartans 1–1, 2–1; ARSENAL v Walsall 4–1

Sixth Round

Millwall v IPSWICH T 1–6; WBA v Nott'm Forest 2–0; Middlesbro v Orient 0–0, 1–2;
Wrexham v ARSENAL 2–3

Semi-Final

IPSWICH T v WBA 3–1; Orient v ARSENAL 0–3

IPSWICH TOWN **1**
ARSENAL **0**

Arsenal, though strong favourites, soon began to lose their grip on the game after a promising start had seen them gain two corners in the first two minutes. Some of Ipswich's combined movements were a delight to watch, as they gradually overran Arsenal's midfield. Poor Liam Brady, obviously not fully fit, could do nothing right and was substituted after sixty-six minutes.

In spite of their ever-increasing superiority, the East Anglians had nothing to show for their efforts at half-time. They finally got the breakthrough with just twelve minutes remaining, but before then Ipswich had deserved to score from each of three brilliant second-half moves. Wark crashed a terrific shot against an upright after Woods had rolled the ball into his path, and then a similar Ipswich attack gave Wark the chance to hit the same post with another effort. Soon afterwards Jennings made the save of the afternoon from Burley's header.

With Ipswich beginning to wonder what they had to do to score, the long-expected goal arrived. Inside-left Geddis ran with the ball from near the half-way line and fooled both Hudson and Nelson by feinting to cut inside and then using a sudden burst of speed to go outside them. Young merely cleared Geddis' low cross as far as Osborne, standing ten yards from goal, and he promptly dispatched the ball into the net.

Ipswich Town: Cooper; Burley, Mills; Talbot, Hunter, Beattie; Osborne, Wark, Mariner, Geddis, Woods. Sub: Lambert
Arsenal: Jennings; Rice, Nelson; Price, O'Leary, Young; Brady, Sunderland, MacDonald, Stapleton, Hudson. Sub: Rix
Referee: D. R. G. Nippard (Bournemouth)

A Stapleton drive for Arsenal goes wide

1978–9

First Round

Barnsley v Worksop T 5–1; Stockport Co v Morecambe 5–1; Altrincham v Southport 4–3; Scunthorpe Utd v Sheff Wed 1–1, 0–1; Blackpool v Lincoln C 2–1; Carlisle Utd v Halifax T 1–0; Chester v Runcorn 1–1, 5–0; Bradford C v Port Vale 1–0; Hartlepool Utd v Grimsby T 1–0; Tranmere R v Boston Utd 2–1; Rochdale v Droylsden 0–1; Hull C v Stafford Rangers 2–1; Darlington v Chesterfield 1–1, 1–0; Doncaster R v Huddersfield T 2–1; Rotherham Utd v Workington 3–0; Mansfield T v Shrewsbury T 0–2; Wigan Ath v Bury 2–2, 1–4; York C v Blyth Spartans 1–1, 5–3; Chorley v Scarborough 0–1; Nuneaton Borough v Crewe Alex 0–2; Portsmouth v Northampton T 2–0; Yeovil T v Barking 0–1; Colchester Utd v Oxford Utd 4–2; Gravesend & Northfleet v Wimbledon 0–0, 0–1; Swindon T v March Town Utd 2–0; Southend Utd v Peterborough Utd 3–2; Walsall v Torquay Utd 0–2; Hereford Utd v Newport Co 0–1; Wealdstone v Enfield 0–5; AFC Bournemouth v Hitchin T 2–1; Barnet v Woking 3–3, 3–3, 0–3; Aldershot v Weymouth 1–1, 2–0; Leatherhead v Merthyr Tydfil 2–1; Worcester C v Plymouth Arg 2–0; Maidstone Utd v Wycombe Wand 1–0; Watford v Dagenham 3–0; Dartford v AP Leamington 1–2; Swansea C v Hillingdon Borough 4–1

Second Round

Droylsden v Altrincham 0–2; Barnsley v Rotherham Utd 1–1, 1–2; Doncaster R v Shrewsbury T 0–3; York C v Scarborough 3–0; Darlington v Chester 2–1; Tranmere R v Sheff Wed 1–1, 0–4; Crewe Alex v Hartlepool Utd 0–1; Bury v Blackpool 3–1; Stockport Co v Bradford C 4–2; Carlisle Utd v Hull C 3–0; Barking v Aldershot 1–2; Watford v Southend Utd 1–1, 0–1; Maidstone Utd v Exeter C 1–0; Portsmouth v Reading 0–1; Wimbledon v AFC Bournemouth 1–1, 2–1; Swindon T v Enfield 3–0; Newport Co v Worcester C 0–0, 2–1; Swansea C v Woking 2–2, 5–3; AP Leamington v Torquay Utd 0–1; Leatherhead v Colchester Utd 1–1, 0–4

Third Round

Sheff Wed v ARSENAL 1–1, 1–1, 2–2, 3–3, 0–2; Notts Co v Reading 4–2; Nott'm Forest v Aston Villa 2–0; York C v Luton T 2–0; Hartlepool Utd v Leeds Utd 2–6; Coventry C v WBA 2–2, 0–4; PNE v Derby Co 3–0; Wimbledon v Southampton 0–2; Middlesbro v Crystal Palace 1–1, 0–1; Bristol C v Bolton Wand 3–1; Newcastle Utd v Torquay Utd 3–1; Brighton & H Alb v Wolves 2–3; Sheff Utd v Aldershot 0–0, 0–1; Swindon T v Cardiff C 3–0; Shrewsbury T v Cambridge Utd 3–1; Man C v Rotherham Utd 0–0, 4–2; Ipswich T v Carlisle Utd 3–2; Orient v Bury 3–2; Swansea C v Bristol R 0–1; Charlton Ath v Maidstone Utd 1–1, 2–1; Southend Utd v Liverpool 0–0, 0–3; Millwall v Blackburn 1–2; Birmingham C v Burnley 0–2; Sunderland v Everton 2–1; Stoke C v Oldham Ath 0–1; Leicester C v Norwich C 3–0; Spurs v Altrincham 1–1, 3–0; Wrexham v Stockport Co 6–2; Newport Co v W. Ham 2–1; Darlington v Colchester Utd 0–1; Fulham v QPR 2–0; MAN UTD v Chelsea 3–0

Fourth Round

ARSENAL v Notts Co 2–0; Nott'm Forest v York C 3–1; Leeds Utd v WBA 3–3, 0–2; PNE v Southampton 0–1; Crystal Palace v Bristol C 3–0; Newcastle Utd v Wolves 1–1, 0–1; Aldershot v Swindon T 2–1; Shrewsbury T v Man C 2–0; Ipswich T v Orient 0–0, 2–0; Bristol R v Charlton Ath 1–0; Liverpool v Blackburn R 1–0; Burnley v Sunderland 1–1, 3–0; Oldham Ath v Leicester C 3–1; Spurs v Wrexham 3–3, 3–2; Newport Co v Colchester Utd 0–0, 0–1; Fulham v MAN UTD 1–1, 0–1

Fifth Round

Nott'm Forest v ARSENAL 0–1; WBA v Southampton 1–1, 1–2; Crystal Palace v Wolves 0–1; Aldershot v Shrewsbury T 2–2, 1–3; Ipswich T v Bristol R 6–1; Liverpool v Burnley 3–0; Oldham Ath v Spurs 0–1; Colchester Utd v MAN UTD 0–1

Sixth Round

Southampton v ARSENAL 1–1, 0–2; Wolves v Shrewsbury T 1–1, 3–1; Ipswich T v Liverpool 0–1; Spurs v MAN UTD 1–1, 0–2

Semi-Final

ARSENAL v Wolves 2–0; Liverpool v MAN UTD 2–2, 0–1

ARSENAL **3**
MANCHESTER UNITED **2**

Arsenal seemed to be coasting home, 2–0 in the lead with only five minutes of a fairly undistinguished match left, when three almost un-believable events occurred, so that in the end it all added up to one of the most fantastic and dramatic Finals of recent years.

United had clearly decided that Brady was their most menacing oppo-nent, and Macari attempted to mark him closely. But Brady lost his shadow in the twelfth minute and swung out a long pass to Stapleton. A through-pass to Price, a quick centre, and three Arsenal players dashed for the ball in the goalmouth. Talbot won the race and put Arsenal one up.

United, apparently unshaken, had most of the play for the next half-hour, but they went further behind just before half-time. Brady was again the architect, as his floated cross from the right was headed in with the minimum of fuss by Stapleton.

An eighty-fifth minute substitution – Walford for Price – may well have upset Arsenal's rhythm. First McQueen was on the spot to score for United following Coppell's free-kick, and then, improbably, United drew level through McIlroy.

But they had hardly finished congratulating themselves when Brady produced a perfectly controlled diagonal run before feeding Rix out on the left, and the latter's curving centre to the far post was shot home by Sunderland for a last-minute Arsenal winner.

Arsenal: Jennings; Rice, Nelson; Talbot, O'Leary, Young; Brady, Sunderland, Stapleton, Price, Rix. Sub: Walford
Manchester United: Bailey; Nicholl, Albiston; McIlroy, McQueen, Buchan; Coppell, Greenhoff (J.), Jordan, Macari, Thomas. Sub: Greenhoff (B.)
Referee: R. Challis (Tonbridge).

McIlroy equalizes for United in the eighty-eighth minute

1979–80

First Round
Carlisle Utd v Hull C 3–3, 2–0; Kidderminster Harriers v Blackburn R 0–2; Morecambe v Rotherham Utd 1–1, 0–2; Altrincham v Crewe Alex 3–0; Barnsley v Hartlepool Utd 5–2; Darlington v Huddersfield T 1–1, 1–0; Grimsby T v Chesterfield 1–1, 3–2; Rochdale v Scunthorpe Utd 2–1; Tranmere R v AP Leamington 9–0; Brandon Utd v Bradford C 0–3; Stafford Rangers v Moor Green 3–2; Burscough v Sheff Utd 0–3; Blyth Spartans v Mansfield T 0–2; York C v Mossley 5–2; Sheff Wed v Lincoln C 3–0; Port Vale v Doncaster R 1–3; Nuneaton Borough v Northwich Vic 3–3, 0–3; Chester v Workington 5–1; Blackpool v Wigan Ath 1–1, 0–2; Halifax T v Scarborough 2–0; Walsall v Stockport Co 2–0; Burton Alb v Bury 0–2; Portsmouth v Newport Co 1–0; Fareham T v Merthyr Tydfil 2–3; Peterborough Utd v AFC Bournemouth 1–2; Enfield v Yeovil T 0–1; Aldershot v Exeter C 4–1; Barking v Oxford Utd 1–0; Wealdstone v Southend Utd 0–1; Reading v Kettering T 4–2; Wycombe Wand v Croydon 0–3; Swindon T v Brentford 4–1; Hereford Utd v Northampton T 1–0; Gillingham v Wimbledon 0–0, 2–4; Salisbury v Millwall 1–2; Gravesend & Northfleet v Torquay Utd 0–1; Colchester Utd v Plymouth Arg 1–1, 1–0; Minehead v Chesham Utd 1–2; Slough T v Hungerford T 3–1; Harlow T v Leytonstone & Ilford 2–1

Second Round
Grimsby T v Sheff Utd 2–0; Bury v York C 0–0, 2–0; Chester v Barnsley 1–0; Rotherham Utd v Altrincham 0–2; Darlington v Bradford C 0–1; Doncaster R v Mansfield T 1–2; Northwich Vic v Wigan Ath 2–2, 0–1; Walsall v Halifax T 1–1, 1–1, 0–2; Carlisle Utd v Sheff Wed 3–0; Blackburn R v Stafford Rangers 2–0; Tranmere R v Rochdale 2–2, 1–2; Colchester Utd v AFC Bournemouth 1–0; Torquay Utd v Swindon T 3–3, 2–3; Yeovil T v Slough T 1–0; Reading v Barking 3–1; Croydon v Millwall 1–1, 2–3; Hereford Utd v Aldershot 1–2; Chesham Utd v Merthyr Tydfil 1–1, 3–1; Wimbledon v Portsmouth 0–0, 3–3, 0–1; Southend Utd v Harlow T 1–1, 0–1

Third Round
Cardiff C v ARSENAL 0–0, 1–2; Mansfield T v Brighton & H Alb 0–2; Sunderland v Bolton Wand 0–1; Halifax T v Man C 1–0; Notts C v Wolves 0–3; Yeovil T v Norwich C 0–3; QPR v Watford 1–2; Leicester C v Harlow T 1–1, 0–1; Luton T v Swindon T 0–2; Spurs v Man Utd 1–1, 1–0; Birmingham C v Southampton 2–1; Portsmouth v Middlesbro 1–1, 0–3; Leeds Utd v Nott'm Forest 1–4; Liverpool v Grimsby T 5–0; Rochdale v Bury 1–1, 2–3; Burnley v Stoke C 1–0; Everton v Aldershot 4–1; Chelsea v Wigan Ath 0–1; Carlisle Utd v Bradford C 3–2; Wrexham v Charlton Ath 6–0; Bristol C v Derby Co 6–2; PNE v Ipswich T 0–3; Newcastle Utd v Chester 0–2; Millwall v Shrewsbury T 5–1; Blackburn R v Fulham 1–1, 1–0; Oldham Ath v Coventry C 0–1; Chesham Utd v Cambridge Utd 0–2; Bristol R v Aston Villa 1–2; Swansea C v Crystal Palace 2–2, 3–3, 2–1; Reading v Colchester Utd 2–0; Altrincham v Orient 1–1, 1–2; WBA v W. HAM 1–1, 1–2

Fourth Round
ARSENAL v Brighton & H Alb 2–0; Bolton Wand v Halifax T 2–0; Wolves v Norwich C 1–1, 3–2; Watford v Harlow T 4–3; Swindon T v Spurs 0–0, 1–2; Birmingham C v Middlesbro 2–1; Nott'm Forest v Liverpool 0–2; Bury v Burnley 1–0; Everton v Wigan Ath 3–0; Carlisle Utd v Wrexham 0–0, 1–3; Bristol C v Ipswich T 1–2; Chester v Millwall 2–0; Blackburn R v Coventry C 1–0; Cambridge Utd v Aston Villa 1–1, 1–4; Swansea C v Reading 4–1; Orient v W. HAM 2–3

Fifth Round
Bolton Wand v ARSENAL 1–1, 0–3; Wolves v Watford 0–3; Spurs v Birmingham C 3–1; Liverpool v Bury 2–0; Everton v Wrexham 5–2; Ipswich T v Chester 2–1; Blackburn R v Aston Villa 1–1, 0–1; W. HAM v Swansea C 2–0

Sixth Round
Watford v ARSENAL 1–2; Spurs v Liverpool 0–1; Everton v Ipswich T 2–1; W. HAM v Aston Villa 1–0

Semi-Final
ARSENAL v Liverpool 0–0, 1–1, 1–1, 1–0; Everton v W. HAM 1–1, 1–2

WEST HAM UNITED **1**
ARSENAL **0**

Arsenal started as hot favourites against a team which must have lost a certain amount of confidence after gradually slipping out of the promotion race from the Second Division in the weeks leading up to the Final.

Manager Lyall had taken the gamble of playing Paul Allen in his West Ham team – the youngest player ever to appear in a Final at 17 years and 256 days – and, more than that, detailing him to mark Arsenal's immensely talented Eire international Brady.

Brady pulled out all the stops in the second half, organizing most of Arsenal's attacking movements, but by that time West Ham had taken the initiative, thanks to Brooking's thirteenth-minute goal.

The move that led to the goal began with Devonshire beating Talbot and Rice out on the left and crossing to the far post. Jennings got a touch, Cross's shot was blocked and then Pearson's hard drive from the rebound was expertly glanced into the net from directly in front of goal by Brooking's head.

A lot of the game was dull and featureless, one suspects partly due to the heat and partly due to West Ham feeling that the denial of the ball to Arsenal was their best method of defence. They held out to become the third Second Division club in eight seasons to win the Cup.

West Ham: Parkes; Stewart, Lampard; Bonds, Martin, Devonshire; Allen, Pearson, Cross, Brooking, Pike. Sub: Brush
Arsenal: Jennings; Rice, Devine; Talbot, O'Leary, Young; Brady, Sunderland, Stapleton, Price, Rix. Sub: Nelson
Referee: G. Courtney (Spennymoor)

Brooking on the ground after scoring

Reg Paine
The Referee's Quiz Book No 2 70p

A new collection of perplexing questions to test your knowledge of the Laws of Association Football.

Includes an introduction by Ted Croker, Secretary of the Football Association, and a note by Ron Greenwood, England team manager, in addition to a checklist of answers at the back of the book – which will ensure you finish the quiz knowing a lot more about the game, however many questions you get right!

Michael Raper and Graham Sharp
The Racing Ready Reckoner £1

The essential book for every punter's pocket. To win or for a place – whatever the stake, whatever the odds – *The Racing Ready Reckoner* will work out your winnings in less time than it takes to fill out a betting slip.

Col James L. Anderson and Martin Cohen
The West Point Fitness and Diet Book £1.20

From the US Army's top experts in physical fitness – a complete conditioning programme for every member of the family, enabling each member to enjoy the best of health and top physical condition whether they're involved in competitive sport, relaxing in retirement, or busy at the office or in the home all day. Includes: the walk/run plan – weight control and nutrition – posture: how to look good – sports for everyone at every age – special fitness for women.

compiled by Jonathon Green
Famous Last Words £1.50

'They couldn't hit an elephant at this distance—' last words of an American general . . . Deathbed wisdom, gallows humour, suicide notes, fond farewells, desperate departures – here is a fascinating anthology of exit lines, over two thousand entries featuring the world's leading figures: Lincoln, Oscar Wilde, Bing Crosby, Julius Caesar, Henry VIII, Noel Coward, Hitler, Van Gogh, Billy the Kid.

'Compulsively entertaining' SUNDAY EXPRESS

J. H. H. Gaute and Robin Odell
The Murderers' Who's Who £1.95

An illustrated anthology of 150 years of notorious murder cases: Manson, the Boston Strangler, the Acid Bath Murders, the Brighton Trunk Crimes, the Brides in the Bath, the Hammersmith Nudes and the horrific cannibalism of Albert Fish – plus countless lesser-known but equally horrendous and bizarre murders. According to Colin Wilson's foreword, 'Perhaps the most valuable single volume ever published on murder', fully indexed for reference use.

'One of the best-organized encyclopedias of crime' DAILY EXPRESS

'Compulsive reading' DAILY MIRROR

Charles Panati
Breakthroughs £1.95

Astonishing advances coming in your lifetime, in medicine, science and technology. By 1984 a liquid will spray away tooth decay; by 1989 physicists will have harnessed fusion power, a clean and near-limitless energy source; by 1994 hurricanes will be tamed and production of rainfall over arid lands will be commonplace. And more: electric cars, flying trains, drugs to prolong life, people/plant hybrids and awakening the (clinically) dead.

'A ten-course banquet for the imagination' NEW YORK TIMES

James McClure
Spike Island £1.95

'A' Division is known as 'Spike Island' in the trade – the trade being policing in that bit of Liverpool that's like a band-aid stuck over where they ripped the heart out – the toughest inner-city area in Europe.

'Shows us the truth of the policeman's job through the eyes of the men and women who actually do it . . . also a book about ourselves, about the society we have created, and about the precariousness of the bridges . . . over the chasm of poverty and crime' P. D. JAMES, NEW YORK TIMES

'Brilliant reportage' EVENING STANDARD

John Slater
Just Off for the Weekend £2.50

Slater's hotel guide

The bestselling author of Just Off the Motorway has selected more than a hundred places to stay, with details of what to see and walks to take, specially recommended pubs and restaurants – and all within a Friday evening's drive from one of England's big cities. With an introduction by Anna Ford.

edited by Harriet Peacock
The Alternative Holiday Catalogue £1.95

If you're looking for a holiday that you won't find in a travel agent's window . . . if there's something you've always wanted to try your hand at . . . or if you want to take your special interest on holiday with you, this A-to-Z of ideas and information is the book you need. 150 different types of special-interest holiday, from backgammon and Bible-study to Zen, upholstery and giving up smoking. This book tells you where to go, what to take, what it costs, and what you'll find when you get there.